The Economic Imagination

The Economic Imagination
Towards a Behavioural Analysis of Choice

Peter E. Earl

LECTURER IN ECONOMICS, UNIVERSITY OF STIRLING

FOREWORD BY G. L. S. SHACKLE

Wheatsheaf
Books

M. E. SHARPE, INC.
Armonk, New York

First published in Great Britain in 1983 by
WHEATSHEAF BOOKS LTD
A MEMBER OF THE HARVESTER PRESS PUBLISHING GROUP
Publisher: John Spiers
Director of Publications: Edward Elgar
16 Ship Street, Brighton, Sussex

First published in the United States of America in 1983 by
M. E. SHARPE INC.
80 Business Park Drive
Armonk, New York, NY 10504

British Library Cataloguing in Publication Data

Earl, Peter
  The economic imagination.
  1. Economics
  I. Title
  330   HB171
ISBN 0–7108–0164–5

Library of Congress Cataloging in Publication Data

Earl, Peter.
  The economic imagination.

  Bibliography: p.
  Includes index.
    1. Economics—Psychological aspects.   2. Decision-
  making.   3. Uncertainty.   I. Title.
  HB74.P8E27   1983   330′ .01′9   83–486
  ISBN 0–87332–250–9 (Sharpe)

Photoset in 10 point Times by Photobooks (Bristol) Ltd
and printed in Great Britain by
Biddles Ltd., Guildford, Surrey

To Alfred S. Eichner

Contents

Foreword

The mark of the natural-born theoretician is the power to make an integral whole out of many seemingly separate and not obviously related elements. I think *The Economic Imagination* shows this power. Its incisive replacement of the marginal-substitution principle by a process of discrete step by step decisions is drastic but powerfully refreshing in its bold ingenuity. Mr Earl has foraged widely in the modern literature, especially in the new, hardly yet academically acceptable areas such as marketing psychology, whose possibilities were revealed to me by Stephen Littlechild's excitingly original paper 'Advertising, Brand Loyalty and Habit'. He has foraged with unerring insight and judgment, and with daring enterprise. What commends this work to me most decisively is its recognition that business action is taken in face of basic irremediable uncertainty. This is the elemental condition of life, but it appears with sharpest force for the business man in the need to buy costly plant, to cope with oligopoly and to engage in bargaining. Here the author has taken over some hitherto neglected tools but he has used them with his own individual touch and method.

I believe that business is a continuous creative gamble. Since 1942 (*Oxford Economic Papers* first series number 6) almost everything I have written has had at its core the word *imagination*. In using it in the title of his book, Mr Earl has nailed the right colours to his mast. This is a stirring, exciting book of high virtuosity and impressive resource.

G. L. S. Shackle

Preface

This book has been written mainly for academic and intermediate/final year undergraduate economists, though it should also be of interest to marketing managers, consumer protection groups and psychologists. Its primary target audience should find that it is full of surprises, in contrast to conventional works on choice and the theory of value which, in recent years, have come to resemble each other to such an extent that one can almost predict which diagram will occur on which page. The book's contents are arranged in a way that should enable these surprises to be as easy as possible to manage, while sections 1.4, 2.8, 3.8, 3.9 and 4.9 use the device of the dialogue (which is normally confined to works on philosophy) to show how key phenomena can be seen from different perspectives. These dialogues are based partly on conversations I have had with sceptical colleagues and partly on my own internal mental debates.

Readers interested in decision making processes who have no background in economics will probably find it best to look briefly at sections 1.3, 1.4 and 2.9, and then begin to read in earnest from Chapter 3 onwards, ignoring references to pricing policies. They should not be worried if they are not sure of the meaning of some of the jargon phrases from neoclassical (conventional) economics that come under fire. Rather, they should pass these by rapidly and concentrate on the constructive aspects of the new theory. All readers may find it both helpful and entertaining to read this book simultaneously with Robert M. Pirsig's (1974) book *Zen and the Art of Motorcycle Maintenance*. Pirsig's view of the world has a lot in common with the arguments expressed in Chapters 5 to 7, though the present work was in final typescript before I discovered that this was the case.

My main intellectual debts and past influences are outlined in section 1.2, where an account of the genesis of the ideas in this book is given. However, I would like to take this opportunity to thank those who have been most helpful while the book was being put together.

Chapter 2 has benefited a great deal from correspondence that I have had with Frederic S. Lee, whose depth of research into the evolution of Post Keynesian price theory I have found quite remarkable. Professor G. L. S. Shackle has given me much encouragement and valuable advice on earlier drafts of Chapter 4. Like any economist, I have been somewhat fearful of straying into unfamiliar disciplines such as psychology, though, unlike most, I have found this unavoidable. Hence I am pleased to be able to record my gratitude to Sharon Axford for extensive discussions on the psychological aspects of the theory proposed in Chapters 5 to 7; these have enabled me to avoid making some unnecessary errors and excessively sweeping statements. Professors Mark Blaug, Stephen Littlechild and Brian Loasby read the entire penultimate draft and provided many useful suggestions. For any errors and ambiguities that remain I naturally take full responsibility.

Finally, I would like to thank my secretary, Mrs Eleanor Bruce, for her patience, speed and accuracy when typing successive drafts of this book, and the American Marketing Association for permission to reproduce, as Figure 5.1, material entitled 'Eight Male Psychographic Segments' from page 201 of W. D. Wells (1975) 'Psychographics: A Critical Review', *Journal of Marketing Research 12*, May, pp. 196–213.

1 Introduction and Methodological Statement

1.1 The Nature of *The Economic Imagination*

The Economic Imagination is concerned with the ways in which people think as they make choices, particularly those concerning which goods to consume or use as stores of wealth, how to behave in the workplace, and which prices to charge. Its subject area, then, is in the very heartland of economics. It is far from being the first book to investigate how these key kinds of choices are made. This is one of the chief reasons why it may prove to be highly controversial. It is different from previous books on choice to such an extent that it may seem to represent a threat to most of them and, by extension, to their authors' reputations. If its arguments are accepted many of the thousands of pages written by the neoclassical economists who dominate the profession will seem to have been a misdirected waste of time.

The fundamental differences that set this book apart from orthodox works on choice are as follows.

(1)   The concept of the 'demand function' is rejected.
(2)   The concept of the 'marginal rate of substitution' is nowhere to be found in the theory that is proposed.
(3)   There is no use of calculus, no 'equalisation at the margin'.
(4)   Instead of continuous preferences there are hierarchical priority systems.
(5)   Consumers are not assumed to be sovereign.
(6)   The theory that is proposed can be used by firms in a practical way, to attempt shape consumer behaviour to suit their own ends.
(7)   No one is assumed to maximise anything.
(8)   Much material comes from the work of psychologists and sociologists.
(9)   Choosers are not assumed to seek 'utility'.

s may alarm mainstream economists but there is a of theorists with whom they will strike a welcome p is difficult to classify without using a cumbersome simplicity we shall call the typical member a BPKE: a st Keynesian economist. However, some of the e tend to think of as BPKEs are more commonly lab utionalists, Neo Austrians or subjectivists, rather than either beha iouralists or Post Keynesians.

BPKEs should find that this book enables them to fill something of a void in their research programmes. Hitherto these economists have specialised in the investigation of macroeconomic phenomena and the behaviour of individual firms. In doing so, they have rather played down the role of individual decision making in the determination of the occurrences they seek to understand. The *Guide to Post-Keynesian Economics* (Eichner (ed), 1979) does not contain a chapter on consumer theory. Similarly, behavioural theory, which treats the firm as a coalition of individuals with a variety of interests, devotes scant attention to the nature of individuals' emotions and motivations, or their effects on decision making. *The Economic Imagination* attempts to fill these gaps and to bring out policy implications of the proposed theory for corporations and politicians.

The BPKE shorthand may cause surprise to some readers, for it has not been common to treat Post Keynesian and behavioural approaches to economics as being essentially one and the same. Certainly, the former concentrates on price theory, income distribution and macroeconomics, while the latter confines attention to the internal organisational aspects of firm behaviour. Post Keynesians often treat firms as if they are 'black boxes', just as do equilibrium theorists. Behavioural theorists tend to leave rather imprecise the nature of the market contexts in which they assume firms to be operating. But the fact the Post Keynesian and behavioural economists have chosen to address different questions and largely ignore each other's work should not be seen as implying that their contributions are inherently incompatible. It is simply a consequence of the ways they have specialised as researchers. Slowly economists from both subgroups are beginning to realise that their approaches are complementary rather than competitive, as is evident in Tylecote's (1980) analysis of inflation, and the work on corporate strategies by Moss (1981) and Kay (1982, 1983).

The two groups of economists comprising the most obviously receptive market for the ideas in the pages that follow have travelled different pathways as they have conducted their researches. However, they share two basic presumptions about the way in which economic problems should be approached. These presumptions are, first, that choice involves uncertainty and the formation of expectations about the future, which means that it is irreconcilable with the notion of equilibrium; and, second, that before hypotheses are applied to historical and contemporary experience they should be examined for logical consistency and *a priori* plausibility. BPKEs necessarily find the axiomatic and positivist methods of mainstream equilibrium theorists hard to stomach. They also take issue with the overriding emphasis given by equilibrium theorists to the notion of substitution and the idea that choices are constrained by exogenously determined endowments. In the real world, it can be dangerous to neglect the importance of complementarities and the fact that choices are frequently constrained by success in bargaining, either between class groups or within coalitions. Bargaining involves differences in perceptions of a situation and is inherently at odds with the mainstream view of determinacy where results are taken to bear some clearcut relationship to 'objectively' defined initial conditions. In *The Economic Imagination* the origins and forms taken by perceptions of decision makers become a subject for serious investigation.

The structure of the book is as follows. The rest of this chapter is spent explaining the evolution of the ideas that are proposed, justifying the methodology employed, and explaining how the analysis differs from some other recent, unorthodox work on choice. In Chapter 2 there is an examination of behavioural/Post Keynesian (BPK) approaches to pricing. The main use to which orthodox choice theory is put is the justification of the Law of Demand, a significant component of neoclassical value theory. It will be argued that the Law of Demand is both unnecessary to explain how prices are determined and trivial as a tool for practical policy. In BPK theory conjectures of costs play the key role in price determination; static demand functions are not used. Hence the choice theorist needs to be able to offer economists (especially those in the real world of business or government) who are looking for policy insights rather more than the 'commonsense knowledge' that if prices are lowered sales often increase somewhat. If prices are cost-determined (with costs taken to include marketing costs) it is the product itself and its marketing package which is the variable of interest. We need a means of deciding what are appropriate market research questions to ask, and of interpreting the answers we get, so that we can understand how variations in the product package determine quantities sold. Only then does it become possible to form conjectures about which product and marketing scheme may be most appropriate to a firm, or which government policy might be appropriate for increasing consumer welfare.

With the conclusion of Chapter 2 having suggested the need for a reorientation of economists' efforts and purposes in the area of the theory of choice, Chapter 3 goes on to argue that the existing neoclassical theory cannot provide an appropriate starting point if the new orientation is accepted. This inadequacy arises because of the kinds of assumptions it makes. In order to develop a practically applicable theory for use in the formulation of industrial and consumer policy, whether private or public, it seems to be necessary to start at an earlier stage in the choice process than does the orthodox theory. In particular, we shall argue that, to analyse situations of structural change that characterise oligopolistic markets, it is necessary to examine how individual choice processes are affected by the inescapable unknowns and complexities of everyday life, underlying motivations, and sources of inertia, without forgetting the social contexts in which people are brought up and act out their lives. These issues are tackled, successively, in Chapters 4 to 7, which comprise the body of the new theory.

1.2 The Genesis of the Analysis that will be Presented

Intellectual autobiographies are generally thought of as the prerogative of the emeritus professor rather than the relatively young scholar. But the conventional view is perhaps unfortunate. Readers of such autobiographies in, for example, the *Banco Nazionale del Lavoro Quarterly Review* cannot fail to notice how some background material makes it possible to see the works of great economists, such as Hicks, Kindleberger and Machlup, in a new light. By seeing where they have been, by whom they were influenced, and which intellectual struggles they have had, we find it much easier to see where they were trying to go in the works that they published over their long careers. There is no necessary reason why readers of lesser economists' works should not profit from similar accounts of their evolutionary paths. It is in this spirit that the present section is offered.

The unconventional approach to choice that this book sets out has its origins firmly rooted in my second year studies for the Cambridge Economic Tripos. In my very first essay I was invited to discuss the proposition that 'The Hicks-Allen theory of consumer behaviour is utterly useless because it yields no testable hypotheses.' During this, my first, examination of the theory, I was not worried about the effects of uncertainty on choice. Nor was I terribly concerned with the lack of testable hypotheses in the theory, despite having read Friedman's (1953) essay on positive economics. What did disturb me, however, in addition to the assumptions necessary to ensure continuity and convexity, was the lack of *any* results, beyond the idea that demand curves usually slope downwards, which could usefully be *applied*, even if accepted only on faith.

It was thus with some concern about the adequacy of neoclassical theory, and with what constituted a good theory, that I went along to Frank Hahn's lectures. The exposition was brilliant but it left me in doubt as to what had been exposed beyond the conditions required for Pareto optimal positions of stable general equilibrium, a few examples of applied welfare economics, and some points about the theory of monopolistic competition in relation to the unsolved problem of oligopoly. The real world seemed to bear little relation to the perfectly competitive world of his general equilibrium analysis and it was unclear where his system would go if the conditions required for equilibrium were not present. I was also left wondering what was the point of *general* analysis, for it yielded no policy conclusions. All of the comparative statics results were defined in terms of *partial* equilibria and they seemed suspiciously to rest on tacit assumptions to the effect that traders had identical preferences and did not indulge in opportunistic behaviour.

Running parallel with Hahn's course was a set of lectures by John Eatwell, which looked at the same subject—the theory of value and distribution—from a Neo Ricardian/Post Keynesian perspective. These lectures tended to reinforce my scepticism with regard to neoclassical equilibrium theory, but they only partially filled the void that had been opened up.

It transpired that Eatwell's alternative paradigm did not, as yet, have a choice-theoretic foundation which would permit an analysis of the turbulent 'short periods' in which individual investment projects and disequilibrium product life cycles work themselves out. This did not seem to worry him too much, for he was concerned with the question of how an economy evolves in the long run. In this context it was argued that the study of aggregates was more worthwhile than the neoclassical approach of focusing on individuals' choices. A system of Sraffa equations was used to explain how prices came about at the industry level, but in order to do so quantities had to be taken as given. Sales and worker productivity levels were said, somewhat vaguely, to be 'socially determined'. It was encouraging to see that firms were recognised to be oligopolistic, yet the problem of oligopoly was dealt with in a way that was not completely satisfactory. Prices were said to be set by firms according to their costs, plus a mark-up, the size of which depended on either the 'degree of monopoly' (Kalecki, 1943) or, if firms were seen as attempting to maximise long run sales revenue, the long run need for investment funds.

Demand functions did not figure in this explanation of pricing; yet an impression was given that firms on the one hand could exercise discretion in working out which price to charge, and, on the other, operated in a highly competitive environment. It was all rather too vague to be convincing, or, worse, seemed logically inconsistent. No one referred to work a quarter of a century before by Andrews, which had attempted to deal with the puzzle of competitive oligopoly, and which Eichner (1978) has since commended to Post Keynesians as the seminal work on microfoundations for their long run macro models. It was another two years before I discovered it. Eichner's own work in the area, which, when coupled with Andrews' contribution, makes the analysis of mark-up pricing so much clearer, was only just achieving publication around this time (1975–6). My Cambridge tutors, however, set great store in Wood's (1975) home-grown theory of the mark-up, which brought out the investment funding idea yet said little about possible competitors' reactions as they might be seen by corporate decision makers.

While I was attempting to cope with these omissions I was asked to read Leijonhufvud's (1968) book on the nature of Keynesian economics. Most people who read it come away noting two things: the difference between Keynes' own work and standard textbook expositions of it, and Leijonhufvud's characterisation of macro-economics as 'Walras without the auctioneer'. The latter is taken by most readers in a very nonchalant way: the fact that there is no one to ensure equilibrium prices before transactions occur means that trade often takes place at prices which are in some sense wrong; not all markets clear, and subsequent attempts to clear one market may merely disrupt another. The typical reader of Leijonhufvud's massive book does not make very much of his discussion of *why* coordination problems arise if there is no *deus ex machina* to ensure that they do not: when they choose, individual decision makers often do not know what *other* people are going to do, yet the actions of others will often bear on the sequels to their own choices. It was Leijonhufvud's discussion of the coordination issue, coupled with my reading, shortly after, Shackle's (1967) *The Years of High Theory*, that turned out to be decisive in my rejection of equilibrium economics in favour of the economics of processes evolving in uncertain, historical time.

Leijonhufvud's discussion of coordination was mainly concerned with the problems faced by firms trying to work out how much to invest, when they could not know how much consumers would spend, and workers trying to decide what to do if they lost their jobs, because they could not see clearly where job opportunities lay. At this time I failed to see it had a structural dimension too—I would have done so had I spotted and followed up his (1968, pp. 69–70) footnote reference to the work of G. B. Richardson—but, a few weeks later, I saw the light for myself, and then, unknowingly, proceeded to reinvent much of Richardson's heretical contribution. My insight came as I was attempting to do an essay involving a quote from Ricardo about the nature of the difference between economies which produce commodities, and those which merely exchange existing assets. In a production economy firms have to decide how much to produce of each feasible commodity. They do this by deciding whether or not particular quantities will be saleable without opportunity loss. But, unless prices are equilibrium prices, as in the world of general equilibrium theory, firms cannot know how much they should produce unless they can know future prices *now*, or can find out the investment plans of other firms and the expenditure plans of consumers. And many of these plans will not exist in concrete form until *after* their decision deadlines have elapsed.

Only in discussing the cobweb problem did most economists come anywhere near to addressing this issue of structural coordination. But they treated the cobweb as a curiosity affecting merely agriculture and the construction industry. They did not seem to think to ask how it might usually be avoided in other sectors. Nor did they consider how the economic system as a whole could operate in a manner which did not entail frequent kaleidoscopic changes and plunges into chaos. After reading Shackle's book I found it hard to see how such 'catastrophic' changes could be avoided if there were no bounds on what decision makers might imagine; on the ability of firms to enter markets; or on the combinations of goods that might be chosen for exploration by consumers who, because of uncertainty, lacked given preferences. Unknowingly, I was driven to the same conclusion as G. B. Richardson: in the real world economic systems function coherently, insofar as they do, *because* of the bounds produced by imperfections of knowledge rather than, as in conventional theory, *despite* them.

When I raised my worries about uncertainty in a tutorial on general equilibrium theory I was told by Oliver Hart that Debreu (1959) had shown how the orthodox paradigm could 'handle' the problem with the aid of the concept of the 'contingent commodity economy'. In this highly abstract sort of economy *all* trade takes place prior to any production. The transactional future is collapsed into the present by an implausible institutional arrangement in which traders on both the supply and demand sides insure themselves against all contingencies by arranging for the delivery of particular goods and labour services if, and only if, particular environmental states come about. For this arrangement to be possible there must be a complete knowledge of technological details and possible environmental states, no births of new traders, and markets which are costless to operate. The 'future' in a contingent commodity economy is the time to come when people get on with production and the receipt of goods for consumption, along lines specified in complete detail in the contracts that they conclude in the present, and which are irrevocable.

It is necessary to assume constant returns to scale and, implicitly, perfect divisibility to guarantee a stable equilibrium in such a system. These assumptions also ensure that all goods can be physically distinct and, in effect, custom-built (as indeed they might have to be if futures markets are assumed to be complete, for contingent wants might be very highly specialised). Intuition suggests that the real world, of indivisibilities and increasing returns, is fundamentally different. Most products necessarily have to be less than ideal to many consumers in order to be available at all at prices they can afford. Obviously, if firms can market and design their products to make them *seem* less flawed than their rivals' offerings, they may enjoy better fortunes than their rivals. However, I saw no suggestion that neoclassical choice theory can be used by firms attempting to do this in the real world. The theory simply assumes that firms know the nature of 'given' preferences and supply perfectly appropriate products. I wanted a theory that could be practically applied and which did not assume all of the interesting informational issues out of the way in order to reach determinate solutions in a highly formalised manner. Since no one lecturing on microeconomics ever considered informational matters I was largely left, in my final undergraduate year, to explore them for myself, simultaneously with meeting the demands of weekly essays on academically more popular topics.

At this stage I was greatly influenced by some lectures on industrial sociology, and Kornai's (1971) book *Anti-Equilibrium*, which led me to the literature of behavioural economics (especially Cyert and March, 1963), and organisation theory. Downie's (1958) disequilibrium analysis of the competitive process, and Leijonhufvud's (1973) investigation of why effective demand failures do not always lead to multiple departures from an economy's evolutionary path, also played a big part in forming my view of how economic systems functioned. It differed fundamentally from the neoclassical perspective in respect of the question of how much slack could be assumed to be present. A taut system of the neoclassical kind only made sense in a world of perfect information. In my world view decision makers did not maximise anything in particular, while there were response thresholds and forces of inertia which might often make changes sluggish, and occasional sudden expectational shifts which could be highly disruptive if they caused response thresholds to be crossed.

In various ways, the disequilibrium authors whose works I was beginning to read were all addressing the question of why economic systems, despite not working perfectly or achieving *equilibrium* positions of Pareto optimality, were often relatively *stable* while evolving and tended to operate as if in some sense channelised. It was rather as if economic systems could be seen as moving, somewhat blindly, down corridors littered with minor obstructions, occasionally taking discontinuous changes of direction up or down flights of stairs (or high speed elevators in mania or panic situations) to other corridors of relative stability. The economic systems these economists were investigating were either macro, market or firm level structures; apart from Kornai they devoted little attention to individual behaviour. I resolved to devote my postgraduate researches to the study of economic processes from this kind of perspective, the original aim being to see which kinds of institutional frameworks and corporate policies would be most conducive to orderly structural change.

My first activity as a postgraduate was to read Loasby's (1976a) book and most of the works it cited. It answered a lot of my questions but caused two things in particular to become obvious. First, it made frequent reference to various disequilibrium/behavioural authors, who had similar concerns to my own, that no one else bothered to mention. It was almost as if they had been ostracised. Second, although the ideas of these neglected theorists could be used to plug many of the gaps in the Post Keynesian approach, no one had ever attempted to construct such a synthesis and there was still much to be desired concerning the theory of individuals' choice processes in a world of uncertainty and complexity. So long as this last weakness remained, theories of corporate behaviour emphasising the internal workings of firms would be built on questionable foundations, or no foundations at all, and nothing could be said about corporate policies aimed at affecting, or taking account of, the behaviour patterns of individuals.

A connection between these two issues began to suggest itself not long after I had been reading work by Ansoff (1968) and Chandler (1962) on the difficulties of constructing corporate strategies and getting organisational changes accepted in firms. Ansoff was talking about the ways in which firms could confine their attention spans to avoid wasteful 'buckshot' search. The managers in the firms studied by Chandler often seemed to have become blinkered in their outlooks, not by careful calculation but by their past experiences. I started to see parallels between this behaviour and the behaviour of economists: the history of economic thought, including the history of the neglect of the ideas of Richardson and the other economists to whom Loasby's book referred, is a history of choices made in conditions of uncertainty and information overloading. Long before,

I had read Kuhn's (1970) work on paradigms and the behaviour of scientists. Now managers in companies seemed to have paradigms too, comprising their corporate world views and institutionalised ways of doing things. Scientific behaviour and the ordinary business of everyday life thus became increasingly difficult to separate.

My own emerging world view was rapidly reinforced around the time (mid 1979) that I moved to Stirling. Neil Kay's (1979) behavioural theory of corporate research and development was published and from it I was led to the work on hierarchies and critique of reductionism in Koestler and Smythies (eds) (1969). Brian Loasby referred me to G. A. Kelly's (1963) *Theory of Personality*, which he had been encouraged to read by Charles Suckling, an industrial scientist who had found it helped him to think about complex problems. Kelly's theory formalises, in structuralist terms, the idea that ordinary behaviour has a scientific purpose, namely, to discover how to cope with the complex and uncertain world that must be confronted in everyday life.

As I had just been reading Koestler's attacks on mainstream behaviourist psychology, which seemed to have parallels in my own dissatisfactions with neoclassical economics, I was amused to find that Kelly's work occupied a place in psychology entirely analogous to BPK theory in economics. The restrictions the behaviourists were prepared to tolerate in order to preserve their methodologies and conduct controlled, and supposedly objective, experiments were on a par with those made by general equilibrium economists. Behaviourists were often restricted to studying the observable behaviour of rats and pigeons because they rejected the notion that the concept of the *thinking* person (as opposed to the *responder to stimuli*) was worthy of investigation; general equilibrium theorists confined their attention to institutional structures which logically could not exist, because they could otherwise see no way of producing states of equilibrium in their atomistic economic models.

The remaining key references in this book were discovered very much by chance. I was led to investigate the Kelly-like work of ethnomethodologists in sociology and education as a result of sharing a university house with two of Stirling's practitioners in these fields. I was encouraged to read Steinbruner's (1974) related contribution by my former pupil Roland Clarke, who shared my interests and happened to see the book in the LSE bookshop (at the time neither Stirling Library nor the Marshall Library in Cambridge included it in their catalogues). Since there is a complete absence of cross referencing between these works I was indeed lucky to mix with fellow academics with much more polymathic tendencies than one usually finds in mainstream economics. Such cross referencing as I have since discovered only occurs in secondary material which would not have caught my attention had I not been aware of the primary sources—Eden *et al.*'s (1979) *Thinking in Organizations* is the only work that cites simultaneously Kelly, Steinbruner and the ethnomethodologists, and it was only the word 'thinking' that gave the clue as to the perspective from which it had been written, thus causing me to select it as worthy of investigation. My own experiences are, to judge by conversations with colleagues, not at all atypical in respect of the inefficiencies they display in the process of inquisitive activity. Indeed, as I have argued elsewhere (Earl, 1983), it seems that the methods used by scientists to choose what to read are not fundamentally different from those that they use in their guises as consumers trying to make choices on a shopping expedition. *The Economic Imagination* can thus be used to aid studies of economists' behaviour; its ideas are reflexive and in this sense it clearly dominates over neoclassical theories of fully-informed 'choice', which it would be absurd to use to study scientific behaviour.

I had originally planned to write a synthesis of these subjectivist ideas and BPK theory of the more conventional kind, which would cover individual, firm, and macrolevel aspects of modern economic systems. But it soon became apparent that such a synthesis would require a book of a thousand pages—a modern version of Marshall's *Principles* that could not be used for elementary teaching and would obviously not represent a viable publishing proposition. A partitioning of the ideas seemed unavoidable. The macroeconomic and monetary theory part of the synthesis has already appeared (Dow and Earl, 1982), while the sequel to the present book, to be called *The Corporate Imagination* and which will take many of the ideas of the present book into a detailed analysis of the evolution of large firms, is already under preparation for publication in 1984.

1.3 The Economic Imagination, Marketing, and *The Joyless Economy*

All of the core novel ideas in this book had taken shape before I ever investigated the literature of marketing. It was only when the need arose to give a lecture course on consumer behaviour, to economics students taking a marketing option, that I did so. When I first discovered the leading marketing texts which proposed theories of consumer behaviour, my first reaction was to think that there already existed a theory of choice that might form a foundation for BPK theory, and that I had perhaps been wasting my time. However, a close examination of the 'start of the art' text (Engel *et al.*, 1978) soon led to an alternative impression.

The 'theories' of choice in marketing are actually little more than flow diagram relationships between almost any of the variables that might conceivably be relevant to the process of choice. In the case of Engel *et al.*, which is not at all atypical, this indiscriminate approach results in the wedding together, as a huge metatheory framework, subtheories that are often at odds with each other in their underlying philosophies. Furthermore, when there is a dispute between rival subtheories, Engel *et al.* often leave unclear precisely which subtheories they are actually combining in their model: for example, it is never clear which theory fills their 'personality' box or precisely how it impinges on the rest of the choice process. This approach is avoided in *The Economic Imagination*: the interdisciplinary coverage is selective but throughout it is subjectivist in outlook, concentrating on questions of knowledge, complexity and uncertainty.

Marketing theorists, unlike conventional economists, have already heard of Kelly's theory of personality, but they do not use it as the basis for the components of their 'theories' that refer to motivation. The only part of Kelly's work they use is the 'repertory grid' questionnaire technique he deveoped (which is outlined in the works by his followers, Bannister and Mair (1968) and Bannister and Fransella 1971)). This is very helpful as a device for mapping the world views of people with broadly similar lifestyles. In Chapters 5 to 7 in the present work I make extensive use of Kelly's conception of what people are trying to do as they choose, and of their emotions, and thus take the economic application of Kelly's ideas much further than hitherto.

This book is both a challenge to and extension of various ideas used in marketing. Mainstream economists will therefore ask whether it is a contribution to economics at all. They will rightly point out that many of the policy implications drawn from the theory are of a kind that would usually be accorded the adjective 'marketing'. I would prefer these to be seen as 'applied economics'. The conventional tendency to push marketing research aside as a separate discipline seems, notwithstanding some of the often lax research tendencies of marketing practitioners, to be both undesirable and somewhat hypocritical. When economists discuss, for example, the problems of getting particular kinds of incomes policies accepted by workers, or trade policies accepted by foreign governments, they believe themselves to be talking about applied economics. But the issues they discuss are of precisely the kind discussed in marketing: how to *persuade* people to behave in a way different from that in which otherwise they might have behaved.

Underlying the attitudes of conventional economists to 'marketing' questions is probably a component of their world views which insists on the sovereignty of the individual chooser; for once sovereignty is rejected the neat equilibrium results and welfare conclusions that depend on the notion of 'given preferences' all begin to crumble away. It is not clear what Pareto optimality means if people's perceptions of their own well-being are to some extent malleable.

While it is inevitable that comparisons will be drawn between the present book and works on marketing, it is just as predictable that economists will point out that it is not the first book of recent years to attempt to incorporate within economics ideas from psychology. That honour goes to Scitovsky's (1977) work *The Joyless Economy*, which was critically acclaimed by some reviewers but which has yet to make much of an impact on the practices of economists. Scitovsky's analysis differs from the present work in two important respects. First, it is based on behaviourist psychology rather than personal construct theory. Scitovsky's consumers *respond* rather than *think* as they act. But a given form of overt behaviour may be underlain by a variety of thoughts. To discover these, observation may not be enough; it may be necessary to ask subjects questions. This is something that most behaviourists have been loathe to do. The second difference is that Scitovsky does not tell his readers very much about decision processes. He notes (1977, p. viii) that there are

two main types of human satisfaction, comfort and stimulation, [and these] are to some extent mutually exclusive. One can get more of both up to a point; but beyond that point, more of one can only be gotten at the sacrifice of the other.

But he does not take the analysis of how people make the choice between them much further than this, even though he does point out that people can only handle limited amounts of information at any moment.

Despite these important differences, I think it would be most unfortunate if the present book and *The Joyless Economy* were seen as wholly competitive rather than partly complementary. Scitovsky may have used an entirely different set of source materials from psychology but that has not stopped him from coming to see certain aspects of human behaviour in the same way as *The Economic Imagination*. This is particularly evident when he discusses novelty, culture, and the arts. At other times, particularly when attention is given to habits, personality traits and social aspects of behaviour, the two perspectives are more conspicuously different. The differences arise very largely because Scitovsky analyses personality differences mainly in physiological terms, whereas this book treats them as differences of world view. Whatever the differences between them, it is clear that the two works agree more with the psychologist's approach to choice than that of the conventional economist. Neither are content to take observed differences in behaviour as revelations of different preferences; both wish to look 'beneath the surface to find the causes and explanations of the differences' (Scitovsky, 1977, p. 28).

1.4 Methodology: A Dialogue

(*Introductory Note*: This section is an attempt to justify the somewhat unconventional methodology employed in this book. Ideally, it is a section which a reader should examine twice: once as numbered, and once as a postscript. This is because it is not easy to argue about the methodology that has been used without making some reference to the content. In this and subsequent dialogues, the views of 'The Proponent' are those of the author; the views of 'The Critic' are an attempt to encapsulate the likely reactions to this book of an orthodox, positivist, neoclassical economist with an outlook similar to that of Friedman (1953).)

THE CRITIC: Having read the rest of this book I find that I have two major objections to what you have done. The first concerns the type of theory you have constructed. The second concerns the absence of conventional econometric material to test your proposals. Perhaps we might discuss these objections in turn?

THE PROPONENT: By all means; fire away!

THE CRITIC: You have constructed a theory of words and graphs, drawing on material from a variety of disciplines, particularly from psychology. By the end of the book, I was far from certain what the final proposed theory consisted of, and certainly a simple and coherent new theory did not seem to emerge in the way that might have been expected. My overall impression is that it is complex and cumbersome, and not really an economic theory at all.

THE PROPONENT: I don't see it as being at all cumbersome. However, this is because I see it not as *a* theory but as what Lakatos (1970) calls a scientific research programme, i.e. a *set* of interconnected theories formulated from a common perspective. To compare my analysis with the orthodox Hicksian model of choice, as an alternative means of explaining the origins of the Law of Demand, you only require the 'characteristic filtering' decision model (sections 4.6 to 4.8), whose roots are firmly within the realm of economics. The psychologically-based theories of motivation and perception have to be incorporated, however, if we wish to begin to make practical use of the model in a predictive as well as a descriptive sense.

Neoclassical theorists, such as yourself, can only keep their models simple, avoiding elements from other disciplines, because they build them as means to relatively simple ends. Their models were never designed as tools for managers to use in making assessments of their markets. If we confine ourselves to situations where my basic choice model is commensurable with the orthodox one, I would contend that mine is the easier of the two to grasp. Priority systems, aspiration levels and potential surprise curves seem conceptually simple enough to me; there is no need in my model to make restrictive assumptions about divisibility to permit the use of calculus, or to presume that values of uncertain outcomes are added together.

I am rather unclear as to why you should wish to insist on compartmentalising everything into neat disciplinary boxes. It is only a *sinking* ship that needs watertight compartments! Are you afraid that if economics begins to incorporate elements from psychology it will rapidly become swamped by them and lose its own identity? I don't think that this should be a major worry. It is bounded rationality which keeps distinctive disciplines afloat. Otherwise economics would be reduced to psychology; psychology to biology; biology to chemistry; and chemistry to physics. But as science grows problems of information overload become more acute and scientists have to specialise. This means that, where there is scope for research on a disciplinary interface, a new subdiscipline tends to emerge rather than one discipline tending to overwhelm the other. Psychologists find it even harder to be generalists within their own discipline than do economists, so there is little reason to expect them to invade the traditional territory of the economist.

Although I incorporate material from psychology I do so in order to deal with economic issues. As I understand it, economics is concerned with choices about the allocation of scarce resources between competing ends, and economic policy with ways of avoiding socially undesirable allocations. If a failure to take account of how psychological matters impinge on choice leads to bad policy advice and misallocations of resources, then the exclusion of psychological content from economic theory can hardly be said to be furthering the ends of economic science. The incorporation of such material makes my behavioural analysis more complex than it would have to be were I only concerned to justify the Law of Demand, but does not make it unmanageable.

THE CRITIC: But your psychological material, for all its jargon, still seems to me to be rather imprecise. A lot of the time you speak of people having 'world views' which 'blinker' them and make them behave in particular ways. You claim that there exists a method of mapping a person's world view but I find it difficult to believe that one can really pin down such a fuzzy concept. And if you cannot measure it I can't really see how in fact you can actually use it in practice.

THE PROPONENT: It's really quite easy to map someone's way of looking at the world. The repertory grid system of analysis, to which I make frequent reference, is, it must be emphasised, a *technique* for constructing such maps; it is not a single set of questions for doing so. To start off a repertory grid investigation and discover the set of blinkers a person uses in the context in question, all we need do is to get our subject to compare and contrast several features related to our particular context. Since we're presently arguing about whether or not *The Economic Imagination* is a contribution to economics, it might be appropriate for us to consider how I might discover your own set of 'economic perspectives'. I would probably start by asking you to describe the likeness and differences you see between, say, this book, Debreu's (1959) *Theory of Value* and Kelly's (1955) *Psychology of Personal Constructs*. If you have only seen and not actually read Kelly's book, this does not matter. You might at least be able to say that, compared with the first two books, Kelly's work is: 'long' (since it runs to two volumes); 'lacking in mathematical notation'; 'older'; and 'heavier'. If you said that Kelly's book was 'about psychology, not economics', I could then ask you to compare and contrast these two disciplines as best you can. This would bring out other things and dimensions to interrelate. For example, you might talk about 'economics' and 'psychology' in terms of 'science/non-science'; 'what I do for a living'; and so on. But this process of bringing out dimensional blinkers will not go on interminably; sooner than you might expect, we will run out of new dimensions in terms of which you make comparisons. For example, when you compare 'science' with 'non-science' you might do it in terms of the 'mathematical' dimension or 'what I do for a living', which you have used in previous answers.

The data obtained by this technique can be arranged as a matrix —the 'things' which have been compared and contrasted on one axis and the dimensions used to describe them on the other. We fill in each box on the matrix with our data in a binary manner. For example, if Debreu's book is characterised as 'light' and this book and the two volumes of Kelly are characterised as 'heavy', I mark a numeral '1' in the Debreu: light/heavy box, and '0' in the *Economic Imagination*: light/heavy and Kelly: light/heavy boxes; and so on. Factor analysis can then be used to check the extent to which, when *you* are using them, the dimensions really are separate or are simply a few dimensions masquerading under different names. It could be the case, for example, that good/bad; scientific/non-scientific; and mathematical/worded all reduce to the same thing.

The matrix also enables one to see which things you view as similar and the number of dimensions you can use for describing differences between things. Your answers might have revealed that you can see complex differences between various 'economics' books, but not between books on 'psychology', because you have not yet read them or even more general books related to them. When you encounter economics books you may attempt to 'see' whether their authors are 'behavioural or neoclassical theorists', but when faced with psychology books you may find this dimension utterly irrelevant and lack an alternative one such as 'cognitive/developmental'. Without an intensive study of the literature of psychology, your repertoire of tools for thought would be too restrictive for you to 'see' very much at all in psychological works. If you are confronted with them you will not see the same things as a trained psychologist, but, then again, she would only be able poorly to discriminate between different contributions to economics.

This, then, is how one can pin down fairly precisely a person's world view. Having discovered the dimensions in terms of which a person views the world, one can work out how she will be disposed to see particular things, how she will behave when confronted with them. For example, if I discover that you see yourself as both a scientist and as an economist, and if the factor analysis reveals that you see 'science' as synonymous with 'formal model-building and testing', I predict that you will not be able to see as an economic scientist someone who comes along and attempts (as I have attempted) to show that henceforth it is important that 'economics' should involve the use of non-mathematical ideas from subjectivist psychology. By challenging your view of economics in this way, that person will by implication, be challenging your view of yourself as a scientist unless you can begin to separate 'science' and 'formal model-building and testing' into genuinely independent constructs. You, in turn, will then attempt to challenge that person's claim to be contributing to economics.

THE CRITIC: But if this technique exists for mapping world views and making predictions of behaviour, why have you made no effort whatsoever to test your theory? You seem to be quite prepared to accept the validity of your theory on the basis of claims, themselves theory-laden, that your assumptions are more realistic, in some sense, than those normally made in theories of choice. But it is never enough to judge theories in this way, for we are always dealing with partial models that are incomplete representations of reality. I see that frequently you say that *if* such-and-such is the manner in which a person processes information or sees a particular situation, then she will be likely to behave in a particular way. But there are many different ways a person *might* use to reach a decision, and many ways she *might* see any particular situation, as you say yourself. So, when I see the situation in question, I may be able to use your theory to present all manner of rationalisations of what is observed to happen next. How can I know that any particular one of them is more likely to be correct than any other of the infinite variety of hypotheses I might construct? Unless we test narrowly-specified hypotheses, we can never know whether a model based on allegedly 'realistic' assumptions is telling us no more than the fact that there seem to be quite a few cases which can be interpreted in the light of this model (see further Popper (1962), pp. 34–7, and Friedman (1953), p. 7).

My charge, then, is that until your work has been subjected to attempts at falsification and has emerged as something which is not obviously incorrect, it can at best be seen merely as an interesting and provocative act of *storytelling* (cf. Ward (1972), Chapter 12). You have bound together, in a coherent narrative, carefully selected facts, supportive documentary evidence, value judgments, high-level theories and low-level generalisations. But that is all. You leave it up to the reader to decide for herself how convincing she finds your stories. *She* is the one who seems obliged to go away and seek out possible counter examples and omitted facts, or simply to perform the sort of empirical investigation which is conspicuous by its absence from this book.

THE PROPONENT: My point in emphasising the case for assumptive plausibility in this area of inquiry is to make people hesitate and consider whether or not they have in the past been getting seemingly 'right' answers for 'wrong' reasons, and whether or not their existing models could be blinding them to certain important issues. It is not my intention to suggest that assumptive plausibility is the *only* ground on which theories can, or should, be accepted or rejected. Nor is it my intention to use *a priorism* to justify my failure to include the sort of empirical work you seem to have in mind. If, at a later date, someone did attempt to test my propositions and found evidence which contradicted them, I would bear this in mind when reappraising my theory. But I cannot guarantee that such evidence would make me reject it. No matter how 'good' present empirical results may be, they too can only provide an incomplete case for using a particular theory instead of a rival. One can never test theories with regard to future events, with absolute certainty that other things have been held equal, or without taking for granted the adequacy of many other theories. Neither predictive realism nor assumptive realism can logically provide a wholly satisfactory case in favour of a particular theory. At the end of the day, one must have faith in the ability of a theory to serve the ends for which it was designed. One chooses a theory according to some personal criteria and should then use it with caution.

My faith in my own analysis comes in great measure from an examination of the plausibility of my assumptions. It is also bolstered by a number of past studies which appear to support my priorities-based view of choice, but which appear to contradict conventional compensatory models of decision making. Certainly, I could have included empirical work in this book instead of leaving it to others to test my ideas at a later date. But in order to keep the book within its length requirement I would have had either to compress the arguments and risk confusion, or to narrow the scope of my analysis and sacrifice valuable chances for the integration of hitherto unrelated contributions.

THE CRITIC: You might also admit that such empirical work would have involved you in another two years of research and forced you to learn new quantitative techniques.

THE PROPONENT: Yes, I won't deny that. Furthermore, I would have been open to the prospect of hostile neoclassical theorists objecting to any inconvenient findings with comments to the effect that my questionnaire based data were biased and open to a variety of interpretations. I would thus have been driven back to emphasising the plausibility of my analysis as a ground for faith.

Your objections to my failure to provide an empirical investigation of my new analysis neatly skirt the way you continue to use Hicksian consumer theory despite the fact that, as Simon (1979, p. 507) has observed, 'Evidence that consumers actually distribute their purchases in such a way as to maximise their utilities, and hence to equate marginal utilities, is non-existent' (cf. also Katouzian (1980), pp. 59–69). Your insistence on confining yourself to the axioms of the conventional theory means that you fail to generate specific hypotheses to test. As a result, your econometric work on consumer behaviour is concerned largely with *estimating* demand relationships, not with testing your descriptive theory (cf. Brown and Deaton (1972), pp. 1150–2). We are both guilty of failing to test our theories but, if anything, it is I who deserves the shortest sentence since I have produced a theory which provides concrete policy suggestions and which *can* be tested. I have not merely said that firms may increase their sales if they lower their prices; I have also used my analysis to derive specific recommendations, concerning policies of product design and marketing, which are likely to lead to business success (see especially sections 4.8, 6.2, 6.4 and 7.3). If firms use them in advance of systematic empirical investigations, their proof of my pudding will be in the eating.

If you cannot dispute the logic of my arguments about the role of faith in the decision to use any theory as a device for coping with our world of partial knowledge, you cannot dismiss my analysis as 'mere storytelling' and prove that it is not a meaningful contribution to 'economic science'. As Feyerabend (1975, pp. 197, 297) has argued, 'science' is much more 'sloppy' and 'irrational' than most of its practitioners care to admit. There is no clear-cut means we can use to decide where to draw the line between scientific contributions, stories or even myths. I can never know for certain whether or not my analysis is going to lead me to make disastrous policy recommendations or whether my analysis has been the cause of particular disasters of prediction. The only thing which is obvious is that I have been able to use it to make claims about things, which I could not have made if I only had the orthodox theory at my disposal. If you don't like my analysis you are not obliged to use it, but neither should I be obliged to use your theory.

THE CRITIC: You seem to be saying that anything should be allowed to masquerade as science if it has something to say about the possible reasons for a particular observation. Such a view of methodology amounts to replacing the philosophy of science by the philosophy of flower power.

THE PROPONENT: That is precisely what Blaug (1980, p. 44) said about Feyerabend's book. The only alternative he could offer (1980, p. 45) was to refer to the *ideals* of science. Certainly, if we look for alternative explanations and question ourselves continually, we may be less likely to end up proposing unhelpful policies. If that is science, then this book, for all its lack of mathematical precision and empirical work, is a scientific work, and a contribution to knowledge. But the extent of its contribution can never be other than a subjective impression.

2 Pricing Choices

2.1 Introduction

Behavioural/Post Keynesian (BPK) and neoclassical economists
may both be expected to be surprised to find that we are going to
discuss price formation before we investigate the choice processes of
individuals. But they will be surprised for different reasons: the
former because pricing decisions are often complex and involve
controversy at high levels within firms; the latter because they see
prices as being determined by the simultaneous interaction of the
forces of demand and supply, a view of price formation which seems
to require a prior statement of how individuals decide how much they
would be prepared to buy were particular commodities offered to
them at particular market prices. We have chosen to discuss price
formation first in order to demonstrate that there is a need for a
reorientation of economists' work on the theory of individual choice.
The new orientation that we suggest is likely to be controversial, but
those readers who find it acceptable should then find the theory of
choice that we propose in later chapters easier to judge, because they
will have a context in which to set it.

The case that we wish to make for a reorientation of work on the
theory of choice is outlined in the concluding part of this chapter,
section 2.9. It follows on naturally from the BPK analysis of pricing
and market entry decisions that is presented in sections 2.2 to 2.8.
This analysis is highly critical of mainstream supply and demand
theory, both at the macro/industry level, and at the level of the firm.
In section 2.2 we use the work of Sraffa and Pasinetti to discuss
macro/industrial price formation, without reference to the theory of
the firm. Their work suggests that economists trying to model growth
and structural change in a fairly aggregated way can get along
perfectly well without reference to ideas of 'substitution effects' in
response to interindustry relative price changes: at this level income
effects and priority patterns dominate. Then, in section 2.3, there is
an examination of Richardson's critique of supply and demand
theory, which emphasises that a firm cannot form conjectures about

its likely costs or sales, at *any* price it might plan to charge, unless it can predict the investment behaviour of other firms. This leads us directly to an introduction to the related work of Andrews, in section 2.4. Andrews' critique of marginalist theories of the firm is outlined in section 2.5 and his theory of industrial pricing in section 2.6. Section 2.7 is concerned with retail pricing, while section 2.8 is a dialogue, the purpose of which is to show how the normal cost analysis of price formation works in markets where technical progress or restyling continually disrupts established patterns of sales.

2.2 Sraffa and Pasinetti on 'Natural Prices'

Prior to the marginalist revolution in economic theory economists argued that, in the long run, relative prices of commodities were determined by technological factors, given a distribution of income between workers and capitalists. Prices were seen as indices, in effect, of the relative efforts that society was obliged to put into producing individual units of the various commodities. As the scale of production changed between sectors, economies of bulk production would appear and, with the added advantage of learning by doing as cumulative production increased, the relative efforts required to produce certain commodities would fall, along with their relative prices. Expansions in output over the long run were associated with falling prices. The factors felt responsible for determining changes in the structure of output were the class distribution of a given level of national income and the rate of change of national income (cf. 'Engel's Law' of 1857 which states that the proportion of income spent on food declines as income increases).

All this changed with the marginalist revolution of the 1870s. Economists came to see prices as if they were indices of relative scarcity with regard to consumer preferences. Expansions of output in a particular sector came to be associated with rises in relative prices for the sector's output. These were felt to be necessary in order to call forth the extra production. The focus of investigations into the causes of relative price changes became the notion of consumer substitution, in place of distributional and income considerations.

The work of Sraffa (1960) and Pasinetti (1981) is characterised by a return to pre-marginalist modes of analysis and arrives at conclusions which are very damaging for the marginalist way of thought. Sraffa concentrates on a system with a static structure of production, which is able to reproduce itself and generate a surplus that can be used either for luxury consumption or expanding the means of production. Pasinetti examines an expanding system which is undergoing structural change. Sraffa's economy could be thought of as representing a snapshot of the structure underlying Pasinetti's system at any moment. Their different systems they analyse in different ways, Sraffa using a set of simultaneous, input output equations, while Pasinetti looks at vertically integrated industries with the aid of matrix notation. However, this does not prevent them from offering us similar kinds of implications as regards the necessity of marginal analysis.

Let us examine Sraffa's approach first. He considers a system where the pattern of output and technological conditions (quantities and capabilities of machines and workers) are given, a system which has an exogenously given rate of profit which competition has caused to be uniform between sectors. In the Sraffa system commodities may be used to produce further commodities, directly or indirectly (e.g. steel is used to build new steelmills; steel is used to make wage goods required to preserve the labour force, either in number or willingness to work). The system can be represented simply as a series of simultaneous equations like the ones below (which exclude, for simplicity, examples of joint products):

$$(A_a p_a + B_a p_b + \ldots + K_a p_k)(1 + r) + L_a w = A p_a$$

$$(A_b p_a + B_p p_b + \ldots + K_b p_k)(1 + r) + L_b w = B p_b$$

$$- -$$

$$(A_k p_a + B_k p_b + \ldots + K_k p_k)(1 + r) + L_k w = K p_k$$

in which:

(i) A_a = the amount of commodity 'a' used up annually in 'A', the total production of commodity 'a'.

(ii) A_b = the amount of commodity 'a' used up annually in the production of 'B', the total production of commodity 'b'.

(iii) B_a = the amount of commodity 'b' used up annually in the production of 'A'.

(iv) p_a = the unit value (price) of commodity 'a'; and so on.

(v)   Since the system at least reproduces itself, $A_a + A_b \ldots + A_k \leq A; B_a + B_b + \ldots + B_k \leq B; K_a + K_b + \ldots + K_k \leq K$.

(vi) r = the rate of profit, which is uniform across sectors $a, b \ldots k$.

(vii)   The system produces k commodities.

(viii) L_a is the fraction of the total annual labour contribution used in the production of A. The sum of all such fractions from $L_a, L_b \ldots L_k$ is equal to unity.

(ix) w = the unit value of labour, with workers assumed to be identical.

(x)   Since we know the rate of profit by assumption, this system of k independent equations determines the $k-1$ relative commodity prices and the wage rate.

Now, it is possible to view such a system in several different ways. One is simply to see it as a set of national income interrelationships for an economy in long run equilibrium, which brings the concept of 'value added' out into the open. A second is to see it as a way of showing up a flaw in the neoclassical theory of aggregate income distribution: if r (or, alternatively, w) is not already known, there are k equations and $k + 1$ variables; thus an equation for r appears necessary too. But such an equation as neoclassical theorists would suggest, namely that the rate of profit is determined by the marginal productivity of capital, cannot be constructed except on the basis of a circular argument. To know the marginal productivity of capital it is necessary to know how much capital there is in total. With heterogeneous capital such a total must be expressed in value terms, yet the prices of capital goods, like any others in the system, are not independent of the rate of profit and are not necessarily related to it in a well-behaved way (cf. Harcourt (1972)).

It is a third perspective on Sraffa's equations which is most relevant for present purposes. So long as we have a given pattern of outputs and inputs, as we will do in equilibrium, and we know r or w, the system enables prices to be determined without any reference to demand and marginal revenue ideas, or to any assumptions about returns of scale (scale effects are irrelevant if outputs are given). If competition works to equalise profit rates in all sectors, as neoclassical theorists always assume it does, prices are determined entirely by technological considerations and the given profit rate. If the system is in equilibrium no one has made any mistakes or wishes to expand production in another sector, so Sraffa's 'natural' prices are equal to average costs of production.

It should be emphasised that Sraffa has not provided a theory of how firms come to choose such prices, for it is not his purpose to construct a new theory of the individual business. Nor does his equilibrium system guarantee that, as firms leave and enter markets to compete away quasi-rents, an equilibrium will be approached which will then exhibit convenient stability properties, for he is not attempting to say that the world necessarily has equilibrium tendencies. What he has done is to construct a special kind of general equilibrium structure which his readers can use to show that, if one *must* play the static equilibrium game, it is possible to study price formation from the cost side alone and without reference to demand functions, the principle of substitution, marginal conditions, or concepts of returns to scale with respect to given production functions. If we know what outputs and the conditions of production are, and if we have a conventionally given profit rate/target rate of return, we can say what equilibrium prices are without reference to any microeconomic theory of price. The rate of return which investment schemes are required to meet may be related to the opportunity cost of finance foregone from speculative uses in money markets, where a 'normal' rate of interest prevails so long as expectations are not subject to severe shocks (cf. Sraffa (1960) p. 33). Alternatively, it may be dependent on the opportunity cost of other physical investment projects if shortages of managerial expertise, rather than finance, are the constraint (see Andrews and Brunner (1952), Chapter 10; Penrose (1959) and Richardson and Leyland (1964)).

In Pasinetti's multisector model of a growing economy, long run, 'natural' prices are cost-determined, as in Sraffa's system. Unlike Sraffa, however, he has to mention consumer preferences since he is attempting to explain how prices and quantities change through time. Central to Pasinetti's view of structural change is his argument that the substitution effects of relative price changes at the industry level are trivial compared with income effects. He suggests that consumer preferences only affect directly the quantities that get sold, not prices. Preferences affect prices *indirectly* through their effects on costs, which arise *subsequently* to the quantity effects. He has in mind the disequilibrium chain shown in Figure 2.1. This chain of self-perpetuating disturbances is a modern version of Adam Smith's original theory of the interaction between the division of labour and

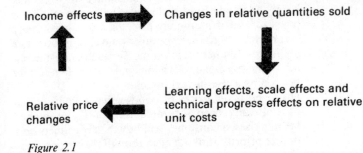

Figure 2.1

economic growth, which BPK theorists have for long been trying to persuade neoclassical economists to take seriously (see Young (1928), Wu (1946), Kaldor (1972), and Richardson (1975)). Unfortunately, this is precisely the sort of diseqilibrium process which drove Hicks (1939, pp. 83–5), and theorists who have followed his general equilibrium lead, to confine their attention to perfectly competitive economic systems in which it is possible to guarantee the existence of stable states of rest.

The chain of events shown in Figure 2.1 only unfolds in historical time. Hence, in order to understand the determination of natural prices at any moment, it is necessary to take quantities as given. Either this, or an historical analysis, utterly alien to the equilibrium methodology of orthodox economists, must be employed.

Pasinetti's (1981, Chapter IV) case against the neoclassical view of the importance of substitution effects to the theory of industrial prices is based on an analysis of consumer behaviour which is in many ways an embryonic version of the theory proposed in the present book. But it must be emphasised that the unimportance of substitution effects between industries does not mean that firms *within* oligopolistic industries can neglect them. At the level of the firm, as is shown below in the discussions of Andrews' work, the BPK critique of the role of demand functions in price determination works rather differently. Pasinetti's industry level critique comprises the following elements:

(i)   Econometric observations of Engel curves can be argued to imply that the absolute levels of utility (a word which Pasinetti uses simply as a shorthand) do not depend on all the consumption which has taken place so far, but on the order in which goods are consumed. That is to say, consumers have a priority ranking in their wants, and although certain wants may become saturated very rapidly they must at least be saturated before the consumer will move on to choose other commodities. A consumer who only has barely adequate food and shelter will not purchase a television set if its money price falls and her money income has not risen, since this would compromise her ability to meet her basic wants. For such a consumer a fall in the price of a television could not meaningfully be seen as a rise in real income.

(ii)   However, if the prices of goods serving wants which have already been saturated fall, or if her money income rises, a consumer will buy those products next on her priority ranking even though their prices may not have fallen. She will not buy larger quantities of the goods that only serve saturated wants. In a growing and technically progressive economy real incomes will be continually rising in this second, relevant, way. Hence price reductions on goods serving lower priority wants for people who otherwise could not afford them, or who have not yet saturated their needs, will only cause an expansion of the sales of these goods which, sooner or later, would have occurred *anyway*. Therefore, over the long run, for which meaningful econometric samples can be gathered to predict changes in industrial structures, real income is the crucial variable, not the price structure. This is so even though not all consumers will be at the same stage in satisfying their wants.

(iii)   In affluent societies consumers will continually be finding that they are able to satisfy extra wants for which they do not feel themselves to possess well-defined preferences of a neoclassical kind. Choice in new situations is more a process of learning than of rationality. In the process of exploring new activities to educate themselves about their characteristics, the best initial strategy for consumers may be to imitate other consumers who are in the immediately higher income bands. Choices will thus be guided not by price but by the choices of others, while new choices become possible due to the expansion of real incomes.

With his discussions concerning priority patterns for wants, emphasis on the social context in which consumption takes place, and plea for economists to recognise that uncertainty and the prospect of learning cause consumer choices to become complexly motivated, Pasinetti points more clearly than most of his fellow critics of neoclassical economics to the direction in which he believes BPK choice theory should proceed. But he does not develop things any further. We follow his implied pathways in subsequent chapters.

2.3 Richardson's Critique of Supply and Demand Theory

Whereas Sraffa and Pasinetti's theoretical contributions have become part of the core of the Post Keynesian research programme, George Richardson's (1956, 1959, 1960) critique of neoclassical economics, and of the orthodox competition policies derived from it, is known and used only by a tiny group of BPKEs. Richardson was concerned with the informational requirements for the coordination of economic activities in the real world, where futures markets do not exist for most commodities. He demonstrated that the informational and institutional arrangements necessary for the attainment of economic equilibrium were incompatible with the neoclassical view of atomistic competition.

Richardson wanted to know how firms worked out whether or not it was worth investing in particular markets, and he found that orthodox supply and demand theorists offered the following, simple, story. A firm considering entry into a perfectly competitive market observes the current price and examines its opportunity costs. If an adequate margin exists between price and cost the firm will enter the market. It does not need to know anything about consumer demand, so long as preferences are not changing, since, being a perfectly competitive producer, its effect on the total supply, and hence on price, will be trivial. It does not need to know about the investment intentions of producers of intermediate inputs, or supply conditions for skilled workers, since, being a tiny producer, its input purchase decisions will not make much impact on the prices of inputs. (It is worth noting at this point that orthodox theory often conflates the analysis by treating each firm as fully vertically integrated, thus reducing the apparent significance of the question of coordination still further.)

This vision of the decision puzzle confronting the firm, and how it gets solved, only makes sense if all other firms are absolutely fixed in their activities. To remove this implausibly strong *ceteris paribus* assumption, and allow other firms to be making investment plans too, is to create a recipe for complete chaos. If there is free entry and markets are not institutionalised—i.e. if markets are impersonal and unorganised, with no regular trading relationships existing between particular buyers and sellers—firms can have no means of knowing what their marginal cost and revenue functions are going to be. In the absence of collusion, futures markets, or the mythical Walrasian auctioneer, firms have no basis for expectation-formation and investment decisions, even if consumer preferences are known and stable.

Having spotted a niche in the market—an area in which customer requirements are being catered for imperfectly—a firm cannot immediately conclude that it should make an investment commitment in this area. The amount of the product which it will be possible to sell at a given price in the future depends on the (as yet unknown) prices at which other firms will be offering substitute goods. Similarly, the prices it will be necessary to pay to obtain inputs in the desired quantities will depend on whether or not other firms bother to create enough capacity despite not knowing the scale of demand for *their* products. Thus, before it can take a sensible decision, a firm needs to have some idea of the likely volume of competitive and complementary investment that *other* firms will undertake.

Once the need for firms to be concerned with the investment activities of other firms is recognised, it becomes necessary to reject the analytical separation of supply and demand functions which is so central to neoclassical economics. The upshot of Richardson's analysis of the investment problem is that, even if consumer preferences are given and known, and are of a neoclassical kind, firms cannot act as if given demand functions exist for individual products unless they know which *supply* decisions are being taken by other firms.

The 'cobweb' cycle of price and output instability, which is often observed in agricultural markets, is an example of what happens in situations where firms have to act without much idea of the investment plans of others. If there is free entry to a market in which a margin presently exists between prices and costs, the entry of all able firms will cause a glut and losses. No one would enjoy the profits by whose potential they had been attracted. However, if all able firms are afraid to enter such a market, the profit opportunity will stay unrealised. Agricultural markets are particularly prone to suffer from inappropriate supply decisions because the nature of the growing season is such that everyone has to make their investment (i.e. planting) decisions at the same time. But, in the absence of collusion, capacity growth is far from guaranteed to be 'just right' even in markets, such as those for chemicals, which are dominated by a relatively small number of large firms undertaking *conspicuous* investment schemes at different times (see Beck (1972) on coordination failures in the world chemicals industry). Large industrial complexes take a long while to become conspicuous and substantial capacity additions may be commissioned before others, commissioned earlier, begin to be constructed.

Given that a free market economy suffers from this coordination problem—which deserves to be known as 'the Richardson Problem' —there is perhaps cause for surprise that matters are not more chaotic than is actually the case. Richardson argued that coordination failures are attenuated because the world is full of market 'imperfections' that help to produce coherence. Exchanges of information between firms and their suppliers, and the fact that firms will continue to use the same suppliers so long as price and delivery conditions are competitive, give the latter confidence to invest so long as they feel that they cannot be undercut by anyone else. If firms have an incomplete knowledge of market niches, or of production processes in other firms, entry will be limited. A pattern of experience will be generated in which firms already in a market observe that usually they are only doing battle with a select band of competitors, whose performance and likely investment potential they can monitor. The smaller the number of firms involved, the more scope there may be for forming conjectures and making appropriate investment decisions.

To the extent that these departures from the neoclassical vision of impersonal, atomistic, competition fail to guarantee adequate *ex ante* coordination, the problem must be solved *ex post*. Marketing activities may have a socially useful role to play in this context, insofar as they help to mould the pattern of spending into conformity with presently existing productive potential (cf. also section 3.7).

Richardson's analysis of market coordination throws into doubt the conventional view of firms investing so as to fill in, *ex ante*, given gaps in demand while constrained by given supply conditions. But it needs to be considered whether his view of imperfections and the institutional aspects of trading opens the door to a reconstituted form of supply and demand analysis that could be used to explain how prices are determined and investment decisions are reached. In the next five sections we will use Andrews' alternative critique of neoclassical theory to show why such a reconstituted supply and demand theory is likely to be inappropriate; and we will use ideas from Andrews' own constructive analysis to provide an explanation of how firms will come to choose prices that correspond broadly to the long run prices of the Sraffa and Pasinetti systems. The analysis which will be proposed will also help explain why we may frequently observe a relatively small number of actual competitors in an area of production despite the potential for entry by a much larger group which seems to be implied by the presence of two modern imperfection-reducing features, namely, the management consultant and the conglomerate corporation.

However, before we move on to consider Andrews' contribution to BPK theory, a word needs to be said about the contribution to price theory made by Alfred Marshall (1920). Without it, there is scope for confusion, since Sraffa's work has often been used to attack Marshall's ideas, whereas Richardson and Andrews both are writers who admit strong Marshallian influences (cf. Andrews, 1951). Marshall had something of a split personality as an economist. In attempting to embrace formal analysis, he discussed pricing within a comparative statics, supply and demand equilibrium framework. In attempting to write down in words a theory of the processes he could see at work in the real world, he outlined a *dis*equilibrium, cost of production, theory of pricing that was more in the classical tradition so beloved by Sraffa and Pasinetti. Richardson and Andrews both emphasise Marshall's disequilibrium theory, the neglect of which has been highlighted in work by Loasby (1978), Clarke (1980) and Levine (1980). Post Keynesians, by contrast, have normally attacked the equilibrium strands in Marshall's work in the course of criticising neoclassical supply and demand theory, rarely mentioning his disequilibrium analysis. Clearly, Richardson, Andrews, Sraffa, and Pasinetti are all on the same side, at least in the sense that they all reject static supply and demand theories.

2.4 Andrews' Theory of Competitive Oligopoly: Introduction

Like Pasinetti and Sraffa, Andrews proposes a theory of price formation in which prices are determined by costs, with no direct role being played by 'demand functions' of the conventional kind. However, whereas Pasinetti argues that substitution is not important in the determination of relative prices and quantities, Andrews' analysis is heavily dependent on firms being exceedingly aware of the prospect of consumers switching from buying their output to purchasing similar products from other firms who quote cheaper prices. This does not mean that Andrews and Pasinetti are proposing incompatible theories, since the latter is concerned with the determination of typical prices at the industry level, while the former is providing a theory of how individual firms decide at which prices they might best sell their products given the industrial context in which they operate. Within any industry, competition is seen by Andrews to be a very powerful force, even if there are only a few producers actually selling at any one time. Monopolistic, protected markets, where a producer's sales or earnings are independent of the investment activities or availabilities of rivals, are really very rare—even amongst public utilities. Railway routes compete with road and air transport; electricity competes with gas and oil; Samuelson's introductory economics text competes with Lipsey's; opera superstar Pavarotti competes with Domingo; and so on. In all but the short run, all markets should be seen as oligopolistic, since, to obtain satisfactory long run returns, suppliers must at all times keep the likely responses of their rivals in mind. Etymology aside, the essence of oligopoly is structural interdependence, and in Andrews' vision of modern capitalism, as in Richardson's, such interdependence is all-pervading.

Despite the fact that Andrews was one of the first post war theorists to attempt to write a theory of competitive oligopoly (Andrews, 1949a, 1949b) and criticise marginalist theory from a disequilibrium perspective (Andrews, 1951, 1964), his work is nowadays only slightly better known than that of Richardson. This is unfortunate, since his arguments are complex and difficult to reproduce in a short space. Readers are therefore urged to consult the original works and rely not merely on a reading of the compressed analysis we offer below: the rest of this chapter should be seen only as a personal interpretation and guide to the main elements of Andrews' thinking. Our exposition includes a somewhat different treatment of cost curves from that found in Andrews' own work, which we believe helps to make clear the relationship between prices, the mark-up and the investment decision. We also offer a discussion of pricing policies in markets for 'fashion goods' (by which we mean any product whose design is prone to change every few months or years) which develops, in the light of his theory, an area rather thinly discussed in Andrews' work.

Andrews developed his theory of the firm in response to deficiencies he came to perceive in the theories of imperfect competition which appeared in the 1930s. For this reason it seems as well, before proceeding to discuss his critique of such theories, to remind ourselves of the bare bones of the original contribution, made in 1933 by Joan Robinson.

At the time *The Economics of Imperfect Competition* appeared, many economists did not spot the deliberate irony in the use of the adjective 'imperfect'. In the introduction to the (1969) edition of the book, Joan Robinson explains that her intention was to show that, if one attempted to construct a logically coherent marginalist theory of the firm, conclusions at odds with the neoclassical world view would emerge. Her analysis suggested that, in contrast to conclusions of the theory of perfect competition, workers are not paid the value of their marginal products and consumers are not sovereign. The free working of market forces results in an economic structure in which unsatisfied wants and excess capacity may coexist.

The need for a new approach to the theory of the firm had been highlighted in 1926 by Sraffa, who demonstrated that the analysis offered in the theory of perfect competition was logically flawed. A horizontal demand curve at the level of the firm would provide no limit to the size of a firm enjoying continuously declining average costs. Constant returns to scale would leave firm sizes undetermined. In this situation, decreasing returns to scale are essential for imposing a determinate size on firms, but there is no inherent reason in engineering why a doubling of all factors should lead to less than a doubling of output. Furthermore, perfectly competitive firms, by assumption, cannot bid up factor prices against themselves by demanding more in factor markets. Sraffa suggested that what stops the unlimited growth of a firm is not a rising cost curve but a falling demand curve.

A perfectly competitive producer can sell as much as it wants without affecting the price of its product because its rising cost curves ensure that it never wishes to produce more than a trivial share of the market output. However, a large firm with falling cost curves that wants to expand its sales cannot do so unless it lowers the price of its output. Its extra sales will come partly at the expense of other firms and partly because a lower industry price for the type of products it is making will encourage more people to buy the industry's outputs. If firms' demand curves are downward sloping so, too, are their

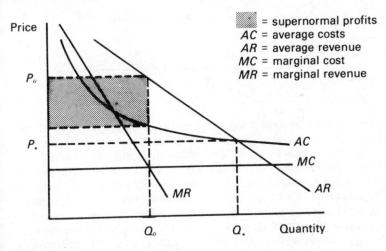

Figure 2.2

marginal revenue curves. Beyond a certain point, extra sales result in negative marginal revenues. But before this point is reached marginal revenues will begin to fall below marginal costs. In such a situation, attempts to expand sales reduce the profits a firm makes, so it will not be in its own interests to try to drive other firms out of the market. It was this restrained type of competition that Joan Robinson set out to formalise in her book, using conventional, marginalist equilibrium tools.

Although *The Economics of Imperfect Competition* is a long and detailed work, the 'theory' it outlines is compressed in textbooks into a terse, two diagram caricature, which we reproduce here as Figures 2.2 and 2.3. Figure 2.2 shows the short run equilibrium of the firm (P_o, Q_o). If there are barriers to the entry of new producers this is also the long run position of the firm. Here supernormal profits are

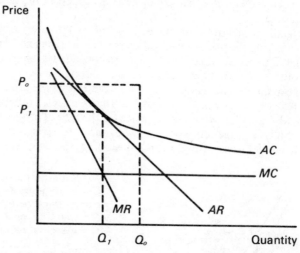

Figure 2.3

possible since average costs are less than average revenue at the output level (Q_o) where marginal cost equals marginal revenue.

Figure 2.3 shows what is often called the 'tangency solution', the long run equilibrium of the firm after other firms have entered the market in response to the lure of the supernormal profits it earns in the short run. In long run equilibrium no one wishes to enter or leave the market: somehow the Richardson Problem has been overcome. The extra production of the new entrants causes prices in the industry to fall. Individual firm demand curves shift to the left until average costs and average revenue are equal and there is no longer an incentive to enter the market. At the output where the average cost and revenue curves are tangential (Q_1), the new marginal revenue curve for the firm cuts its marginal cost curve and its profits are maximised subject to the constraint imposed by the new market conditions.

The welfare implications of this use of equilibrium analysis are, as Joan Robinson set out to show, rather disturbing. In the theory of imperfect competition, capitalism not only fails to pay workers their marginal value products, it also works against the interests of consumers. Figure 2.2 shows that firms do not give consumers the low prices that economies of scale make possible. Instead they extract supernormal profits by restricting output and raising prices above the level sufficient to permit viability. Figure 2.3 shows that consumers still lose out if such profits are eventually removed by new entry: firms then produce with spare capacity, as an excess of firms in the industry causes resources to be wasted. If prices were set in the first place so that average costs and revenues were equal (as at (P_*, Q_*) in Figure 2.2), neither the supernormal profits of the short run nor the waste of resources in the idle capacity of the long run would occur. However, according to the theory, the profit-seeking tendencies of firms prevent this from happening.

This aspect of the welfare content of the theory, if not Joan Robinson's remarks about wages and marginal value products, has had a significant influence on competition policy in many countries. Even where several 'imperfectly competitive' firms already dominate an industry, the theory suggests that, if barriers to further entry exist, action is likely to be necessary to prevent overcharging and the restriction of output by existing firms. If there is easy entry it seems better to tax employment in the industry to discourage a wasteful use of resources in excess capacity, while simultaneously removing any short run supernormal profits. (Such was the thinking behind the Selective Employment Tax introduced by the Wilson government in the UK in 1966, at which time it was felt desirable to shift resources from the service sector to manufacturing.)

If the notion of the downward sloping demand curve is rejected at the level of the individual firm, orthodox competition policies become highly questionable. Andrews rejected such demand curves and, in consequence of this, spent much of his time as an applied economist using his alternative view of the competitive process as a basis for defending companies charged under conventional monopolies legislation (cf. Andrews and Brunner (1975), Chapters 4 and 5). Like Andrews, we are wary of aspects of competition policy founded on the notion that firms face downward sloping demand curves and thus enjoy considerable discretion in the prices they can charge. But this does not mean we believe that modern capitalism cannot threaten consumer sovereignty. Everything in the garden is not quite as rosy as Andrews sometimes suggests, but it is important that we identify the right things as weeds and are not lured, by an inappropriate view of the competitive process, into making the wrong policy recommendations.

2.5 Andrews' Critique of Theories of Imperfect Competition

The distinctive view of the competitive process that characterises Andrews' writings is one that he evolved after carrying out lengthy case study investigations of the behaviour of firms in, particularly, the UK textile and footwear industries. These studies were never published by Andrews and he was criticised for his failure to do so by reviewers of his main book, *Manufacturing Business*. Case study work is impossible without the goodwill of managers and it may well be that Andrews realised that it would have been rather tactless to reveal how the firms he had been allowed to investigate operated, for at this time (the late 1940s) Labour politicians were thinking about nationalising these industries. However, if we are prepared to take his claims about the broad behaviour of firms on trust, or are swayed by the commonsense logic that lies behind the justifications that managers gave for their practices, we can see that the conventional marginalist view of price formation, embodied in the theory of imperfect competition, may be grossly misleading. There are several reasons for this:

(a)   The short run pricing behaviour which leads to the (P_o, Q_o) result on Figure 2.2 is only plausible in cases where firms are very short sighted or new entry difficult. Managers repeatedly told Andrews that it was not worth raising prices to increase short run profits because, if they did so, other firms with a capacity to produce duplicate products would soon start to undercut them. The 'long run' is not a long time coming if suitable capacity already exists in other firms and, even if it does not, it is foolish not to recognise that the gestation period of new plant is only a fraction of the time that capital equipment may be expected to last, except in circumstances where technical progress is exceedingly rapid. A 'snatcher' type of policy of the kind shown in Figure 2.2 can only make sense to the owner of a company who intends to sell it in the near future to someone who does not realise that its current profits are being achieved at the expense of its long run position.

(b)   Andrews found that firms did not seem to set their prices over short periods by finding the output at which their marginal costs and revenues would be equal, and then offering in the market *no more than this* in order to ensure the emergence of a particular market clearing price.

On the contrary, prices were fixed over considerable periods, on the basis of notions of 'normal' production costs that were firmly rooted in their accounting practices, and *were not intended to be market clearing* (cf. Lee, 1981). Firms expected sales to fluctuate but they only changed their prices if industrial cost conditions changed. If orders increased firms supplied more, and vice versa. There was no attempt to relate the marginal costs and revenues at any particular time; it is not rational to do so if it is recognised that today's sales are dependent on yesterday's price, and today's price affects tomorrow's sales. Instead, firms set prices that they expected would be competitive in the long run.

(c) It is conventional to suggest that the main barrier to breaking into a market is the investment funding necessary for doing so on a scale big enough to permit competitive costs. This view arises from the tendency to see the typical potential entrant as a newly established firm. It is a view which makes markets seem less competitive than is actually the case. Andrews found that firms were aware that potential entrants were often existing large firms with a similar technological base to their own. The main entry barrier is the charging of an inconveniently low price by existing firms, and the inability of potential producers to see a way of designing a superior substitute product that *they* could afford to sell at a price which would be inconvenient to existing producers. There is, of course, no guarantee that existing producers will always judge correctly which price and product strategy will be successful in the long run. In a world of partial ignorance mistakes are bound to be made and entry may be attracted. Entrants, too, may be overoptimistic, or fail to see that they could enter without opportunity loss—prices may be set too high or too low if information is incomplete.

(d) In many markets there are several actual competitors who can produce an identical physical product. There is no obvious reason why customers should prefer one source of supply to another, if prices and delivery conditions are identical. In such a situation a firm will be well aware that it may be able to win customers from its rivals if the latter do not come up to satisfactory standards. But if it is lax itself, it will lose custom. This is particularly the case in situations where customers (be they final consumers, retailers, or users of inter-mediate goods) require regular supplies. It is *goodwill* that keeps them coming back to the same supply source in a situation where several firms may be known to be able to supply a satisfactory product at the market price. If a mistake is made today and a customer's goodwill lost, the present value of future lost sales may be huge.

In order to keep their customers in the long run, firms are not merely constrained to watch the prices their rivals can quote. They must also at least match them on delivery, consistency of product quality, and so on. If they fail to do so they will soon find their goodwill vanishing, particularly if word spreads about their deficiencies. So long as they match their rivals, the amount of goodwill they have seems to depend on the luck of the draw, on initially being discovered by chance or by a word of mouth recommendation that they are an acceptable supplier. Once goodwill is incorporated in the analysis of markets it cannot be other than misleading to argue that firms who produce (or could produce) identical products, to cater for a non-trivial section of the market, enjoy individual downward sloping demand curves.

Andrews' analysis of goodwill led him to propose a different explanation of observations of 'excess' capacity from the one supplied by imperfect competition theorists. Firms are always hoping to pick up extra business, partly from their rivals when these make mistakes, and partly as a result of changes in the population of customers or total number of buyers in their markets. To ensure that they can satisfy new customers without disappointing their existing, regular ones they will keep a margin of spare capacity that allows immediate delivery or, if waiting lists are a conventional feature so that advance orders reduce business risks, permits them to quote delivery dates no worse than those of potential producers of similar products. For imperfect competition theorists, spare capacity is a long run result of short run 'snatching' policies and is a waste. For Andrews, by contrast, it is a necessary element in policies aimed to attract and preserve goodwill, without which long run profits and sales would unnecessarily be jeopardised.

The objections that Andrews raised against theories of imperfect competition should not be seen as amounting to a claim that it is necessarily impossible for firms to perform marginalist calculations at the start of each 'short period'. Rather, he was suggesting that this is not a sensible thing to do if they want to maximise profits over the long run. In oligopolistic markets, where competition is possible from extra production offered by existing producers who have similar facilities, such marginalist calculations are inevitably over-shadowed by the problems of the future that might arise from the policies of the present.

2.6 The Full Cost/Normal Cost Theory of Price Determination

Andrews' theory of how firms set their prices in competitive oligopolistic markets is based on the concept of entry prevention. His conclusion can be stated very simply: a firm sets its prices just below what it conjectures to be the opportunity costs of production of other firms who could produce duplicates of the products it supplies. It should be added that usually those products which are not pure services will comprise a mixture of physical and service-related characteristics, such as reliability of quality, an after sales maintenance facility, or helpful sales advice. If firms decide that a different bundle of such features may enable them more easily to meet their goals they can change the product they offer but it will still be necessary, for long run success, to adhere to the same pricing rule.

At the price it sets according to its conjectures, the firm sells as much as it can, though the volume of orders it receives will fluctuate with changes in the general state of demand and its share of goodwill. It only changes the price it quotes when the expected costs of potential producers change, and not as a result of changes in the state of its order books. Unless it has good reason to believe that the cost conditions enjoyed by other firms are different from its own (e.g. unless it is aware that another country's producers are benefiting from a falling exchange rate or an incomes policy) it will use the behaviour of its own costs as a guide to the entry-forestalling price level. Given its capacity, it will have some expected 'normal' level of capacity utilisation and its price can be expressed as its average direct costs at this normal level of output plus a mark-up. But it is important to remember that although a firm may talk of a mark-up of *its* costs, the size of its mark-up is limited by the costs of *other* producers, potential or actual, plus the mark-up that *these* firms would require before thinking the market sufficiently attractive to enter.

Before we consider the conditions for entry and exit, it may be helpful to illustrate what has so far been said with the aid of a diagram, Figure 2.4, and then with a practical example.

The following points should be borne in mind when Figure 2.4 is being examined:

(1) Andrews assumes average direct costs constant over a wide range of output, because this is what is observed in the real world. Somewhere, to the right of Q^N (the normal rate of output), these costs may rise in the short run due to the need to meet overtime payments, and the

use of less efficient, older machines usually kept in reserve. In the long run, learning and technical progress reduces costs generally.

(2)   The difference between the price, P, and average direct costs at Q^N, is the mark-up, or gross profit margin.

(3)   If average fixed costs are added to average direct costs we get average total costs and the firm's net profit margin at Q^N can thus be inferred. Average fixed costs

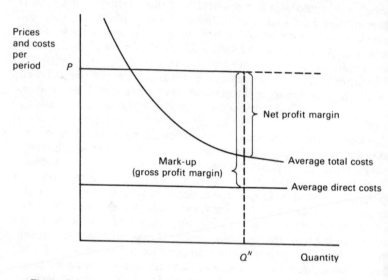

Figure 2.4

include the cost of the capital equipment rig that has actually been installed and contributions to the firm's overheads that have been allocated to the product in question.

(4)   The horizontal line from P must not be confused with the horizontal demand curve of the perfectly competitive firm. *It is not a demand curve*. It represents the maximum price that the firm thinks it can charge without provoking production by rivals, existing or potential. In Andrews' theory of price determination at the level of the firm there are, strictly speaking, no demand curves, only cost curves. If the firm is lucky or its sales staff are more than usually competent it will sell more than Q^N; if not, it will sell less.

(5)   Since average total costs fall as output rises, profits rise in a boom and fall in a depression, or with corresponding shifts in goodwill.

Now, suppose that a retailing chain, that does not own producing capacity, wants to sell skirts of a particular kind. Clearly, a skirt producer will not be able to win a contract from this retailing chain if it quotes a price higher than that which another firm might quote for the same carefully specified product. However, if it is selected to produce the initial batch of skirts for the retailer's own brand, it will be given repeat orders for these skirts and for new patterns so long as it always charges a competitive price. Not only will the retailing chain have a 'preferring the devil you know' type of reason for continuing to deal with the firm—it has not experienced the output of other firms to know whether their quality or delivery reliability is better, but it knows that its targets for what is *satisfactory* are being met at a price no higher than other firms are quoting—it also needs the goodwill of its producers so that they will be prepared to make future investments in new capacity (cf. Richardson, 1972). If the retailing chain over-orders at first, and causes its suppliers to invest in new plant that, it turns out, cannot be used, it will be the kind of customer that these firms can do without.

The skirt producer may lose orders if the retailing group charges too high a price and attracts entry from a boutique chain. However, it could also be lucky enough to win alternative orders from the boutique chain. Just as consumers change the products they buy, so firms that buy from other firms change their buying patterns as their fortunes change: the market is in a constant state of disequilibrium. But the disequilibrium does not manifest itself in price changes so long as firms' conjectures about their rivals' costs are correct and unchanging; it simply leads to shifts in relative sales levels. Where costs are reduced by technical progress and learning by doing, firms will have to lower their prices if they think that their rivals are enjoying similar cost reductions, otherwise they can increase their profit margins.

If inappropriate prices are charged and entry occurs, prices will then fall to the 'correct' level. However, not all cases of entry into established markets are the result of mistakes being made by existing producers. For example, in the case of the UK petrol retailing industry, discussed by Shaw (1974), the major existing operators realised that a conventional entry-forestalling policy would be very expensive in terms of the profits that would have to be sacrificed for the several years it would take independent retailers to acquire and develop outlet sites. The leading companies preferred these short run (but in *this* case relatively long-lived) excess profits, which they could plough back immediately, to the less certain long run profits. As a result, a system of price leadership developed which lasted until the independent retailers grew and forced prices to the normal cost level.

The high level managers responsible for important pricing decisions may often be fairly near the end of their careers in a firm. As a result, calculated sacrifices, in which future profits are to some extent discounted, may be more common than Andrews seems to have imagined. But the planned risking of entry in conditions of uncertainty in no way invalidates the arguments he raised against the marginalist conception of the way in which firms actually decide what prices to set. It simply means that, to apply generally, the theory he proposed needs to be amended to take account of managerial attitudes to distant as opposed to near profits when profit plough-back is the main source of investment finance. This modification to Andrews' basic idea forms part of the contributions to the BPK theory of the firm made by Eichner (1976) and Moss (1981).

If the prices charged in an industry are not 'correct' entry-preventing prices, a potential producer has to conjecture what the appropriate price really is and work out the sales volume that would be possible at this price. The would-be entrant then investigates the full costs of producing, over its planning period, at the expected normal level of output. In the case of a complete new plant being necessary, full costs include all the sums that must be paid out to factors to produce the planned normal output, and a target net rate of return to take account of foregone net earnings from other uses of the investment funds. Paying out costs include rates, factory rent, costs of overheads, costs of production labour and materials, and, as far as managers are concerned, the payments to shareholders that are conjectured to be necessary to prevent the company being taken over and a new management team installed. Overheads include contributions to research and development, and to marketing. Where plant already exists and costs of capital have already been sunk in money terms, the full cost is effectively the opportunity cost of using the equipment to produce for another market. In either case, if the full cost per unit at the conjectured normal quantity level is no greater than the conjectured 'correct' price for the market, entry will be considered worthwhile.

If full costs are less than the 'correct' price and fall as output expands, the firm will not usually attempt to sell more at a lower price, but will simply take a bigger margin. The reason for this is that, at the level of the industry, the quantity sold is not very responsive to the price that firms charge (recall section 2.2 above, on the dominance of income effects), while at the level of the firm it is very responsive indeed, due to the fact that products are identical or arranged in a chain of close substitutes. Thus a firm knows that, if it charges a lower price than the entry-preventing one, other firms will follow since they will lose sales in a big way and conclude that they have guessed the normal cost price incorrectly. But the fall in price would not leave the entrant, or other producers, with a greatly increased sales volume. It will simply have removed its extra 'efficiency' margin of profit.

The above discussion implies that entry is most likely if a competitive level of full costs can be achieved at a normal output level which is only a small fraction of the total market volume. To attract sales the entrant could quote a lower 'correct' price but this would, in causing the industry price to move to this level, only add a small amount to total industrial sales. This small amount is all the entrant can expect to get, unless it has good reason to believe it will be more than usually successful in picking up goodwill. The exception to this is the situation in which the firm realises that the establishment of the 'correct' entry-preventing price will lead to the departure from the market of a group of less efficient producers. This may leave a big enough 'space' for entry to take place on a large scale. Similar considerations will be borne in mind by existing producers who are investigating the possibilities of re-equipping with a new vintage of plant whose viability rests upon a large increase on sales.

Exit from a market only occurs in the relatively short run in the orthodox theory if a firm cannot cover its average *variable* costs and if there is no prospect of using the equipment to produce something else. The shutdown condition in Andrews' theory is the situation when the firm can no longer cover its 'average paying out costs' and sees no prospect of things improving. The orthodox theory implicitly treats all overheads as if they are machines whose money costs have already been sunk. However, Andrews recognised that overhead staff involve current payouts of cash. He also emphasised that much production line employment is in the nature of overhead labour because production lines often still require the same volume of labour to run them when they are slowed down. These factors mean that firms using relatively high numbers of workers per unit of output will be the most vulnerable when sales contract, unless their production processes happen to be less integrated than their rivals and can be shut down in stages instead of merely being run at a slower pace.

2.7 Retail Pricing

If there is any industry to which we could point as one where both entry and exit are common features and can occur rapidly it must surely be retailing. The frequency of entry and exit is an indication of the frequency with which entrepreneurial mistakes are made in this industry. It also reflects the attempts of Local Authorities to gather revenue. By varying their rating charges they can extract excess rental earnings from site owners and ensure that premises are occupied by the shops that are most profitable. Given that entrepreneurial over-optimism and rating valuation policies make retailing a highly competitive industry, it is perhaps surprising that identical physical commodities often sell for different prices in different shops. Conventional theory explains this by pointing out that standards of service differ and that no two shops can stand on the same site, so each shop supplies a slightly differentiated output and thus enjoys its own downward sloping demand curve. Andrews, by contrast, adapted his normal cost theory of price to explain the observed behaviour. This adaptation is to be found in Andrews (1950), (1964, Part B) and Andrews and Friday (1960).

Andrews argued that the conventional emphasis on location is misplaced since it treats consumers as paralysed when, in fact, they often enjoy walking around shopping centres to explore what is available. While he did not presume that consumers are perfectly informed he saw no reason to suggest that they are not canny shoppers, and he emphasised the importance of window shopping and contact between consumers in the social setting as means of acquiring information. As Andrews saw it, it does not matter that *all* consumers might not be canny shoppers: competition will still hold prices generally down to normal cost levels since, even if only, say, 10 per cent of consumers are avid seekers of bargains, a shop which can attract all of these by offering lower prices than elsewhere may acquire an important share of the market. The failure of identical commodities (identical, that is, with regard to demonstration, after sales facilities, and so on) to sell for identical prices in a given locality has to be explained in a different way.

Andrews' starting point was to suggest that the unit of analysis in retailing should not be the individual commodity, but the basket of things bought on a particular shopping expedition. Many goods from a given shopping basket will be stocked by a number of shops, each of whom is trying to get customers to use themselves rather than their rivals. If, on average, they all set prices to deter entry by even more shops catering for their kind of customer, they have no way of picking up goodwill at the expense of each other except by chance unless they can somehow differentiate the 'baskets' that they sell.

The ease of entry in retailing means that margins are often very low, especially in general stores or supermarkets where the concept of the basket is most obviously important. Thus, unless a general price cutting exercise would knock out smaller producers and leave a larger market share, a retailing group will not attempt to expand its sales by starting a general price war. (It must be added that, even if a general price war *is* worth starting, the shops that survive it because they have lower costs are then constrained to keep prices at the new low level and to do battle with each other, which they cannot do by a further general price war unless there is *still* scope for knocking out higher cost outlets.) Instead of general price cuts, shops attempt to use loss leader policies and their choices of stocking mix and service qualities to win extra customers. With loss leader schemes the average basket's cost is determined in the usual way, though some of its components do not cover their costs and others earn higher than normal margins. Sometimes the losses are borne by the manufacturers rather than the retailers. This happens either when a product has recently been introduced and the manufacturer is attempting to break customer inertia by making smaller the risk of trying an unknown product, or because the manufacturer sells a 'basket' of goods too and is trying to encourage shops to stock its ranges of products, in the knowledge that its sales volumes depend to a great extent on the number of shops displaying its products.

Loss leader schemes attempt to create illusions in situations where it is simply not possible to display all prices simultaneously. Even if consumers are not fooled and purchase only the bargain offers, there is still the possibility that they will become regular customers because they discover that the service or variety of goods stocked fits their image of 'the ideal' in ways which they had not expected. A variant on the loss leader idea is the situation common at times when a newly introduced product is in short supply and immediate delivery is possible only from unorthodox supply sources at black market prices. Regular retailers release their stock slowly, at the list price, rather than parting with it immediately at the black market price. They do this in order to generate 'floor traffic' from customers who otherwise would not bother to enter their premises to see what else they are selling. They forego higher revenues on the new, fashionable product in the hope of selling their usual lines to people who enter their showrooms not planning to do anything except inspect the new product, and whose attention may be drawn to other possibilities for expenditure which they had not been considering. A refusal to be seen to be charging the black market price may also be a useful way of presenting an image of fairness to customers, with long term beneficial consequences for goodwill.

Shops will continually be seeking to improve their stock and price-mix policies, since any policy which is conspicuously successful will rapidly be copied. The pattern of retail prices will change continuously, even though, aside from retailing innovations and inflationary pressures on wholesale prices, the price of the average basket of goods will not change unless shops have misjudged the costs of their actual or potential competitors.

2.8 Normal Costs, Fashion Goods and Pioneering Products: A Dialogue

THE CRITIC: This normal cost theory of pricing is interesting, but I have some doubts about its generality. Its emphasis on the long run consequences of short run pricing decisions makes eminent sense if we are dealing with firms that supply intermediate inputs, or supermarkets that wish to pick up a regular clientele of shoppers. But once we start considering dynamic markets where the product is always changing it begins to look rather shaky. If the life cycle of a product is only a few months (as in the case of clothes) or, at most, say, five years (as in the case of a car), the emphasis on the long run seems misplaced.

THE PROPONENT: I think you've got two issues muddled together here. When you talk of a typical product life cycle you're rather putting the cart before the horse since you neglect the relationship between a firm's pricing policy and the length of time it will attempt to sell a product. Quite apart from this issue is the question of what happens if, over the product life cycle as a whole, the firm earns supernormal profits. To attempt to maximise net revenue over a product life cycle without regard to the consequences for the returns to future products would be as foolish as to attempt to maximise net revenue over any period of a product life cycle without regard to the consequences for the returns during the rest of the product life cycle. In order to deter entry, existing producers must manage their pricing strategies so that their products *seem* likely to earn net revenue streams over their life cycles which are slightly less than those which would make entry an attractive proposition. Each product life cycle must be seen, in effect, as a separate product *entity* which cannot be sold in a way which gives other firms the impression that the market is worth entering, since to do otherwise would jeopardise the prospects of subsequent product life cycles.

THE CRITIC: I'm still not convinced. Take the case of the car market. Here it seems that if one firm produces 'a winner' there is not a sudden influx of new car producers selling *duplicate* products. What we usually see is a proliferation, over a period of time, of *differentiated* substitutes. Not only this but there are often reports that decisions over pricing policies in such markets are the subjects of considerable debate—for example, the divergent views in the British Leyland boardroom over the appropriate price for the Mini-Metro car were very widely reported in the UK press in 1980. These two points must surely mean that in this kind of market firms can be thought of as acting as though they enjoy discretion as to which point they choose to occupy on a demand curve determined by consumer preferences.

THE PROPONENT: The firms that produce new substitutes for 'a winner' are not driven to do so necessarily because the firm that makes it is attempting to price in excess of normal costs, or has made a mistake in guessing what normal costs are. The successful producer is threatening their market shares and profits by producing a superior product which it thought of and introduced first. This product hastens the end of the life cycles of their own products, *forcing* them to think about a retaliatory strategy. The successful producer may have been driven to develop its product for similar reasons. It stayed in the industry because it saw a way of doing better than those firms whose products presented a threat to its own, earlier model. Firms which sell deficient products at, on average, their competitors' full costs are providing an incentive to entry (or, in this case, an incentive to stay in the market and design a better product) as surely as if they were producing ideal products and charging prices which their rivals believed they could undercut without opportunity loss. If no one knows what the ideal product is, or, to put it another way, if there is always scope for invention and innovation, it is not surprising that firms should attempt to try something different if they spot deficiencies in current 'winners'. Firms which never launch products unless they seem free of all possible flaws will fail to generate the profits necessary for designing the perfect product.

THE CRITIC: Are you saying that ultimately, for example, the Model T was a very crude car but that the Ford Company could not have been able to develop the cars it sold after the Model T had it not obtained know how while making it, or used some cf the profits for funding R and D?

THE PROPONENT: Yes, and that retaliation by rival producers was inevitable even despite the fact that Ford kept their prices down in line with costs.

THE CRITIC: I think you've rather fallen into a trap I was setting by using the Model T as an example. It is well known that Henry Ford wanted to produce cars as cheaply as possible and, in setting prices, even took account of the cost reductions he *thought* he could get before they were realised (cf. Smyth, 1967). This is rather difficult to square with your belief that a firm does not attempt to boost sales volume by lowering prices, because it realises that producers of substitutes would follow and the increase in total sales would be trivial.

THE PROPONENT: No, it isn't. Ford was trying to break the chain of substitutes by creating something which no one else had offered—a car which the typical American could afford. The early success of the Model T fits in perfectly with Pasinetti's arguments about income effects, that were discussed in section 2.2. By creating a car for everyone before any other producer, Ford hoped to gain cost advantages, partly through economies of scale and partly through learning by doing, that no one else would be able to match. And the more cars he sold, the more damage he could inflict on other producers and the more secure his long run position would seem to be. In the early stages of a market a highly aggressive policy of this kind, which has nothing to do with marginalism, makes perfect sense. His policy made it unprofitable for other firms that offered cars as crude as the Model T to continue to produce them. Without his production line technique he would have been foolish to charge prices below the typical producer's normal costs. To do so would have been to spark off a price war that benefited no one.

THE CRITIC: But in the long run Ford's aggressive strategy of price leadership went wrong. . . .

THE PROPONENT: Yes, though this was because Ford failed to realise that rising US real incomes meant that car purchasers could be more discriminating and could afford to buy cars which catered for lower priority wants than mobility. His competitors—at least, those who were still in business—began to use the production line technique, though in a less extreme way than Ford, to mass produce technologically superior, more comfortable and more stylish cars. In this situation further price cuts would not affect sales in the saturated market for basic transportation, and would no longer damage his competitors. The most profitable course of action was to change the product, to move 'up-market' and try to produce a better product than those that were already being offered. To me, this product life cycle seems perfectly consistent with the views on long run pricing associated with Andrews and Pasinetti.

THE CRITIC: You haven't yet explained why, if firms do normal cost pricing, there can be boardroom disputes over the appropriate pricing policy.

THE PROPONENT: These disputes arise either because board members have in mind different time horizons and different goals, or because they perceive potential sales and competitors' responses differently. For example, if the head of one division is going to retire in a few years time, and cannot be given investment funds immediately unless current profitability is increased, she is going to be keen that a new product in one of her colleague's divisions is launched with a price that generates profits now, even at the cost of shortening the lifespan of the product. The head of the division producing the new product might have a far longer time horizon in mind and wish to go for an aggressive, low price policy, rather than attempting to exploit any temporary 'monopoly advantage' that the new product might have in terms of design. Yet another director might have a similar long term view but argue that the new product is so superior that if priced in line with its rivals it would cause such a dramatic collapse of their sales that these producers would be forced to speed up their product redesign programmes. If this director is right a low price policy may result in a shortening of the life cycle of the new product and a failure to earn a normal level of profit on the investment.

THE CRITIC: You would concede, then, that with dynamic markets, unlike, say, markets for nuts and bolts or 'own brand' cans of beans, the basic normal cost theory of pricing is too simple, and so, too, is the modified version suggested by Eichner (1976) and Moss (1981), which was mentioned in section 2.6.

THE PROPONENT: I would stick by the basic normal cost idea as applying for successive product life cycles taken as 'wholes', but concede that it is not going to be so obvious how to manage each product life cycle so that, as a whole, it does not attract new competitive production. The Eichner/Moss theory rather tends to proceed as if the managers involved in a price setting decision are, to use a phrase from Loasby (1967), 'fully conditioned organisation men', who have identical interests and perceptions. Often it will be a useful approximation to think of corporate behaviour in this way—indeed, management induction programmes are often designed to engender a common corporate imagination—and in such situations the Eichner/Moss contributions, or Andrews' original theory as a less general case, seem fine. At other times, however, we must recognise that pricing decisions are reached collectively, by a process which involves an element of bargaining.

In a world of uncertainty individual managers in a firm may not all interpret information in the same way and may be able to conceal their true motives behind what they propose, even if they all understand the basic rationale for normal cost pricing as a device for ensuring the long run survival of the firm in which they are presently employed. If we recognise this we must see that behavioural theory (e.g. Cyert and March, 1963) and Post Keynesian Theory (e.g. Eichner (1976) or Moss (1981)) are ripe for integration to form a general theory of the firm, instead of remaining as separate theories which either emphasise internal bargaining, and neglect external market constraints, or vice versa.

2.9 Conclusion: The Implications of the Normal Cost Theory of Prices for the Orientation of Consumer Behaviour Theory

In this chapter we have attempted to present a BPK analysis of price formation, in which prices are set without reference to conventional demand functions. We began by showing that prices at the industry level could be explained from the cost side alone, so long as quantities were known, and we argued that at this level shifts in relative quantities are brought about primarily by changes in real incomes, not by substitution effects associated with relative price changes *per se*. Having shown that a set of compatible industrial prices *could* be inferred without reference to demand functions, we went on to suggest that individual firms within industries *could not* plausibly be thought of as setting prices in the light of a knowledge of timeless demand functions of the sort central to neoclassical value theory.

We have suggested that markets generally are most appropriately to be seen as oligopolistic, as least so long as the term is taken to denote the fact that firms recognise the interdependence of their decisions with those of other producers, actual and potential. The existence of large numbers of potential producers means that it is misleading to think of 'oligopolistic' as referring to the smallness of the number of actual producers, whatever the etymological basis of the word. We argued that in such markets prices will be set with reference to the *cost* positions of actual and potential producers of similar products. Demand only affects prices indirectly, and through time, insofar as it determines quantities sold and thus affects normal costs of production through scale and learning effects. How much a firm can sell, and the price it can charge for a given product/ marketing package, depends on the opportunity costs of other firms. If a firm sets its price above the normal costs of its rivals, it will encourage them to produce substitutes. If a firm sets its price according to normal costs but produces a product which sells very successfully in the present, it will affect its competitors' innovative activities, and hence its future sales. If its product is so successful in the present that its competitors are starved of profits and cannot innovate, its sales will expand in the long run; but if its competitors are able to retaliate by using up financial reserves and bringing forward their product development schemes, its long run sales will tend to fall.

This view of the nature of markets and the process of price formation leads us to believe that there should be a reorientation of economists' efforts in the context of the theory of choice. We are led to this conclusion by the chain of arguments that follows.

A firm will not be able to enjoy long run survival and growth in competitive oligopolistic markets unless it is successful at choosing product/price/marketing packages which generate current cash flow, do maximum damage to rivals presently in the markets for which it produces, but do not attract entry. To make such choices a firm needs to be able to *predict* the size and time profile of sales which will result if a particular product/price/marketing package is put together and the crucial, one-shot decision is taken to try it in practice.

Firms cannot make these predictions simply by looking at past price/quantity data and then using econometric techniques to estimate demand functions. Such demand functions may exist at the industry level in stable markets, but they do not exist at the level of the individual firm. Furthermore, a firm which breaks into an established market will not wish then to *experiment* to discover a price/quantity relationship. It may be attracted to enter because existing producers have mistakenly set prices too high, but, if its own initial price is also too high, other firms may follow it in and jeopardise its long run position. It will also not wish to see what happens if it lowers its prices after entry, because of the risk of starting an expensive price war. Once a firm has become established in a market, there is no guarantee that lower prices for its outputs will lead to increases in sales: customers may interpret price cuts as signs of a weak trading position or a recognition by the firm that its products have fallen behind in terms of quality. In such a situation, a price cut may lead customers to postpone even those purchases that they would have made at the original price, on the expectation of further price cuts, and vice versa for price increases (cf. Andrews (1958), p. 38).

Matters are even more difficult when a firm is contemplating the introduction of a new product. No prior sample exists from which a demand function can be estimated, notwithstanding competitors' reactions. However, once a 'pioneering product' has been launched, increases in sales will be due more to the diffusion of information among consumers than to changes in relative prices (see Bain (1964) and Ironmonger (1972)). A firm that is developing new products normally cannot perform trial marketing exercises for every product it has in mind as a possible winner before it makes its irreversible investment commitment. The firm needs a theory of how its potential customers think and choose, which it can operationalise with the aid of market research data in order to assess the potential sales patterns for possible product/price/marketing packages. And it is one of the duties of the economist to provide such a theory.

In the orthodox analysis of value there is no obvious need for the theory of choice to do any more than set inquiring minds at rest by providing a possible explanation of the origins of demand functions. Demand functions are timeless and reversible in the orthodox theory, while the list of products on offer is given. If a firm can discover the nature of such demand functions by experimenting at zero cost, it has no need at all for a theory of how individuals choose. Such costless experiments cannot be conducted in the real world, since past, present and future sales are interlinked, and capital is often highly specific with regard to the sorts of outputs it can be used to make. There is thus a need for a theory of choice which is not only a reasonable explanation of how people decide what to purchase, but which also can aid prediction.

3 Behavioural versus Neoclassical Theories of Choice

3.1 Introduction

The neoclassical analysis of choice used by the great majority of today's economists was never intended to serve as a predictive tool in the hands of business managers. This analysis owes its origins largely to the work of Hicks (1939), who was quite explicit about his reasons for including an analysis of choice in a book whose primary concern was to develop 'a technique for studying the interrelations of markets' (1939, p. 2). His aims were much more modest than our own. What he sought in the main was a plausible *justification* of the Law of Demand; his work on the theory of choice 'began with the endeavour to supply a needed theoretical foundation for statistical demand studies' (1939, p. 5). He made no attempt to suggest that economists should attempt to discover the preference maps of samples of individual choosers prior to estimating demand relationships. It is hard to conceive of a workable *questionnaire* technique which *could* be used to discover n-dimensional preference orderings of the kind assumed in his theory. However, if price/quantity data can be observed directly, there is no need to discover individual preference mappings before attempting to estimate demand relationships.

Since Hicks was writing as if his economy had a static technology and perfectly competitive firms, it may have seemed adequate to develop a theory which could provide a possible description of the origins of downward sloping demand curves—and hence the prospect of convergence towards market equilibrium—yet which had little practical significance for managers trying to come to terms with market uncertainty in turbulent, oligopolistic environments.

Given the origins of the conventional analysis it would perhaps seem rather unfair to criticise it for its practical limitations, were it not for the fact that it has had a powerful blinkering effect on the attitudes of most economists to the functions of *any* theory of choice. Having used it to 'explain' the origins of the Law of Demand, the typical economist then becomes rather complacent. She rarely considers the possibility that the Law of Demand could be justified with other theories of decision making, theories which might point to a need to investigate new topics of importance for policy and to question many of the results of conventional welfare analysis. It is the aim of this chapter to examine the procedures, the logic and the assumptions of the conventional theory of choice from a behavioural standpoint, to show just how misleading a form of analysis it may be to use.

The form taken by the chapter is a series of short sections, each of which is concerned with a characteristic central to our alternative behavioural analysis and which is ignored or rejected by neoclassical treatments of choice. However, before we proceed to these detailed discussions it may be helpful, since our readers may include psychologists and managers who have no training in the neoclassical theory of choice, if we present a quick sketch of the barest essentials of this theory. A modern neoclassical theorist will no doubt object that in doing this we are deliberately setting up a 'straw man' to kick down, and that the theory of choice has come a long way since Hicks developed the 'essentials' we are about to reproduce. This objection is unjustifiable. Inspection will reveal that any advanced neoclassical text—Deaton and Muellbauer (1980) must surely be the most comprehensive and scholarly representation of the 'state of the art'—which shows how propositions can be derived graphically, and not merely with mathematical notation, is replete with two dimensional diagrams showing indifference curves, budget lines and points of tangency. Modern sophistication in the neoclassical analysis of choice has been concerned with the use of formal techniques and with points of detail; the fundamentals have not changed.

The essence of the neoclassical theory of choice is as follows. A consumer, in attempting to choose between mutually exclusive schemes of action, faces three constraints. The first is the size of her endowment of physical and human capital, i.e. the property and skills she possesses at the start of the trading period in question. The second constraint is the limited amount of time she has to spend in consuming goods and services: if she wants more leisure she can only get it by working less. Finally, she faces a given set of market prices for commodities that she might wish to buy or sell, and for labour services. Given these constraints, her choices are determined by her preferences. The consumer knows what she wants and how to get it. She does not dither in a state of indecision. She is assumed to wish to maximise her utility and to have a convex preference ordering over all goods. This means that she is prepared to give up units of one commodity in order to obtain more of another, though at an ever-decreasing marginal rate of substitution.

The preferences of a neoclassical consumer can be represented graphically as a set of indifference curves. An indifference curve shows possible combinations of commodities that the consumer would find equally satisfactory. On a two dimensional diagrammatic simplification, such as Figure 3.1, indifference curves located further

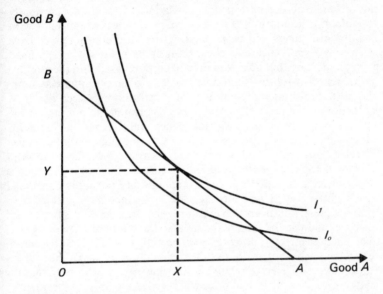

Figure 3.1

and further to the north east represent increasingly desirable combinations of commodities. On Figure 3.1, all points on the indifference curve I_1 are superior to points on the indifference curve I_0. Given her endowment and the set of market prices, there will be a maximum quantity of one good which the consumer could choose if she chose to consume nothing else. There will also be a set of possible combinations of goods which she can choose. On Figure 3.1, she can choose OA units of good A and none of good B; or OB units of good B and none of good A; or any one of the possible combinations traced by the line AB. To maximise her utility she chooses a combination of goods such that there is no other combination available to her which is on a higher indifference curve. On Figure 3.1 she chooses OX units of good A and OY units of good B. Her indifference curve I_1 is tangential to her budget line *AB* when she chooses this combination of goods. If she alters the mix of goods slightly in either direction she finds herself losing utility, moving on to a lower indifference curve.

By moving the positions of budget lines to represent shifts in incomes or relative prices it can be shown how the consumer will change her behaviour. An increase in income, with relative prices of goods *A* and *B* unchanged, is shown by a rightward shift in the budget line, parallel to the original budget line *AB*. A relative cheapening of good *A*, with total spending power unchanged, would cause the budget line to swivel to the right from point *B*, i.e. the consumer could now get more of *A* on its own, or combinations of *A* and *B* not previously feasible, but no more of *B* on its own. New points of tangency with indifference curves will be implied. If the indifference curves have been conveniently located, a cheapening of one good will be associated with an increase in the amount of it that is purchased. But there is no *a priori* reason why this should be the case, given the simple assumption of diminishing marginal rates of substitution between goods. A reduction in the price of a good causes a consumer to purchase more of it, except when it does not. Since indifference curves slope downwards towards the right, a relative price change that does not affect a consumer's real income will always induce substitution in favour of the cheapened commodity. However, if money income is unchanged, a fall in the price of a commodity normally consumed results in a rise in real income. The consumer may well wish to purchase less, not more, of the commodity because of this rise in real income, and use the money she saves to buy more of something else. The 'income effect' of the price change pulls against the 'substitution effect' in such a situation, but theorists typically *assume* that substitution effects are large relative to income effects, whatever sign the latter have. A reduction in price will then lead to a rise in the quantity sold, and neoclassical preference theory 'explains' why this happens.

3.2 Consumer Motivation and Preferences

The neoclassical economic agent is not a thinking, creative chooser in any meaningful sense. She is simply a preference system with a limited endowment, who faces a given set of market prices. Everything she might ever do is written down in her preferences. To know what she *will* do we have simply to discover her preferences and specify a set of prices. The modern neoclassical theorist, however, typically makes no attempt *actually* to discover preferences and plot indifference maps. Sometimes it is conceded that 'the construction of an indifference map may require quite a bit of introspective information from the consumer—he must be able to state his preferences among *all possible* combinations of commodities' (Baumol (1972), p. 221, emphasis in original). The impossibility of using questionnaire methods to do this is then neatly skirted by a discussion of revealed preference analysis, which, it is said,

permits us to find out all we need to know [about the consumer] just by observing his market behaviour—by seeing what he buys at different prices—assuming that his acquisitions and his buying experiences *do not change* his preference patterns or his purchase desires. *Given enough such information*, it is even theoretically possible to reconstruct the consumer's indifference map . . . (Baumol (1972), pp. 221–2, emphasis added).

Having asserted that it is possible to discover indifference maps, *in principle*, neoclassical theorists typically proceed to ignore the practical difficulties of doing this and instead simply *assume* the existence, in general terms, of convex preference orderings. They then focus their attention on the modelling of budget constraints of a more complex form than the linear kind found in Hicks' original exposition (cf. Deaton and Muellbauer (1980) p. xii). Changes or differences in behaviour are increasingly explained by changes or differences in the constraints choosers face, not in their preferences. Thus the modern neoclassical theorist is not interested in how people 'make up their minds' at all: people are preference orderings, and they attempt to maximise utility.

Nowhere does the neoclassical economist attempt to consider precisely what is subsumed under the heading of 'utility maximisation'. The procedure of leaving matters of motivation to psychologists is justified by the suggestion that, so long as the chooser has a preference *ordering*, it is unnecessary for the economist to inquire about the real nature of the motives underlying her choices. If consumers are, nearly enough, sovereign and have well-defined preferences (i.e. if they know what they want and if their wants are not continually changing or being changed by the influence of peer groups and advertisements), this may be a reasonable justification. However, if it is at least possible that consumers are not sovereign, then precisely how firms can affect choices by non-price means is a topic of interest to firms themselves, as well as something which should become a matter for public policy. To justify her assumption that consumer preferences are given, a neoclassical theorist might point to observed patterns of repetitive consumer demand. A policy-oriented behavioural theorist, by contrast, would see a need to study the nature of habitual decision processes, the origins of goodwill, and motivational factors behind persistence, in order to discover how firms can design marketing campaigns to disturb such repeated patterns and whether or not such stability as is observed is indicative of a loss of consumer sovereignty in the face of advertisements.

As was shown in the previous section, neoclassical economists assume that people are always prepared to sacrifice units of one good in order to obtain more of other goods from which they can derive utility, so long as the rate at which the substitution has to be made is acceptable. The assumption that marginal rates of substitution are continually diminishing rules out any possibility of upward sloping, horizontal or vertical indifference curves, despite the fact that they would square nicely with everyday observations of people who appear satiated in respect of particular types of consumption. Perhaps inevitably, this assumption has blinkered neoclassical theorists into placing great emphasis on substitution effects due to relative price changes and to underplay the significance of income effects. But despite such a strong emphasis on substitution effects—against which, as we saw in section 2.2, Pasinetti has provided a powerful critique—orthodox theorists have had little to offer in the way of an explanation of why some goods are closer substitutes than others. If the price of whisky rises, a neoclassical consumer might just as easily switch her consumption in the direction of, say, housing expenditure as she might expand her consumption of gin. If a new product is introduced, neither ordinary indifference analysis nor revealed preference theory can offer any clues as to why it may succeed in displacing existing ones or may fail to do so. About all the conventional theorist can say is that its introduction will cause one set of (hypothetical) indifference curves to replace another. Analogous limitations arise in the conventional treatment if advertising and consumer experience shift preferences over goods.

3.3 Characteristics and Separability

One economist with a neoclassical background is well known for trying to get his fellow economists to see consumer preferences from a new perspective and thereby partly to overcome the problems we have just mentioned. This is Kelvin Lancaster (1966), whose central proposition is that consumers should be seen as wanting commodities not for the sake of possessing them as commodities, but for the characteristics of which they believe them to be composed. This implies that preference maps should be drawn with regard to the characteristics space rather than the goods space; i.e. on indifference diagrams, axes should refer not to particular goods but to the characteristics they contain. Commodities can then be shown as points on indifference curves that refer to alternative, equally satisfactory bundles of characteristics. Products which are perceived as containing similar sets of characteristics may thus be expected to be closer substitutes with each other than those which do not—e.g. whisky and gin can both produce intoxication, but do not, unlike a house, help to provide shelter. In Lancaster's analysis, change in the list of goods available or in perceptions of goods, no longer requires preferences to be redrawn, merely the location of new goods, or the relocation of differently perceived goods, as points in characteristics space (cf. Archibald and Rosenbluth (1975), p. 572).

Although Lancaster's 'New Theory of Demand' retains the core neoclassical ideas of utility maximisation and multidimensional, convex preference orderings, most economists have adopted a 'wait and see' approach to it, wishing to see what results others can derive with it before adopting it themselves. It is difficult to find documentary evidence showing why they have taken this attitude. We suspect that the following three reasons may be among the most important, and they have a bearing on the kind of behavioural analysis we shall later construct. First, there may be a fear among positivist researchers that any relationships they estimated in the light of a knowledge of the 'objective' characteristics of commodities might predict very badly as a result of actual consumers perceiving them differently.

Another obvious objection to Lancaster's theory is that the list of characteristics in a consumer's preference system might change as fast as, if not faster than, the list of feasible commodity choices. Experience will cause consumers to become connoisseurs and add to their lists of desired characteristics. A neoclassical theorist who adopts Lancaster's idea thus may simply be jumping 'out of the frying pan and into the fire'. If preferences are assumed to be convex and non-separable, connoisseurship seems to imply a need continually to redraw preference maps in the characteristics space, not at all unlike the need to redraw convex preference maps in the goods space as new products appear or perceptions change. One way round this problem is to abandon the notion of a convex utility *function* in favour of a hierarchy of wants. A new characteristic can then simply be assumed to be slotted in at a level dependent on the priority assigned to it by the consumer, without having any effect on the relationships between characteristics above this level, or between those lower down. This is one of the modifications to Lancaster's theory which is proposed in the next chapter.

But perhaps the most powerful bar to the widespread use of Lancaster's amended neoclassical theory is the concept of the 'utility tree' (see Strotz (1957), Simmons (1974, pp. 69–89) and Green (1976,

Chapter 10)). This concept provides another means of exploring differences in substitution rates and permits novel products to be incorporated into a chooser's preferences with only a partial change in their structure. The existence of literature on the utility tree is the reason why Katzner (1970, p. 156), for one, decides to 'wait and see' in respect of Lancaster's work. Other economists appear less open on this matter. The utility tree analysis specifies preferences in the goods space but separates them out into various branches and levels. For example, the work/leisure choice may be made independently of consumption plans that are dependent on the income realised at work, and while broad categories of consumption expenditure may compete against each other (e.g. food, shelter, entertainment), expenditures *within* broad categories do not compete with those in other categories (e.g. meat is substituted against cereals but not against records). The appearance of a new product will only affect part of the utility tree: e.g. if a person discovers a new type of cheese this may affect the way in which she divides up her food budget, but it will not affect the size of her food budget or the ways in which she divides up her shelter and entertainment budgets.

Although the utility tree idea *may* help explain why new products only have limited effects on patterns of choice, it does little to help explain why particular products succeed or fail. Furthermore, it tends misleadingly to distract attention from complementarities—linkages between activities—which Lancaster had hoped to highlight with his characteristics analysis. For example, alcohol may be consumed in the context of entertainment, but a person who drinks a lot may then feel it necessary to diet. Similarly, a person who chooses a job with much scope for overtime earnings may expect to come home feeling so tired in the evenings that she will watch much more television, as a form of relaxation, than otherwise she might have done. When someone chooses a job she does not select it without regard to the sort of broad lifestyle it will enable her to attain, even if she does not choose between alternative, completely specified, bundles of work and consumption activities, or equalise marginal rates of substitution and price ratios simultaneously across all goods. The utility tree approach of 'top down' resource allocation picks up the latter point about marginal substitutions but is prone entirely to miss the lifestyle issue.

3.4 Reductionism, Holism, and Structuralism

Apart from such occasional departures as the utility tree, neoclassical analyses of choice are ostensibly highly reductionist in their method.

The neoclassical theorist sees aggregative concepts as if they are simply the sums of their component elements, with properties that can be inferred from a knowledge of the properties of these elements. It is this approach which explains why neoclassical theorists have little time for macroeconomics: macroeconomic phenomena, from such a standpoint, are 'no more' than aggregations of the outcomes of individual decisions by household and firms to buy and sell goods and services, including labour services. Unemployment is seen by the reductionist as the result of individual choices, not as a consequence of some 'overall' system failure: hence the recent search for microfoundations for macroeconomics (cf. Weintraub, 1979).

The modern behavioural theorist, by contrast, uses an approach to economic analysis that is either holistic or, increasingly, structuralist. The former approach recognises that reductionism may be misleading if resources are allocated in a 'top down' manner, as Kay (1979) has argued in the context of the budgeting of resources for corporate R and D, and as proponents of the utility tree quite clearly believe. Perhaps more important still is the point that reductionism may generate misleading results because of the simplifications that have to be made to permit the aggregation of the base entities. In common parlance: reductionists may end up 'failing to see the wood for the trees'. Taken literally, this metaphor helps us to see the problem very clearly. Suppose we wish to depict a forest on a map and we have the choice of using aerial photography or ground surveys to construct our image of it. To view it from an aircraft may preclude the identification of individual trees, yet it may lead rapidly and cheaply to an adequate representation for a map. The reductionist method, of plotting the positions of thousands of trees and then adding them up, may produce a very distorted image if the measuring devices are inaccurate or are not used with sufficient care. Thus the holistic technique may yield more accuracy for less input of resources (cf. Hofstadter (1979), pp. 310–36).

But we recognise that holism is not without its own limitations. This should already be apparent to some extent from our objections to the neglect of complementarities in work on utility trees. These limitations lead us naturally to follow Kay (1982) and favour a structuralist methodology, particularly for dealing with dynamics. Structuralism focuses attention on the *linkages* and interactions between components, rather than merely on the characteristics of the components considered as entities. It also recognises, after Koestler (1975b), that the universe is a complex hierarchical system in which every 'component' or 'whole' is double faced: a 'component' is an aggregate of other, lower level components; a 'whole' is a 'component' of some yet higher level structure. The 'bottom' levels of neoclassical theory—the household, the firm and the commodity—can all be seen in this way. So, too, can forests and trees: in terms of our forest example, structuralism is akin to taking an ecological approach in order to predict how the shape of the forest is going to change on maps in the future. The structuralist perspective suggests that it may be dangerous to focus wholly on one level of abstraction and neglect higher and lower level connections, constraints and implications. Let us now, therefore, consider the traps into which reductionism leads the neoclassical choice theorist.

The first difficulty arises from the fact that households and firms are composed usually of more than one decision maker. People with interests that are partly competitive and partly complementary often take decisions jointly and participate jointly in the activities they select. The neoclassical analysis treats firms and households as if they are 'black boxes' and does not examine how collective choices are made. In the neoclassical theory of the firm the pressure of market competition, and the fact that the production function and market prices are usually assumed to be perfectly known, might provide a justification for neglecting individual choices. Under these assumptions everyone must see things in the same way and is forced to pursue a common goal: the maximisation of profits. In the case of the household it is less obviously possible to use the pressure of competition as a way of justifying paying no attention to the question of collective choice, of how household indifference curves might be inferred from the preferences of individuals in a household. As Humphries and Rubery (1981) have observed, the neoclassical theorist often adopts a blatantly sexist escape route when pressed on this issue, and says that household preferences are imposed by a benevolent dictator, namely, the husband. The behavioural approach, by contrast, prefers to see firms and households as coalitions of people with different interests, which are viable so long as enough resources are available to satisfy all the parties involved. Resource allocation is seen as the outcome of a bargaining process that is affected by organisational structure and past experience. Hence it seems necessary to construct a theory of choice and motivation applicable to bargaining processes (see section 7.5).

It is evident from the work of Kay (1979, pp. 210–1) that eminent neoclassical theorists such as Koopmans and Arrow are exceedingly hostile to holistic methods of research. However, there is a sense in which such theorists are actually using an aggregative, 'top down' analysis in their work on choice, despite their claims to be 'bottom up' reductionists. The neoclassical household is usually portrayed, at least implicitly, as if it is a microcosmic representation of the market phenomenon that is to be explained. Households are not divided into classes or groups with common lifestyles; they are regarded as identical. In effect, neoclassical theorists start with market level observations and divide them by the number of households in order to get a picture of the 'typical' consumption bundle. The representative consumer chooses a bit of everything and, like the market, is thought to be in, or near to, equilibrium.

Such an abstraction makes the assumption of convex preferences seem deceptively plausible and removes inconvenient corner solutions from the analysis. The deception is all the more powerful because of the tendency to label axes with neatly divisible goods that most people consume (apples and oranges, not Cadillacs and swimming pools). It can be a very misleading form of analysis, albeit a mathematically tidy one. For example, if most individuals (households) are not actually trading in more than a few markets at any one time, it may be unreasonable to expect them to act 'as if' they are aware of all prices. Such partial knowledge may cause them to find it difficult to distinguish between absolute and relative price movements as they re-enter markets where recently they have not been transacting (e.g. as they replace worn out durables). In times of unanticipated inflation this may produce a distortion of their spending patterns compared with those observed during periods of stable prices (cf. Deaton, 1977).

Coddington (1976, pp. 1258–63) has observed that crowd behaviour in financial markets is not easily to be analysed by a reductionist methodology. He depicts it instead as an economic equivalent of riotous behaviour or mass hysteria. A similar characterisation might be offered in respect of imitative behaviour and attempts to maintain relative status ('keeping up with the Joneses') in consumption choices (cf. Hirsch, 1976) and labour markets. These kinds of behaviour are clearly incompatible with timeless, equilibrium analysis. What we need is a dynamic analysis that concentrates on the *network* of interactions within populations of potential customers. (Chapter 4 of Marris' (1964) *Economic Theory of 'Managerial' Capitalism* is a curiously neglected attempt to provide such an analysis; see also Bain (1964) and Ironmonger (1972).) But what we get in neoclassical theory is an assumption, for reasons of mathematical tractability, that utility functions are independent: it would be impossible to represent household preferences as stable features if they were allowed to be shaped by social and family interactions. The neoclassical assumptions make it possible to study the properties of equilibrium states, but where individual units take their behavioural cues from each other, as well as from price signals, we are unlikely to be near or moving toward such states. To understand what holds the system together and prevents continuous kaleidoscopic change, and to predict where it might move, it seems necessary to explore the nature of the linkages between the elements, rather than merely to add together the recent positions of elements to obtain a snapshot of an aggregate pattern.

3.5 Global Versus Bounded Rationality

The simplifying assumptions that neoclassical economists make reflect the fact that these scientists, like any others, suffer from what Simon (1957) has called *bounded rationality*: the capacity of their minds for formulating and solving complex problems is tiny relative to what is required for objectively rational action. Indeed, Marschak (1968, p. 12) has quoted the psycholinguist George Miller as saying that, compared with television or telephone systems, human beings are more like bottlenecks than channels for the efficient flow of information. There is only so much information that people can absorb or dispense, and only so many interdependencies of which they can take account at any one time. A skilled pianist or typist can transmit twenty five 'bits' of information per second, but most people find ten bits per second an upper limit.

A paradoxical result of the neoclassical theorist's bounded rationality is that she is driven to construct a theoretical world in which economic agents behave as if blessed with global rationality. This world functions as if it is populated by information handlers at least as adept as, say, Franz Liszt, who had no difficulty in sight reading piano concertos by Mendelssohn or Grieg when confronted with them for the first time. Neoclassical consumers are typically assumed to be able to equate the ratios of price and marginal rate of substitution for 'N' goods, with 'N' not necessarily a small number. Consumers in Lancaster's adaptation of the theory deal with 'N' characteristics in a related way. It is as if they can take account of all of the available bits of information in all of the ways that might possibly be necessary.

It might be argued by a neoclassical theorist that the reference to pianistic virtuosity is unfairly chosen, and that her theory is adequate for analysing simple, everyday, tasks like the purchase of a bundle of conveniently divisible goods in a supermarket. Here, shoppers seem to be held up not by the task of taking decisions about what to buy, but by the queues that result from the slowness with which goods can be checked-out and packed at the tills. However, the possibility that in this situation consumers are actually taking their decisions in an entirely different way—e.g. by using simple rules of thumb—is one which is difficult to dismiss, especially in the light of the observation by Ries and Trout (1981, p. 77) that

[The average supermarket today] has 10,000 different products or brands on display. This means that a young person has to sort out and catalogue 10,000 different names in his or her head.

When you consider that the average college graduate has a speaking vocabulary of only 8,000 words, you can see the problem.

The kid spends four years in a university and ends up 2,000 words down.

Some of the more sophisticated neoclassical economists have, with the aid of such notions as the utility tree, started to try to deal with some of the consequences of bounded rationality. But their work is very much a modification of theories that begin with global rationality. This may be blinding them to some fundamental issues. For example, in the work on utility trees it is the notion that people consider simultaneous marginal substitutions between *all* goods that is rejected in favour of substitution only between goods in particular categories. But the notion of substitution itself is left unquestioned, despite the fact that real people often speak in terms of *priorities*. In the chapters that follow we shall attempt to grapple with the fact of bounded rationality as a central matter of concern rather than as a cause for belated modifications of detail.

3.6 Non-Existent Information

Despite their bounded rationality, real world decision makers often wish to have more information than they presently possess, in order to avoid making mistakes due to uncertainty. Neoclassical work on choice under uncertainty characteristically deals only with the impossibility of knowing about future environmental states (the weather, health, and so on) in the present. But a much more significant informational gap concerns information which does not presently exist in the system because its existence is contingent on transactional decisions which other people have not yet taken. The Keynesian savings and investment problem, for example, arises because people are unwilling or unable to make advance orders for goods to be delivered in the future. An act of saving today does not represent a demand for any particular good at any particular point in the future. Hence a decision to invest is often very much in the nature of a leap in the dark.

Consumers have to take investment decisions too. When they purchase expensive consumer durables they may take considerable risks if their expenditure involves them in substantial increases in their credit repayment commitments, or reductions in their financial reserves. If they cannot know whether or not they will have jobs in months to come, because no one has yet decided their fates, their decisions to purchase expensive durables will be taken in recognition of the possibility that, if they lose their jobs, they may either have to trade in what they have bought and suffer a capital loss, or find themselves severely constrained in their other activities. Their behaviour will thus be highly speculative and affected by the news of what is going on around them, or by the predictions of pundits who may be little better informed.

This speculative element in consumer behaviour, which has been emphasised by Reddaway (1937), Townshend (1937), Katona (1960), and Smith (1975), is particularly important in wealthy economies, for here expenditure on durables will be proportionately significant and wealth will be more likely to be held in securities, of inherently uncertain value. In wealthy economies there will also be a greater tendency for durable goods to be replaced long before they are completely worn out, and hence greater discretion in the timing of replacements. Thus, even if stable long run preferences exist for the services yielded by particular durables, their demand patterns can be exceedingly unstable in the short run and prone to fluctuate in response to 'the news'. But although the importance of avoiding capital losses is most obvious in the case of expensive durables, there is, in principle, no reason why this 'liquidity preference' view of demand cannot be applied to *all* goods that are not perfectly perishable: people may postpone even minor purchases *in case* these are not really needed, or could be got more cheaply elsewhere. Subsequently they may be distracted by other unforeseen contingencies and end up purchasing altogether different bundles of goods. (See Dow and Earl (1982), Chapter 8, for a more detailed analysis.)

This emphasis on the flimsy, speculative foundations of much consumer demand is not based merely on *a priori* reasoning. It is strongly supported by Smith's (1975) study of the US car market and Katona's (1976) work with data from OECD countries, in which he correlated shifts in rates of expenditure on consumer durables with shifts in confidence among voters concerning the ability of their governments to control inflation. The policy implications of this analysis are not trivial. It would appear that social security provisions which guarantee hire purchase and overdraft interest commitments may serve not merely as *ex post* macroeconomic stabilisers, preventing a multiple spread of a demand failure. They may also work in an *ex ante* sense, making demand contractions less likely in the first place. If consumer confidence *has* collapsed, and a form of liquidity trap prevails in an economy, our analysis suggests that there may be considerable scope for macroeconomic stimulation by means of *propaganda* designed to shift consumer confidence. If firms can attempt to control their sales by advertising, there is no reason why governments should not also think of using propaganda measures to shape consumer savings behaviour. If such measures work when nations are at war with each other, they may equally well be applied in the war against poverty and unemployment. To design appropriate propaganda, policy makers need an understanding of how people think and take significant decisions under uncertainty. It will be argued in section 3.8 that neoclassical theories of choice provide inadequate representations of how such decisions are taken (see also Dow and Earl (1982), pp. 199–201).

3.7 Information Impactedness and Organisational Slack

Information pertinent to choice, and which might not overload the boundedly rational decision maker, may exist somewhere in the system, yet be unavailable at an affordable cost, if at all. Parties possessing such information may be unwilling to transmit it to those who would like to have it, because it is not in their interests to do so. Consumers do not tell firms that they would be prepared to pay more or tolerate reductions in quality. Workers do not tell their superiors that they would be willing to work harder for the same wage. The finance controller of a company will find it hard to know where a problem really lies, and how resources should be allocated, if heads of sales, production, design, and stock control, all blame each other for any failings and, on the basis of their 'specialist knowledge', attempt to justify their claims for resources. Boards of directors do not tell shareholders that dividends could be higher, without harming the long run growth of the company, if their own claims on resources were reduced to the undisclosed minimum that they would tolerate. Shareholders, likewise, do not make known any possibility that they would tolerate a particular cut in dividends without attempting to have the board removed. Potential shareholders do not usually reveal the conditions under which they would consider making a takeover raid. Potential producers do not make public their investment intentions. Where information exists but is compressed into inconvenient pockets in the system, from whence it may only be obtained by some form of bribery, coercion or espionage, a state of *information impactedness* may be said to prevail (we owe this term to Williamson, 1975).

So long as people are specialists in some sense, they may be able to achieve returns to particular activities in excess of the minimum return necessary for their participation. Where several parties to an exchange enjoy informational advantages over each other a bargaining situation exists. If the parties are prepared to reveal sufficient information to each other as to make a complementarity of their interests become apparent they will form some kind of coalition and a transaction (market or otherwise) will emerge. The difference between the returns the members of a coalition receive and the minimum they would find acceptable as a basis for continuing the relationship has been termed *organisational slack* by Cyert and March (1963, p. 36).

With experience, a specialist's knowledge of a system may increase. This may increase or reduce the level of slack. Consumers may become more attuned to the real nature of the products they are buying, *vis à vis* rival products. Their minimal requirements may thus rise (if the usual product has fallen in their estimation) or fall (if other products are found to be more inferior than first thought). Similarly, learning by doing may give the incumbent of a job an informational advantage over potential raw recruits, so she can now take life rather more easily. A worker may also come to see more clearly how her part of the organisation operates and thus be better placed to bargain with her local rivals, unless her gain in knowledge is outstripped by *their* idiosyncratic learning. The scope for opportunistic behaviour is restricted by the existence of potential and actual competitors who could provide similar services above a particular price, the social transmission of information—at least so long as opinion leaders in a social grouping are not themselves ill-informed and making a pretence of expertise—and the presence of consultants. But these factors need not eliminate it entirely.

An economic system characterised by specialisation and the dispersion of knowledge inevitably contains some measure of slack, and its behaviour therefore cannot be seen as conforming to a precise pathway determined by underlying 'objective' data of preferences and technology. In fact, information impactedness makes technology very difficult to isolate from preferences. A technology can only be specified if people bound up with it are willing and able to divulge their idiosyncratic knowledge. It is often rather hard to draw a precise line between information impactedness, the nonexistence of information and bounded rationality. A person may cease being opportunistic and do her best to dispense information to, say, a new colleague. But the latter's learning may only be possible in full measure with actual experience, because the 'teacher' is insufficiently articulate to be able to convey all of her idiosyncratic knowledge. If something cannot be conveyed but requires experience to be appreciated, and if there is no guarantee that everyone will experience the same things in a particular situation, it is very hard to think of the technology of an economy as something that can be written down as a 'book of blueprints'.

Important areas of policy are ruled out of court if we do not face up to the existence of information impactedness, and attempt to construct instead deterministic theories of choice 'as if' it does not exist. Let us first consider consumerism and consumer welfare. To assume there is no information impactedness is to divert economic analysis away from consumerism and, more generally, from the need to construct a new welfare economics that abandons the study of the perfectly sovereign consumer and disinterested policy maker in favour of an analysis concentrating on bargaining processes, the origins of power, and the constraints on its misuse. The welfare losses that may be associated with advertising cannot be analysed with a theory of choice that assumes preferences are given and does not consider how consumer perceptions are formed or how people think. A neoclassical theorist is thus singularly ill-equipped to make any meaningful pronouncements about the work of critics of modern capitalism such as Galbraith (1958, 1975) or Joan Robinson, when they make claims such as the following:

Consumer's sovereignty can never be established so long as the initiative lies with the producer. For the general run of consumer goods the buyer is necessarily an amateur while the seller is a professional. To make industry genuinely serve the needs of the public, as it is supposed to do in the textbooks, would require a monopsony of consumers, equipped with their own experts. Some slight efforts are being made nowadays to protect the consumer interest, but they cannot make much head against the power of advertisement (Robinson (1969) pp. xi–xii).

This comment recognises a possible consequence of the prevalence of information impactedness. But it is one which might be countered by another, which recognises the problem of bounded rationality. For example, the Neo Austrian objection to the sort of attitude displayed by Joan Robinson begins by noting that

Consumers do *not* always know what products are available and even if they do know of their existence they are not always aware of their properties. And consumers cannot, of course, seek further information about a product or property of whose existence they are unaware (Littlechild (1978, p. 32), emphasis in original).

What may sound like a *persuasive* advertisement may be the form of advertisement necessary to attract the consumer's attention and make a product *stand out* as being of interest in a world where too much information can, paradoxically, lead to ignorance. This sort of argument makes it clear that we should be much more open-minded than Joan Robinson or Galbraith often appear to be. Unfortunately, many Neo Austrian economists tend to write from a standpoint in which everything in the garden of modern capitalism is seen as more rosy than it would be if there were more public intervention. This causes them to argue as if the point made by Littlechild is sufficient to justify the approval of *any* advertising, and the retention of the assumption of consumer sovereignty.

Two examples may help to illustrate why we should beware of jumping to conclusions in the area of consumerism. Take first the sale of deodorants, one of Galbraith's favourite examples of a heavily advertised, highly successful, but intrinsically worthless product. Deodorants are sold, in part at least, as devices that help the user become more attractive to members of the opposite sex. But the natural odours which they suppress are actually human pheromones: secretions which are natural chemical attractors and which only repel if present in excessive amounts due to a failure to wash regularly. An Austrian economist would doubtless argue that there is money to be made by pointing this out and discrediting the product. Certainly, popularist sexologists have done very nicely by writing books that make this point (amongst many others), and consumerist magazines are growing in circulation. However, much more money has been made by cosmetics firms that continue to *smother* consumers with 'information' to the effect that deodorants are an essential device for coping with everyday life. And now some of these firms are beginning to sell aerosol cans of 'natural pheromones' to put back what their other products take away!

Secondly, we must note that even if information impactedness and persuasive advertising combine to result in consumer choices being controlled, to some extent, by firms, we cannot, in a second best world of unemployment, say that this loss of sovereignty is *a priori* a bad thing. Consumers may prefer to have incomes to purchase goods, knowing that they may have fallen victim to advertisements, than to be unemployed and have a more restricted ability to pit their wits against firms in the market place. If UK and US car firms, for example, were more adept at controlling the behaviour of their potential customers, their market shares would have been less compressed by imported substitutes. Unemployment in their industries, and as a result of the multiplier, would be lower.

Ideally we might wish to see such unemployment prevented by import controls or devaluation (coupled with a domestic demand expansion so that unemployment is not exported to the rest of the world). But, if there are political barriers to the use of such policies, an economist who can advise on propaganda-related ways of controlling demand may, somewhat paradoxically, be performing a socially useful function. Lower unemployment may be achieved at the cost of more consumers being deceived or made to think differently. If there is no such thing as objective knowledge or given preferences, it is by no means obvious that such 'distortions' of choice are *always* undesirable distortions when seen in isolation from their employment effects. Deodorants can be shown experimentally not to make people more 'attractive', and, to give another example, energy economists can explain why double glazing is unlikely to save money. But who is to say how the different, and not always quantifiable, characteristics offered by, say, a Chrysler and a Datsun car *should* be appraised?

The tendency of the typical neoclassical economist to assume away the problems of information impactedness and bounded rationality has led to bias in industrial policy too. The neoclassical theorist implicitly treats firms as if all of their personnel work according to perfectly detailed job contracts that cover all contingencies; there is no scope for discretion and no need to consider decision processes within firms. As Loasby (1967) points out, with firms thus treated as black boxes their efficiency can only be discussed with respect to their sizes, locations, and the prices they charge.

In addition to this overly restrictive mainstream approach there is a growing (but as yet minority interest) literature, on a modern variant of the neoclassical paradigm, which *does* plead that policy makers should recognise that job contracts in the real world are not perfectly specified and hence that questions of motivation and control may be rather important. This is the work on *X*-efficiency spawned by the (1966) paper of Leibenstein. While this is a welcome improvement on the standard neoclassical approach, it is insufficiently radical in its philosophy to serve as a foundation for BPK theory. We agree with the objections raised by Loasby in his review of Leibenstein's (1976) book *Beyond Economic Man: A New Foundation for Microeconomics*. Leibenstein tends to write as if production functions are knowable and efficiency is to be improved by making the real world conform with the neoclassical ideal. However, as Loasby (1976b, pp. 914–15) points out, 'in a world of ignorance, unexpected change, and significant transactions costs, imperfectly specified contracts are essential.' An '*X*-efficient' state with zero workplace discretion thus is not an appropriate reference optimum for welfare economics or industrial policy making. Organisational slack may exist as a result of incompetence. However, it is also a result of choice and its removal will not usually be without distributional implications. There is no presumption in BPK theory that it is necessarily undesirable.

If job incumbents are unable or unwilling to spell out precisely what it is that their experience enables them to do, and what is the maximum that they are prepared to do in return for a particular remuneration, then it may often be appropriate to allow them discretion. To specify what *is* generally known about the technology, and arrange for the delivery of a precise output in the light of this, may lead to less output than in a situation of discretion where the same remuneration package is being offered. In the real world the worker is told neither precisely how to do her job, nor precisely what her reward will be for what she does. Her promotion prospects are usually as loosely specified as her present task. To understand whether any given employment relationship could be improved upon we need to understand how workers think and how the competitive process operates inside organisations.

It would be unfair on mainstream economics to conclude this section without considering some of the formal neoclassical work on bargaining problems and the market failures that may arise as a result of information impactedness. We have in mind the literature on game theory and the theory of the core (Chapters 8 and 9 of Weintraub's (1979) book are an accessible introduction to recent work on 'the core' and the essential references), as well as that associated with Akerlof's (1970) work on quality uncertainty. Much of this looks likely to be of limited practical application. This is because there are several features of real world bargaining situations with which highly formal analysis cannot cope.

The problem with most bargaining situations is that they lack a well-specified structure or, if well-structured, are complex. Game theory and the theory of the core are not very useful to decision makers in game situations—such as property selling, haggling over trade in allowances against a new car, or in attempts to extract promotion—where the opponent's possible set of options is far from clear. Nor does game theory tell us much about how to play successfully games like chess where all the interest arises from bounded rationality.

The works on market failure in situations of quality uncertainty are perhaps more helpful. They are concerned with what may happen if good or bad quality products, of the same outward appearance, cannot be distinguished by buyers, and cannot, therefore, trade at different prices. Owners of 'good' used cars may be unwilling to trade them in if they can get only the price of an average quality car, yet risk trading up to a 'lemon'. This may bring about a shortage of good used cars, and a quality of *traded* cars which is lower on average than the average quality of all examples of the marque of the same age in existence. Even owners of 'objectively' average quality cars may find a price that reflects the average quality of traded cars unattractive and feel similarly 'locked in' to their present vehicles. The end result may be that, in the absence of a system of guarantees, to raise the resale price (and hence permit higher trade-in prices on average), only poor quality cars get traded, and they thus live up to purchasers' pessimistic expectations. Another market where this problem has been identified is that for health insurance. If *only* the accident prone or congenitally unhealthy were willing to take out insurance, and thus could not be cross-subsidised by risk averse pessimists, insurance premia could be so high as to lead to a total collapse of the market. The literature in this area has made a useful contribution by setting up the nature of the problem that needs to be analysed. But to study why market collapses are not usually total in such situations, and to discover appropriate types of guarantee provisions to reduce the extent of the failure, we need a theory of how people are motivated and take speculative decisions—which leads us to the next section.

3.8 Potential Surprise versus Probability: A Dialogue

THE CRITIC: You seem to write as though neoclassical economists always assume traders are perfectly informed. That is simply not the case.

THE PROPONENT: Sorry if I've been giving that impression, though you must surely concede that it is almost a convention in advanced neoclassical texts for uncertainty to be introduced into the analysis only in the final chapter (cf. Debreu (1959); Deaton and Muellbauer (1980)). My reason for wanting to propose a new theory of choice in a world of imperfect foresight arises not out of the failure of theorists such as yourself to provide *any* such theory but, rather, out of my concern with the deficiencies of the probabilistic, expected utility models you typically use.

THE CRITIC: Now you're talking as though you're ignorant of the latest alternative to these models, namely, the 'rational' expectations models.

THE PROPONENT: I've heard vaguely of these. Perhaps you'd better explain how they work before we discuss my objections to the probabilistic models.

THE CRITIC: Rational expectations models are basically very simple. We assume that agents do not know for sure what will happen in any particular situation, for outcomes are prone to stochastic variation. However, they *do* know that these outcomes are normally distributed around a given mean. They also know the real nature of the model underlying the mean result; usually we assume they realise the economy functions as in neoclassical theory. Agents will not continually take decisions that are, on average, biased, for they learn that it is rational to choose the mean figure—it is the best guess they can make. On average their guesses will be correct; windfall gains and losses will cancel out.

THE PROPONENT: I don't think this idea is going to have much effect on the faith I have in my own way of modelling uncertainty. It seems, first of all, and in the light of the work of Joan Robinson and Shackle, to be philosophically unsupportable because it is incompatible with the epistemic foundations of time. In your world of rational expectations the past offers, on average, an accurate guide to the future. Current expectations and behaviour are not logically independent of future events, and each moment is not uniquely knitted into history. Real world decision makers find that, as history evolves through time, the past offers no guarantee of the future. Consequently, they must act on the basis of their imaginations and they are free to imagine anything, including things which have not happened hitherto. Of course, what they imagine may be heavily dependent on their past experiences or thos, of other people in related decision contexts, even if the contextual similarities are rather slim: these experiences may provide a useful basis for forming conjectures of what *could* happen, and of what might potentially block particular outcomes. However, real world decision makers are not trapped, as are your 'rationally expecting' choosers, in a world of preordained equilibrium. Rational expectations models contradict the epistemic asymmetry of time; they seem merely to replace the perfect knowledge assumption with a stochastic euphemism (see Bausor (1981) for a more detailed analysis).

I'm also rather disturbed by the suggestion that people would willingly accept stochastic variations for what they were, *if* they encountered them. My concern here results from my reading of Steinbruner's (1974, pp. 110–1) description of how people behave in binary betting experiments.

THE CRITIC: You mean the sort of experiment they perform in psychology, where subjects are asked to bet on which of two outcomes will come up each time?

THE PROPONENT: That's right. A common ploy is to ask them to choose between A, which rewards by coming up two-thirds of the time, and B, which only comes up one-third of the time. The two-thirds/one-third mix is then generated by a random mechanism. What do you think most people do in this situation?

THE CRITIC: Well, since they are facing a stochastic process, I guess that pretty soon they will learn that the way to generate high winnings is to bet on A every time; they will then win two-thirds of the time.

THE PROPONENT: In fact, people have a strong propensity to choose in variations on a two-thirds/one-third *pattern* and lose nearly all the time. Like somebody who attempts to develop a system to 'break the bank at Monte Carlo', they will not accept that the overall mix has stochastic origins. They seem to be determined to impose patterns of order upon what they see (cf. the discussions of motivation in Chapter 5), and end up producing disastrously biased outcomes. Of course, if they *can* discover an underlying pattern, because one exists to be discovered, they will win every time.

THE CRITIC: As a good positivist I suppose I shall have to admit that such evidence is rather damaging for my rational expectations analysis. So let's turn to my probabilistic theory. In later chapters of this book you seem to replace the notion that there are degrees of probability ranging between zero (certainty that an event will not occur, or, at least, a subjective conviction of complete confidence that it will not occur) and one (certainty that an event will occur, or complete confidence at present that it will occur), with Shackle's (1949, 1955, 1958, 1961, 1979) idea that people think about uncertainty in terms of degrees of *potential surprise*. If people presently think an event cannot possibly have a particular outcome they expect they will be shocked if it does come about, whereas, at the other extreme, if they think there is nothing to prevent it from occurring they will not be at all surprised if it does come about. I rather get the impression that you are making an awful fuss over a mere linguistic change. This impression is reinforced when I look at the curves representing conjectures of possible outcomes in Chapter 4—potential surprise curves as you call them—and discover they look like inverted normal distribution curves.

THE PROPONENT: When he coined the term 'potential surprise', Shackle was trying to break with the idea that if a decision is repeated often enough it will generate a pattern of outcomes distributed in line with a good set of probability estimates. I've always found instructive his (1955, p. 25) example of the problem facing Napoleon as he worked out which strategy to use at the battle of Waterloo. In terms of the conventional probabilistic theory, how would Napoleon have made up his mind?

THE CRITIC: For each strategy he would have assessed the list of sequels that could occur and the probability of each sequel coming about. He would then have assigned an expected utility to each sequel and multiplied this by the probability of the situation actually arising. This would be done for each probable sequel of each scheme and then the values would be summed for their respective schemes. According to the theory, he would have chosen the strategy, amongst those that he considered, which had the highest total value.

THE PROPONENT: But it would have been meaningless for him to perform such an *adding up* operation in this situation—even supposing he could have done so. (Since each sequel might have been thought of as a bundle of diverse characteristics, each of which might have had different 'probabilities' of coming about, bounded rationality could have posed quite a problem. Napoleon's decision was a *crucial* one, for if he lost he might never be able to lead an army again. After losing and being exiled to St Helena he could not have another try to show that his chosen strategy would generate victories more frequently than any other strategy. It was essentially a 'one-off' decision: If it had succeeded he would not have needed to repeat it; because it failed, he was in no position to do so. His decision was a personal disaster, but it was made no less disastrous by the fact that he thought there was some chance that he could obtain any one of a variety of less disastrous outcomes by choosing as he did. The alternative outcomes associated with any given strategy were not meaningfully commensurable. They could only have provided him with some *counterpoise* to any hypothesis of disaster that he entertained if, by seeming themselves to be in some degree possible, they served to make the unpleasant outcome less plausible, making him feel that he would be rather more surprised if, in the event, it did come about.

THE CRITIC: But I understand that Napoleon actually rated his chances in probabilistic terms before the start of the battle and then, perhaps being a good Bayesian, revised them downwards as it was taking place. And people in everyday life often speak in probabilistic terms.

THE PROPONENT: It's the philosophical difference between probabilistic and potential surprise analyses that matters, not the words we use. When someone assigns a possible outcome a particular probability rating we have no reason necessarily to presume she will perform an adding up operation of the kind proposed in neoclassical theory. My behavioural perspective means that I find much more plausible the idea that when a person envisages a range of possible outcomes she will focus on their extreme values, or on tolerable, good and bad values, as she tries to avoid making a mistake. In everyday life a person who says she thinks something has a 'high probability' she means that she would not be very surprised if it occurred, because she cannot see much to prevent it and can see many reasons why it could occur, even if it has not occurred hitherto. It is common for people to say that, while they think something is 'not probable', it is at least 'possible'. By this they mean that they cannot see a good reason why it should *necessarily* occur, and that they would be rather surprised if it did.

THE CRITIC: Suppose that I accept that the probabilistic theory is unsound in the context of important decisions, such as choices about jobs, investment schemes, expensive durables, and whether or not to have children (who might be of either sex or born handicapped). It still seems a useful idea for discussing behaviour in, say, supermarkets where low value purchases are made time and again yet where availability and quality are prone to variation.

THE PROPONENT: That would be quite a concession for you to make given your liking for all-embracing, general models. But I think you'd be rather foolish to adhere to your model even within such a restricted domain—for several reasons. First, it is not always the case that low value items can be purchased without recognition that something of a crucial decision is involved. For example, my father has repeatedly lamented the fact that he lost an entire reel of holiday photographs this year due to the film breaking inside his camera; they cannot be recaptured. Secondly, I notice that your probabilistic model is much more demanding of a chooser's information processing capabilities than is the Shackle-inspired model I propose in the next chapter: my model nowhere assumes that choosers add up rival outcomes. Thirdly, I would contend that, in 'nearly replicable' situations where decisions *are* unimportant and uncertainty exists, it is quite possible that no deliberative thought occurs and, instead, rule of thumb techniques are used for dealing with uncertainty (see sections 6.4 and 6.5). Finally, may I ask you if you ever recall, as a child, being prevented by some last minute hitch from going to a party and, if so, what you did at the time?

THE CRITIC: I can't see what it's got to do with our present discussion, but I do seem to remember that sort of thing happening. I recall screaming and sobbing despite my parents' attempt to console me by saying that there would be plenty of other parties in future months and years. I wanted to go to *that* party.

THE PROPONENT: That ought to clinch the case in favour of a

non-probabilistic analysis of choice under uncertainty. You were displaying the common tendency to treat all but the most trivial events as unique. As Shackle observes, 'We live in the present moment. If I fail to make a success of *this* moment my whole faith in my capacity for dealing with life is to some degree undermined' (1955, p. 65, emphasis in original).

3.9 Satisficing versus Maximising Behaviour: A Dialogue

THE CRITIC: At the start of this book you seem to be going against the grain of the great body of economic reasoning by saying that you do not presume decision makers maximise anything.

THE PROPONENT: I'm simply following Nobel prizewinner Herbert Simon (1957, 1959), who has pointed out that the notion that agents maximise subject to their budget constraints is logically open to question in situations of uncertainty and where the list of options available is not given but has to be discovered. People can never know in advance what might be the payoffs to possible schemes to search for better information. Search may fail to uncover helpful information and such information as is obtained may be worth less than it cost to acquire.

THE CRITIC: But there is a perfectly simple neoclassical way of getting round this problem. The decision maker simply applies the probabilistic method of calculating expected utilities to a list of alternative search strategies, which includes a 'do nothing' option. She then chooses the search method with the highest expected payoff and, in the light of the extra information she obtains, she works out expected utilities for rival schemes of action (including any she discovers in the search process) in the normal way. If she has a correct idea of the relevant probabilities she will undertake the optimal amount of search over the long run.

THE PROPONENT: I thought I'd just shown you that your probabilistic theory of choice left a lot to be desired, and it seems to be no less flawed in this context. To the extent that each search situation is unique, and information is not forgotten once it has been discovered, the process of search does not involve repeatability and cannot have probabilistic foundations. But if I ignore this problem, I'm still rather puzzled as to how you think people choose their lists of possible search schemes in the first place.

THE CRITIC: If these are not already given, decision makers choose between alternative possible ways of searching for schemes of search.

THE PROPONENT: It sounds like you have set yourself a problem of infinite regress. To break it you must either assume given information at some point, or adopt a behavioural approach and assume that people simply will not *bother* to search at some stage if they think that their list includes at least one option which will at least enable them to meet their aspirational targets. That is to say, instead of seeking to maximise under uncertainty, decision makers may be thought of as *satisficing*: they try to meet targets of adequacy rather than pinnacles of attainment.

THE CRITIC: But surely, if you applied such an idea to firms operating in a competitive environment, you would find that satisficing firms would be driven out of business by firms which always searched for the best option before making a choice. Such firms could earn higher profits and use these to finance more research and investment expenditure.

THE PROPONENT: This sort of suggestion ignores the logical problems of infinite regress. It also fails to recognise that decision making can be very expensive if the list of possible activities is not given but has to be constructed, and activities require in-depth evaluation. A firm which does not set its sights too low and which has evolved an efficient set of rule of thumb procedures (cf. sections 6.4 and 6.5) may be able to act more quickly, and at less cost in terms of management time, than one which *attempts* actively to behave in the manner assumed in neoclassical theory. If the environment is reasonably stable, 'simplifying satisficers' may drive out 'deliberating maximisers' (cf. Winter (1964)).

THE CRITIC: You just now mentioned, and have in previous pages also referred to, 'rule of thumb' methods of taking decisions. You're not going to try to say that people never engage in deliberative thought, are you?

THE PROPONENT: No. A lot of work by behavioural theorists in the past has overplayed the importance of such simplifying choice techniques (in contrast to most marketing work, which has tended to treat all choice as deliberative, despite rejecting the neoclassical approach). Steinbruner (1974) is about the only behavioural theorist who has hitherto tried to understand how boundedly-rational choosers take 'big decisions' under uncertainty, but, as will be explained in section 5.6, his own solution is something of a special case.

THE CRITIC: I've also been wondering what happens if people fail to meet their aspirations or find them much easier to meet than they had been expecting.

THE PROPONENT: Behavioural theorists assume aspiration levels tend to move into line with attainments, but emphasise that they do so rather slowly. Cyert and March (1963, p. 38) place this idea at the heart of their work on organisational slack. In situations of information impactedness the demands of coalition members fail to rise in line with the resources available to the coalition in good times. This excess of payments serves as a buffer which permits the organisation to survive difficult periods, within bounds, without fragmentation.

THE CRITIC: If aspiration levels are moving around all the time, how can you investigate welfare issues? An allocation which is Pareto efficient one day may be Pareto inefficient the next if the aspirations of some people move up and those of others are reduced in the light of experience.

THE PROPONENT: If we view preferences as historically-evolving sets of aspiration levels and decision makers as considering only limited ranges of options, we must inevitably approach policy matters in a rather different way from that which you, as a neoclassical theorist, would normally take. I would wish, for example, to pay particular attention to the interactions between advertising campaigns and aspirational shifts. A marketing policy can be used to encourage people to move 'up-market' by suggesting that their aspirations are too low; it *may* thus enhance consumer welfare by causing consumers to discover activities superior to those which they would otherwise have chosen. However, it may also lead to the sort of dissatisfaction about which Hirsch (1976) has written to his *Social Limits to Growth*. If one group cannot improve its position in society without threatening the position of others who see themselves as relatively superior, then, at the end of the day, despite higher consumption levels, no one may actually feel better off, unless the advertising process results in employment being higher than it might otherwise have been. And, if there otherwise would have been full employment, resources devoted to advertising might have been better used in removing public squalor. In a world of satisficing it is also possible that advertisements may be used in attempts to discourage search which might uncover the superior products of rivals. For example, it can be suggested that a company's products meet aspiration levels which in no way should be thought of as modest, and, if consumers accept such a picture of what their preferences ought to be, they may end up choosing from unduly restricted agendas of possible options.

THE CRITIC: Introspection leads me to suspect that my own aspirations are rather more inflexible than you seem to be suggesting, so that the notion of given preferences might still be a useful approximation: if I'm disappointed, I don't give in and accept 'second best' all that easily.

THE PROPONENT: This is an important point, but it is one which leads me even further away from a neoclassical view of things. Hitherto, behavioural theorists, apart from Kornai (1971, pp. 190–202), have rather underemphasised the fact that many aspirational shifts are not merely lagged, they are discontinuous. Response thresholds have to be crossed. This takes time and unusual patterns of behaviour may be observed in the interim. *Euphoria* is a state of over-confidence which occurs where expected attainments run ahead of conventional aspirations and cause insufficient search to be carried out. The results of euphoria can be disastrous; a case in point is in the business of banking, which is discussed in detail in Dow and Earl (1982, Chapters 11 and 12). At the opposite extreme we find *frustration* and disillusionment, which arise from a persistent failure to meet aspirations because search is not successful or initial endowments are inadequate. Here, too, ill-considered behaviour may be the result—people react in a desperate, hostile manner to maintain their views of themselves in the world (see further, sections 5.5, 5.6 and 7.3). Euphoria and frustration are quite clearly disequilibrium (and often disequilibrating) features and are necessarily at odds with the neoclassical paradigm, but they are phenomena which policy makers ignore at their peril.

3.10 Conclusion

The arguments presented in this chapter indicate that, from a behavioural perspective, the neoclassical analysis of choice must be judged to be misleading in two senses of the word. The analysis is misleading as a description of how individuals made decisions. To put it bluntly: real world decision makers possess neither the wit nor the knowledge to act in a way that corresponds approximately to neoclassical optimising behaviour. The analysis is also misleading in the sense that the form taken by neoclassical models of choice is such that the attention of economists who use them is turned away from significant areas of concern for corporate and public policy. By contrast, the behavioural analysis of choice, which is developed in the chapters that follow, places such areas of policy, along with the question of how decision makers cope with ignorance and complexity, at the centre of attention. Not only this, but it is a form of analysis which it is easy to envisage being used, in conjunction with questionnaires, to aid predictions in situations where positivist methods of research are made redundant by the absence of suitable data.

4 Alternative Behavioural Theories of Choice

4.1 Introduction

In the previous three chapters we have discussed our reasons for wanting to propose an alternative theory of choice to the dominant Hicksian approach used by neoclassical economists, and we have outlined the image with which we should like such an alternative to conform. In this chapter we begin to construct the new theory by examining the question of how it is that decision makers choose between mutually exclusive schemes of action, given their motivations and perceptions of these schemes. In Chapters 5 to 7 we shall examine these 'givens' in detail. For present purposes it will be adequate to assume, as neoclassical theorists do as a shorthand, that choosers are 'utility' seekers, and leave aside any detailed discussion of the origins of their perceptions.

It is easy enough to state our own preferences for the characteristics and functions of a behavioural theory of choice. However, with a touch of irony we must confess to facing a problem of choosing between rival non-neoclassical theories of choice that have been proposed outside mainstream economics writings to meet the sort of objections we have been making against traditional models. In this chapter we review the leaders amongst these non-neoclassical choice models and then go on to propose a new model of our own, and some variations on it, before attempting to justify the superiority of our own ideas.

Behavioural economists and marketing specialists producing theories of choice have taken as a common starting point the notion that choices are made between schemes of action conceived as bundles of attributes or characteristics, rather than goods as wholes. In this they are clearly taking a position somewhat similar to that suggested by Lancaster. They also recognise that consumers choose activities from relatively restricted agendas of possible schemes. These restricted agendas have to be used because decision takers have a limited ability to obtain and process information within a given time period. It is further agreed that, just as there are many possible activities, so too are there many characteristics, and boundedly rational choosers may often limit their attention at any moment to a subset of those which might be relevant. But here the agreement stops and theorists then divide into two broad camps.

Closest to Lancaster in approach are the proponents of compensatory choice theories. As we shall show in sections 4.2, 4.4 and 4.5, decision takers are assumed in these models to restrict quite severely the number of product attributes they consider in order to enable themselves to handle attributes simultaneously. The other group of theorists (whose numbers include the present author) suggest variations of a lexicographic, priorities-centred choice model. This work is examined in sections 4.3, 4.6, 4.7 and, with regard to policy implications, in 4.8. In this latter type of model the chooser can consider many more attributes without getting confused because attributes are evaluated sequentially and there are no trade-offs of the conventional kind between them.

Unlike conventional theories based on indifference analysis, these behavioural theories can all be operationalised for use in market planning with the aid of questionnaire data from market research. This property might seem to imply that it ought to be easy to choose between them on empirical grounds. But this has not been the case; there is no general consensus as to which one gives the best predictions. Given this difficulty, it is easy to think that our own introspection should be capable of revealing whether we use compensatory or priorities-based methods of taking decisions. But it is just as easy for us to be misled by our own predispositions, by a process we shall discuss in detail in section 5.6, especially if we have been brought up to believe in the principle of substitution. To illustrate this complication, we present a dialogue concerning the case for and against lexicographic models in section 4.9. This dialogue reveals how both basic theories of choice may be consistent with a body of evidence despite having fundamentally different practical implications. In it we explain why we shall use a lexicographic theory as the basis for all the discussions of choice in the remaining chapters. Section 4.10 is a brief conclusion.

4.2 Compensatory Models: An Overview

Expectancy value compensatory choice models have become very popular in consumer behaviour research since the mid 1960s. In essence they are less restrictive versions of the characteristics approach to choice which Lancaster (1966) has been attempting to encourage conventional economists to use. The market leaders amongst them are the versions proposed by Rosenberg (discussed in section 4.4 below) and Fishbein (discussed in section 4.5). These models differ significantly in the variables they include but share a common view of what a person does when choosing between alternative schemes of action. Though they are often discussed as if they refer merely to choices between particular brands of consumer products in the market place, these models, like the non-compensatory models we also discuss, aim to be generally applicable. Thus a scheme of action may refer to the activity of purchasing or using a particular commodity, the activity of accepting a particular job or performing a particular act in a social situation, the activity of charging a particular price for a commodity, and even the activities of electing to use a particular method of going about searching for additions to an agenda of possible activities or electing to use a set of simple rules of thumb for making 'cybernetic' choices (which we discuss in Chapter 6 and which involve little detailed processing of information).

In compensatory models choices are assumed to be made in the following way, once a decision has been made that sufficient search has been undertaken for possible schemes of action.

(i)   Each scheme is evaluated separately with regard to all the attributes/characteristics considered relevant.

(ii)   Attribute evaluations are carried out in terms of a) the likelihood that the scheme actually possesses the attribute and b) the person's view as to whether the attribute is a good or bad thing.

(iii)   For each attribute the two evaluations are multiplied together in the person's mind (in units which have never been very precisely specified).

(iv)   The totals thus obtained for each attribute are then summed together to give a grand total for the expected value of choosing the scheme perceived by the person. At this point in the choice process some of the models accord weights to the various attributes, related to their importance to the decision taker.

(v)   The grand total for the scheme is stored in the person's memory and the procedure is repeated for all the remaining schemes, including the scheme to make no change in the relevant area.

(vi)   The person then chooses the scheme of action with the highest total expected value.

This choice procedure is easiest to envisage if the decision taker's evaluation of attributes consists of simple 'yes/no' evaluations with uncertain outcomes (e.g. 'How likely is it that I will be able to "double expose" photographs if I buy this camera?') rather than evaluations along a scale, the points of which each have different likelihoods of occurrence (e.g. 'How likely is it that this car has a top speed of (a) 100 mph, (b) 110 mph, (c) 120 mph?'). In the scalar example the person may have to consider individual points on each scale as separate attributes unless only one point on each attribute scale has a greater than zero possibility of actually being a feature of the scheme being considered. This is really what has to be done if Lancaster's choice model is to incorporate uncertainty. The great increase in the number of figures being summed is clearly at odds with our bounded rationality assumption.

To remove this inconsistency when scalar attributes are being evaluated two modifications can be suggested. The first is to conceive of the person as asking herself how surprised she would be if the scheme were to perform best in respect of such attributes (e.g. 'Will this be the fastest, . . . the most economical, . . . etc?'). But the problem with this 'maximisation' type of variation on the model is that the decision taker is often going to be asking herself a nonsense question. She can only choose one of the schemes at any moment and can only test the accuracy of her conjecture if she can, so to speak, 'repeat the experiment' with a different choice later on or observe the fortunes of others who choose, in contextually similar circumstances, the options she now rejects. This difficulty of logic can be avoided by making, instead, a satisficing modification to the basic model. Thus the chooser may be assumed to be interested in obtaining particular target level outcomes for scalar attribute dimensions (e.g. 'How surprised would I be if this car failed to return at least 30 mpg, . . . earn at least N admiring comments from people I know, . . . etc?').

4.3 Non-Compensatory Models: An Overview

Clearly, in the type of model considered in the previous section the idea is that some kind of weighted averaging process is going on in the chooser's head. Even if weights are not explicitly assigned to particular attributes when the grand total for each scheme is being summed, a poor score on one attribute dimension may be compensated by a good score on another and a high total still implied for a certain scheme despite its lack of all-round adequacy. By contrast, the models which we consider in this section all exclude the possibility of compensations between attributes. Because of this they may immediately arouse the hostility of a conventional choice theorist— in just the same way as would a decision to debar a brilliant student from a university degree because somewhere along the way she has failed to pass a minor course that is not obviously of great importance to the student's competence in the main discipline. The failure to take an overall view makes such a decision seem terribly arbitrary. However, while non-compensatory decision procedures may appear unreasonable, they have the compensating advantage (*sic*) of removing the need to engage in the often difficult task of working out a present value for each competing scheme by weighing up and summing its pros and cons. In non-compensatory models an activity will be chosen if it passes a particular test, or a set of tests in the appropriate sequence, the scores of which are never added together. Three types of non-compensatory model warrant discussion here.

(i) *The Disjunctive Model.* In this theory the chooser behaves in a particularly extreme way since she establishes a single attribute as being dominant. A scheme is then acceptable if it meets the target level for this attribute, regardless of how it is perceived to perform in other dimensions. If several schemes pass this test, either of two mechanisms may be used to resolve the conflict. First, the person might select the cheapest scheme. However, this solution makes it sound as if cost is a second *priority* and we have ceased to consider a single attribute, while only in monetary transactions is it obvious what is meant by 'cheapest'. A generally applicable theory of choice quite clearly cannot rely on a cheapness criterion as a conflict-resolving device. Both of these difficulties are avoided if, when a tie occurs, the chooser selects the activity which is expected to perform *best* with regard to the dominant attribute.

The disjunctive theory seems to be a theory of fanatical behaviour and, as such, it contains something of a logical contradiction. A hi-fi fanatic may seek sound reproduction quality regardless of other factors such as the appearance or bulkiness of the equipment, subject to her budget constraint. However, such a fanatic will, unlike the less interested person who vaguely feels she knows what sounds acceptable, construe sound reproduction as having many dimensions, e.g. dynamic range, frequency response, freedom from distortion and speed variations. It seems plausible to argue that the fanatic will use *some* kind of multiattribute choice technique, even if all the characteristics she considers are subordinate to one particular dimension. However, flawed as the disjunctive model seems to be in respect of truly fanatical behaviour, we are not going to reject it outright. It will resurface in Chapter 6 below, when we discuss 'cybernetic' decisions.

(ii) *Lexicographic Choice Models.* Unlike the compensatory models, where schemes are evaluated separately but in respect of all their relevant dimensions, the lexicographic approaches to choice propose that choosers consider all of the schemes, still on their agendas of possibles, with regard to a single attribute at a time. In most advanced undergraduate texts on choice a brief discussion is given to lexicographic preference orderings. Usually, such discussions are not set in the characteristics space but concern choice between competing commodity bundles. Deaton and Muellbauer's (1980) comments are fairly typical, as is the brevity of their dismissal:

The most famous example of discontinuous preferences is the lexicographic ordering. For example, if a bundle q^1 contains more food than q^2, then q^1 is preferred to q^2 irrespective of what else q^1 or q^2 might contain. If, however, q^1 and q^2 have identical food content and q^1 has more clothing than q^2, then q^1 is preferred to q^2 again irrespective of other components. The bundles are ordered according to the principle of words in a dictionary or lexicon; food comes first in the lexicon, clothing second, and so on. In this case, each bundle has no points (other than itself) to which it is indifferent; indifference surfaces cannot be drawn and no utility function exists.

Although lexicographic orderings represent a perfectly reasonable system of choice, it is convenient to rule them out (Deaton and Muellbauer, 1980, p. 27).

Malinvaud (1972) seems to find the concept of a lexicographic ordering much more unreasonable:

Such a preference relation has sometimes been considered; it hardly seems likely to arise in economics since it assumes that, for the consumer, the good 1 [food] is immeasurably more important than the good 2 [clothing]. We lose little in the way of realism if we eliminate this and similar cases which do not satisfy [the axiom of continuity] (Malinvaud, 1972, p. 20).

Outside neoclassical economics, two basic versions of the lexico-graphic choice theory have been proposed. Both are articulated in the characteristics space and assume that choosers rank characteristics in order of importance. We shall label them 'naïve' and 'behavioural'. In the naïve model (e.g. Tversky, 1969) the scheme which dominates in respect of the highest ranked attribute is given the highest rating. If two or more activities tie these are then examined with regard to the next most important attribute. The process continues for lower and lower priority characteristics until only one scheme remains. That scheme is then selected and no more, lower priority attributes are considered.

In the behavioural lexicographic model (e.g. Georgescu-Roegen, 1954; Fishburn, 1974; Earl, 1980) people are assumed to set targets for attributes, as well as ranking them according to their priorities. They then avoid considering trade-offs and attempt independently to pursue as many of these characteristics goals as possible. The priority ranking acts as a conflict-resolving and filtering tool. If they run out of relevant attributes before filtering out all but one of the mutually exclusive schemes, they can resolve the conflict by using the criterion of cheapness (in choices between transactions); choose the scheme expected to perform best in respect of the lowest dimension; or search for other relevant attributes to include in their priority rankings. Choice between the rival methods of conflict resolution may be made by the same filtering method. This type of choice model is discussed and developed further in a novel way in sections 4.6, 4.7 and 4.8 below.

(iii) *The Conjunctive Model*. This is also a behavioural, satisficing model, for the chooser is assumed to set targets for each relevant attribute. However, in this case a scheme is only acceptable if it is expected to possess *each* attribute in at least the target amount. If no scheme passes this test search will take place. If more than one scheme is adequate in all dimensions the tie could be broken by using the cheapness criterion (if choice involves a monetary transaction) or by bringing other attributes into the picture. Where the person does not have to search to discover other pertinent characteristics, but draws them from her existing list in some priority order, we are really dealing with a hybrid conjunctive/lexicographic model. Such a model has been proposed and tested (without suffering an obvious refutation) by Whan Park (1978). The problem with this hybrid model is that it starts somewhat late in the choice process. Different categories of commodities will be subject to different first stage conjunctive tests, but Whan Park does not tell us how the group of characteristics relevant for one class of commodities relates to that for another. It may be adequate to treat them as separate for some market research purposes, but not if we wish to understand the consumer's budgeting (i.e. separation) process itself. However, it may be perfectly reasonable to allow a behavioural lexicographic model of the kind we will later explore in detail (which can be applied to budgeting) to incorporate conjunctive filters at various levels in the priority system. That is to say, a particular characteristic that a scheme may have to offer, to survive to be considered against the next priority filter, is the ability to satisfy a complete group of aspirational requirements, which will not be allowed to compensate against each other.

4.4 Rosenberg's Expectancy Value Compensatory Model

Milton Rosenberg (1956) first proposed a compensatory choice model a decade before Lancaster's somewhat similar characteristics theory was published. Rather surprisingly, it was only after Lancaster's theory appeared that Rosenberg's work, which had appeared mainly in psychology journals, began to receive much attention from consumer behaviour researchers. When, at last, Hansen (1969) and Bither and Miller (1969) examined its predictive properties they found that it seemed to perform fairly well. However, its empirical performance does not enable us immediately to decide to adopt it as the basic theory of choice with which to underpin behavioural economics. This is because the other models discussed in subsequent sections of this chapter have also appeared to be consistent with bodies of evidence. Hence we feel we must examine the assumptive structures of each of the rival approaches for *a priori* plausibility before making our choice.

Rosenberg hypothesised that expected values are dependent on two key variables: first, values (i.e. characteristics or evaluative criteria); and second, the perceived instrumentality of a scheme with regard to the person's values (i.e. the ability of a scheme to help or hinder the attainment of the person's values). The 'perceived instrumentality' term is usually applied in a way which makes it rather unclear how the model handles uncertainty. Usually the term appears concerned with how far an activity seems to go with regard to meeting a target, rather than the likelihood of the scheme enabling the target fully to be attained. The values in question are not restricted to the physical characteristics of the activities being evaluated, but may include, for example, characteristics related to the social context in which the choice is being made.

The form of the model is as follows:

A person chooses the scheme with the highest overall evaluation A_o, where:

$$A_o = \sum_{i=1}^{N} (VI_i)(PI_i)$$

in which

A_o = the overall evaluation of the attractiveness of alternative O.

VI_i = the importance of the ith value.

PI_i = the perceived instrumentality of alternative O with respect to value i.

N =   the number of pertinent or salient values.

VI_i is measured on a twenty-one category scale ranging from − 10 (gives me maximum dissatisfaction) to + 10 (gives me maximum satisfaction).

PI_i is measured on an eleven category scale ranging from − 5 (the condition is completely blocked through undertaking alternative O) to + 5 (the condition is completely attained through undertaking alternative O).

This is the pure form of the model which was tested by the authors cited earlier. They found that VI_i and PI_i were independent and would not predict response when used separately.

The form of Rosenberg's model renders it easy to use in marketing planning for it is, unlike models based around n-dimensional indifference surfaces, amenable to combination with questionnaire data. If sample surveys of consumer attitudes reveal that a market is segmented in a certain way into groups with common value structures and perception tendencies, it will be fruitful to put this data (for a firm's own product and those of its rivals) into the model to see which product typically dominates. An examination of the raw data in the light of the relative total scores would yield information on which product attributes should best be changed, and which aspects of the product should be most heavily advertised to have the greatest impact on the overall evaluation A_o. This is the way in which all of the models discussed in this chapter can be used (though with the lexicographic models the firm's object is to make its product survive more stages in the filtering process than its competitors' offerings, rather than achieve some maximum expected total value). It is not the way in which a conventional economic theorist would normally expect to use a model of consumer choice.

4.5 Fishbein's Expectancy Value Compensatory Model

Martin Fishbein's expectancy value theory of choice was first published in 1963. According to Engel *et al.* (1978, p. 393), this model has in recent years accounted for more published research on consumer behaviour than any other single subject. This is perhaps hardly surprising. Its simple multiple regression form makes it eminently suitable as a means of generating publications for those researchers who have a penchant for 'number crunching' and are willing to gather suitable questionnaire data (often in highly artificial situations using college students and imaginary brands).

The predictive capabilities of Fishbein's model vary considerably according to which study one reads. Reports range from the enthusiastic, such as Tuck (1976), to the critical, such as Ryan and Bonfield (1975) and Warshaw (1980), though increasingly there has been a preponderance of the latter kind. The critical studies suggest that the model often produces weak and inconsistent predictions and typically suffers from a high multicollinearity between independent variables. However, such studies have not prevented Fishbein's theory from acquiring the dominant place amongst models of consumer choice in leading texts, with non-compensatory models frequently being given only the briefest of examinations.

Engel *et al*'s (1978, pp. 403–9) behaviour in this respect is quite astonishing; it is as if they are prepared to slot Fishbein's model into the 'evaluative criteria', 'beliefs', 'attitudes', and 'intentions' boxes of their enormous flow diagram 'theory' because it is fashionable, rather than because it has emerged spotless from testing. They discuss some of the critical studies and say that the problem is that the usual specification of the model does not take account of anticipations of circumstances, or, of changes in circumstances. Claiming that to do so will lead to better predictive properties, they use their revised version as part of their larger model in the rest of their book. Engel *et al*. seem entirely to forget that they had earlier (1978, p. 393) cited the study by Reilly *et al*. (1976) in which a group of consumers were given descriptions of compensatory, disjunctive, conjunctive and lexicographic choice techniques and asked which seemed best to describe how they worked out which model to purchase when buying a car. The vast majority said they used the lexicographic method. Despite this, and despite their recognition that it is easier to process information by attribute (as in lexicographic models) rather than by brand (as in compensatory models), the total attention Engel *et al*. give to lexicographic theories of choice is barely in excess of that given in mainstream economics texts economics texts such as that of Deaton and Muellbauer (1980), whose entire discussion was quoted in section 4.3.

In this section an examination of Fishbein's later, extended model will be presented, since this version, which is found in Fishbein and Ajzen (1975), is the one that has received most attention. Its focus is less restrictive than the original version since it is concentrated on a person's attitude towards an activity (such as buying an object) rather than towards an object itself. It must be emphasised that the model is used as a device for predicting intentions, rather than actual behaviour, when it is tested. The form of the model is a simple linear regression equation:

$$B \simeq BI = (A_B)_{W1} + (SN)_{W2}$$

in which

B = overt behaviour.

BI = behavioural intentions. These are expressed as the person's subjective probability of undertaking the activity (In tests the person will be asked to indicate how likely it is that she will choose the activity by saying where she stands in respect of a scale ranging from 'I expect to undertake it', to 'I do not expect to undertake it'.)

A_B = attitude toward the goodness or badness of undertaking the activity.

SN = The person's subjective norm concerning the activity.

W_1 and W_2 = Empirically determined weights.

$\simeq$ between B and BI indicates that overt behaviour and intentions will only be approximately equal, their degree of correspondence depending on contingencies that occur between expressing intentions and actually taking a decision.

Fishbein suggests that a person's attitude towards undertaking the activity will depend on how the person views the consequences of doing so, what the person thinks will happen and how this is evaluated. The proposed form of the attitude component is:

$$A_B = \sum_{i=1}^{n} b_i e_i$$

in which

b_i = the likelihood (usually written as 'subjective probability', but usually derived in questionnaires on a seven point semantic differential scale of agreement/disagreement about whether or not an attribute will be associated with the activity) that performing the activity will result in consequence i.

e_i = the person's evaluation of the goodness/badness of outcome i (usually expressed as a point on a seven section good/bad scale).

n = the number of salient beliefs the person holds about performing the activity. Fishbein follows Miller's (1956) rule that most people can only keep in mind 7 ± 2 things at a time, so n is usually between five and nine.

The person's subjective norm (SN) concerns her feelings about how people who matter to her will view her intention to undertake the activity. Fishbein proposes that it is determined thus:

$$SN = \sum_{j=1}^{n} NB_j MC_j$$

in which

    NB_j = the person's belief that referent j thinks she should undertake the activity.

    MC_j = the person's motivation to comply with referent j.

    n = the number of salient referents.

Although Fishbein's model is couched in terms of the language of probability we would not wish to group it with the hard-core probability-based neoclassical choice models that we criticised in section 3.8. Its proponents use it to analyse crucial decisions without in practice making more than a linguistic violation of Shackle's possibility-based view of how people think about uncertainty. No presumption is usually made that the set of *BI* values obtained by questioning a consumer (or groups of *n* consumers who have been discovered to have broadly similar value structures) will sum to unity (or, in the group case, to *n*). For example, in the application of the model tested by Tuck (1976), not only was a crucial decision at the centre of the investigation but little attempt was made to identify the precise list of alternatives. Tuck's sample comprised a group of women cadet soldiers who were questioned about their attitude to army life, what their social reference group thought of them being in the army, and *whether or not* they thought they would stay in it after completing their training. There is no reason why, when the Fishbein model is being tested, people should not be asked to say how *surprised* they would be if they did/did not undertake the activity in question, or if it did/did not turn out to be characterised by particular attributes.

Fishbein's model makes a serious attempt to recognise the importance of bounded rationality: for a compensatory model, it seems a world apart from the kind incorporating the *n*-dimensional equalisation of marginal rates of substitution and relative prices, that a conventional economist would instinctively wish to construct. Some kind of separability over activity attributes is implied in preference orderings, as Fishbein assumes that the list of salient attributes will vary according to the type of activity under consideration. When the model is being used choosers are only asked to list the 7 ± 2 salient attributes that immediately come to mind, or to choose the 7 ± 2 attributes that seem most relevant from a long list provided by the researcher: Fishbein accepts that to attempt simultaneously to consider unlimited numbers of attributes would involve information overloading. Whereas Rosenberg requires a rating of relative importance to be assigned by choosers to the attributes with which they are concerned, attribute importance ratings have no role in Fishbein's theory. His view is that the mere fact that an attribute has made the list of 7 ± 2 salient characteristics is sufficient indication of its importance in the context in question. As with Rosenberg's model, however, its specification leaves one rather unclear about how it incorporates scalar attributes (see section 4.2 for a discussion of how this type of problem might be handled).

4.6 The Characteristic Filtering Lexicographic Model

Compensatory models are not the only ones to run into difficulties if attempts are made to use them in situations where uncertainty about scalar attributes cannot be ignored. The behavioural lexicographic model also begins to seem inadequate in such a context, for it is no longer clear what it means to say that a characteristic is conjectured to be present in a large enough measure to enable an aspiration to be met. For example, a particular car might turn out to offer a fuel consumption of at least 30 mpg on average, but, then again, it might not. If we aspire to have a car which offers 30 mpg, should we reject the car in question? If we do choose it we are clearly taking a chance that we will meet our aspirations; we think it represents an *acceptable* gamble in respect of the aspiration in question. A dual form of satisficing seems to be involved here.

To say this rather begs the question of how we should conceptualise this part of the decision taker's thought process. There are several ways of doing so within the lexicographic framework. In this section we shall consider a first approximation, which involves a novel synthesis of the satisficing approach with Shackle's (1949, 1958, 1961, 1979) nonprobabilistic analysis of choice under uncertainty. Shackle's theory is not a multiattribute treatment of the problem, for it was originally designed to deal with profit/loss conjectures in investment decisions where profit was the only thing sought by the decision taker. Furthermore, it is cast in a generally neoclassical framework of convex gambler indifference curves, rather than aspiration levels, and thus it is rather at odds with the fact of bounded rationality. Let us take the synthesis in three easy stages.

(a) Shackle's Potential Surprise Curves. Shackle calls a person's set of conjectures about the distribution of possible sequels to be associated with a scheme of action her *theory* of the scheme. A graphical representation of such a theory he terms a *potential surprise curve*. A decision maker may be thought of as conceptualising a multi-

dimensional scheme as a set of potential surprise curves; as a set of theories.

To find out a person's theory about something we need to ask her how surprised she would be by various sequels in respect of each relevant, dichotomous characteristic scale. Examples of such scales include: profit/loss, economical/wasteful, safe/dangerous, and so on. Degrees of surprise can range from zero surprise (concerning a sequel that the person believes to be perfectly possible), through mild shock, to utter astonishment (the state the person thinks she would be in if a sequel she presently believes impossible—'inconceivable'— occurred). In the case of the fuel consumption example with which we began this section, the person's theory of a particular car's thirst for petrol might be as follows: 'I do not think it is possible that its fuel consumption would average out at more than 35 mpg or worse than 25 mpg. Figures between 32 and 35 mpg, and 25 and 28 mpg, would surprise me in some degree, the more so the closer they were to the inconceivable extreme values. But I think that any value between 28 and 32 mpg is perfectly possible; I wouldn't be at all surprised if its fuel consumption fell into this range.' A diagrammatic representation of her theory is shown in Figure 4.1.

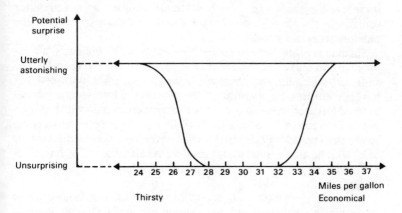

Figure 4.1

The person's theory about a particular characteristic of the scheme in question, encapsulated on a graph as a potential surprise curve, is one dimension of the scheme's *image* (cf. Boulding, 1956) in the person's mind. Such an image will be open to revision in the light of extra 'knowledge' obtained by experience, search, from society, and from advertisements. For example, the car whose uncertain fuel economy we have been discussing may be a new model and, when it has been tested by trade journals, the person may cease to perceive uncertainty in this area because all reports suggest that it returns 30 mpg. In this case the potential surprise curve reduces to a 'T' shape, a line rising vertically from the 30 mpg point on the thirsty/economical axis, combined with the horizontal line that is perpendicular to the maximum potential surprise rating of 'utterly astonishing'.

Alternatively, trade journals might record a wild variety of figures, causing the width of the potential surprise curve to increase at the top (the range of possible sequels to a decision to choose the car widens) and also increase at the bottom of the diagram (the person begins to think that quality control is so dreadful that, within the now-widened range of possibles, hardly any outcome would be surprising). In this case the potential surprise curve might resemble a section through a 'rift valley', i.e. cliffs either side of a broad flat floor. Not only this, but the inconsistent reports of the car's performance may affect the person's theories about its possible performance in relation to other quality control-related dimensions, such as its reliability and standard of finish on delivery. Shifts of potential surprise curves are thus interrelated. Firms attempting economically to shape potential customers' images of their products need to find out the nature of these relationships (i.e. which attribute is used as a proxy for something else, and so on) in order that they exert leverage at the most appropriate point.

Shackle repeatedly emphasises how the 'state of the news' affects the decision maker's confidence. Potential surprise curves may thus shift very suddenly, completely or in part, to the right (optimistic) or left (pessimistic). For example, if the prospect of losing one's job has loomed larger than usual, a scheme of action concerned with buying a new car on credit, to replace an old one, will seem universally worse than before with regard to whichever characteristic dimensions are thought to be related to insolvency and the prospect of re-possession (e.g. 'what the neighbours would think', 'my future credit rating').

The example we have chosen to introduce the potential surprise curve is a convenient one in that the horizontal scale has an obvious, regularly divisible measure—miles per gallon. But an obvious cardinal scale will frequently not exist. This causes a problem when we are trying to specify a scale for our vertical axis of potential surprise: we have points for the extreme values of zero and complete anticipations of surprise, but no immediately obvious way of pinning down intermediate values on a scale with a unit interval. With questionnaire work the researcher can specify, say, a ten point scale of degrees of surprise. If names are attached to each point on such a scale (e.g. 'mildly shocking', 'somewhat eyebrow-raising', and so on) the questions cannot refer to a cardinal scale, merely to an ordinal ranking. For purposes of evaluating opinions it will often be preferable to name such points with everyday expressions, since this is likely to make interpersonal opinion comparisons more reliable. With many dimensions it also seems likely that people naturally think in ordinal terms because outcomes related to the dimensions are in some sense non commensurable.

Take the case of a person's theory about the effects on her health of a particular walking and climbing holiday. One kind of occurrence bearing on her ultimate decision might be the possible sequel that she is 'killed in a fall'. While it is clearly absurd to think of a cardinal scale on which a particular point might represent getting 'severely killed', it is not inconceivable that the person might be worried in different degrees by the prospect of particular kinds of accident, whose consequences would by one means or another turn out to be fatal. She would thus have an ordinal ranking over different ways of getting killed. Next to the least bad of these she might rank the state of being 'confined to a wheelchair as a result of a fall'. Still less bad sequels might include, in order, 'a broken leg, . . . a broken arm, . . . a sprained ankle, . . . blisters, . . . a sufficient improvement in stamina to outlast a particular person on the squash court', and so on. Shackle (1956) has considered whether or not it is always possible to convert an ordinal ranking of this kind into cardinal terms and uses a method suggested by Armstrong (1939) to show a way of solving the puzzle. The essence of this method is a process of progressive bisection. If we are unable to say whether we regard a broken arm as having a 'utility' nearer to that of a broken leg or a sprained ankle, it can be claimed to represent a mid point. Then, as Shackle (1956, p. 214) notes, 'Each half of the interval can be similarly halved, and so on until, perhaps, a limit is set by [our] reaching the smallest difference between utilities which [we] can discriminate.'

When Shackle's work on potential surprise first appeared the issue of specifying precise cardinal axes for the diagrams caused quite a controversy. It was recognised by Carter (1953) that, if the analysis had to be confined to an ordinal framework, continuous potential surprise curves could not be used and the entire calculus-based choice solution which Shackle had proposed would be threatened. The loss of the right to use calculus and depict tangencies is, however, a blow to formalism only, not to his basic idea (see Shackle, 1961, p. 188). The progressive bisection solution thus enabled Shackle's formal apparatus to stand. For our own purposes cardinality is not necessary. Our behavioural solutions to the problem of choice under uncertainty nowhere involve the use of calculus or require continuity and smoothness in potential surprise curves. Furthermore, the ordinal approach to defining the nature of the theories people hold is often conceptually and practically much simpler. However, that said, we shall usually continue to speak of, and depict, potential surprise curves as if they are continuous, for it makes the labelling of axes on the diagrams so much tidier.

The behavioural use of potential surprise curves at no point requires that they should only have a single range through which, as we move rightwards on the diagram, potential surprise falls continuously, and then a single range through which it rises continuously ('continuously' refers here to movements within the bounds of zero potential surprise and utter astonishment). In Shackle's original treatment, the possibility that the course taken by a potential surprise curve might resemble a section through a valley with several subfloors and discontinuous terraces is destructive for his calculus-based solution. The difficulty is just the same as in conventional Hicksian theory where a non-convex indifference curve might have several points of tangency with a given budget line. In our ordinal view of potential surprise, the possibility of multiple local minima for degrees of potential surprise may be particularly widespread. A person thinking about the effects on her health of a climbing holiday may rank a broken arm between a broken leg and a sprained ankle in terms of counter-desiredness. But she may feel more confident of being able to avoid a broken arm than either of these other unfortunate outcomes. Hence her potential surprise curve for the health implications of a particular holiday will have a local maximum of potential surprise in respect of the broken arm sequel.

The example of the climbing holiday may be used yet again to deal with another objection to the scales against which potential surprise curves are drawn, namely, that they seem ill-suited to dealing with 'yes/no' types of conjectures. A person *can* ask 'will I get killed if I go climbing' and conclude it is not inconceivable. In the event, she is *either* killed *or* lives. Clearly, however, this is more than a simple yes/no issue, for either outcome, as we have suggested, can take many forms. This seems to apply with all apparent yes/no issues. To give a second example, a person who applies for a job either gets she does not. But not getting it can include reaching the short list, getting a first interview, or outright rejection, while the offer of the job may involve any one of a variety of characteristics combinations that the person could rank in order of the number of priority-targets that they seem likely to enable her to attain, and all of which rank more highly than simply getting as far as the short list.

Three further comments about potential surprise curves are in order before we consider the second element of our synthesis. First, it should be stressed that, although Shackle invented them as part of a theory of choice for situations where the probability calculus was not applicable, it is not true to say that a potential surprise curve can be defined for all pertinent dimensions of all events. If, for some scheme of action, the range over which the characteristic can vary in degree is thought to be unlimited, so that *any value whatever* can turn out to be the relevant one, then this characteristic cannot be treated as relevant to the choice or rejection of the scheme of action. That is to say, if, for example, shares on the stockmarket were not seen by someone to have *any* bounds on the price movements that they might follow at *any* point, decisions taken by that person in respect of shares could bear no relation to possible changes in their prices. Other criteria (such as the need to hold a particular number to obtain control of a company) would be in use if a person purchased shares in such

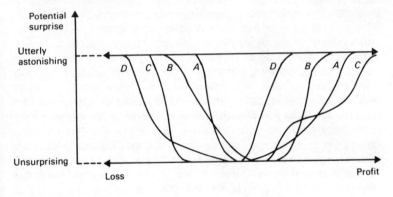

Figure 4.2

circumstances; price speculation requires a *theory* of what will happen to prices *within some range*.

Second, we would emphasise that when several potential surprise curves, associated with a person's theories of the sequels to carrying out a group of schemes (only one scheme of which she can select), are shown on a single diagram there is no reason why these curves should not cross. The curve with the best sequel just-deemed-possible will often not be the one with the least bad sequel just-deemed-possible. The sort of situation shown in Figure 4.2 will be quite common. *AA*, *BB*, *CC* and *DD* are potential surprise curves concerning, say, the expected profits to be obtained from choosing, respectively, scheme *A*, *B*, *C*, or *D*.

The scheme with the least bad sequel deemed just possible (i.e., on

Figure 4.2, scheme *A*) we denote with the term *the neutral scheme*. It is the safest option—in respect, at least, of the characteristic in question. There is no reason why a scheme which is the neutral scheme in one dimension should be the neutral scheme in every respect.

The third point to note is that, although Shackle has always drawn surprise curves that have some section running along the horizontal axis, there is no reason why, in some situations, a person should not expect to be surprised in some degree by all of the sequels of which she can conceive. In such a case nothing would be rated as perfectly possible and the potential surprise curve would fail even to reach the horizontal axis.

(b) A Dual Aspiration Filter for a Single Characteristic. If conceivable outcomes for an activity can be represented by a potential surprise curve which is other than T-shaped, the decision maker is under no delusions that her choice is anything other than a hazardous activity whose outcome is uncertain. The ability of a scheme to enable the chooser to meet her aspiration in respect of a particular characteristic may therefore be in doubt. Behavioural theorists have hitherto rather neglected the gambling aspect of choice. As a result they typically only define a single aspiration level for each attribute under consideration in the choice process. We shall call the aspiration level a person has if she perceives *insufficient uncertainty to make the choice seem hazardous* her *neutral aspiration level*, A_N. An outcome equivalent to A_N we shall call a *neutral outcome*. This use of the term neutral outcome is slightly different from Shackle's coinage of it in a non behavioural context, but it is one to which he seems favourably disposed. As he notes in his (1958) treatment of his theory,

I wish next to define a *neutral outcome*, a hypothetical outcome whose realisation would leave the decision maker feeling neither better nor worse off than he does at present. . . . The neutral outcome of one action-scheme will be higher or lower according to the possible outcomes which he discerns for the other action-schemes which seem open to him. I have for some years now thought that there is some connection between the idea of the neutral outcome and the psychologist's concept of the 'level of aspiration' (Shackle (1958), pp. 48–9, italics in original).

By the phrase 'insufficient uncertainty to make the choice seem hazardous' we mean that the person can conceive of no scheme with a hypothetical outcome which falls short of A_N by such an amount as to fall short of the attainment level A_T, where $A_T < A_N$ on a characteristic scale ranking outcomes left to right in order of desiredness. We call A_T the person's *gambler response threshold* for the characteristic in question.

If the decision maker perceives an action-scheme, which she can choose to avoid, that offers hypothetical outcomes that are at once $< A_T$ and $> A_N$, she will recognise that if she selects it she is taking a gamble. We suggest that she will only regard it as an acceptable gamble if two conditions hold simultaneously. First, the neutral scheme of those on her list of possibles must be perceived to entail a

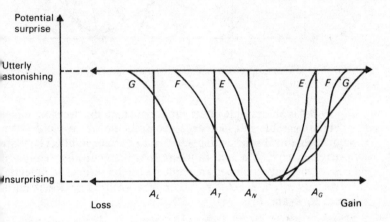

Figure 4.3

hypothetical outcome $< A_T$. Second, if the scheme in question is not the neutral scheme and does offer a hypothetical outcome $< A_T$, there must be at least a barely conjectured possibility that it will enable the chooser to attain her *gain aspiration level*, A_G, where A_G is some particular level $> A_N$, *and* she must not conceive possible an outcome which is so poor as to prevent her from attaining her *loss avoidance aspiration level*, A_L, where A_L is some particular level $< A_T$. This tortuous set of inequalities may be rendered less opaque by the examples in Figures 4.3 and 4.4.

Figure 4.3 illustrates the situation where there is uncertainty but no gamble worth taking and yet the chooser is satisfied. There are three schemes, *E, F* and *G*, where *E* is the neutral scheme, and their hypothetical outcomes are depicted by the respective potential surprise curves *EE, FF* and *GG*. Only scheme *E* is acceptable. In the absence of scheme *E*, a gamble would be faced and only scheme *F* would survive the test (and would also be the neutral scheme), for while *G* offers the best conceivable outcome it also offers a conceivable worst outcome of less than A_L.

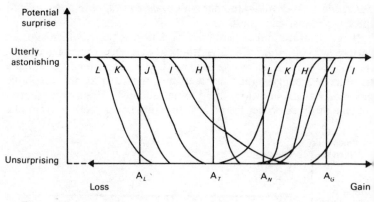

Figure 4.4

Figure 4.4 is an example of the situation where the decision maker has to take a gamble, but some acceptable schemes are available, even though the neutral scheme happens not to be acceptable. There are five schemes, *H, I, J, K* and *L*, where *H* is the neutral scheme, and their hypothetical outcomes are depicted by the respective potential surprise curves *HH, II, JJ, KK* and *LL*. The aspirational filters reject schemes *H, K* and *L*.

(c) Multidimensional Choice. Typically, the schemes of action competing for the decision maker's undivided attention will have more than just the two dimensions 'potential surprise' and a particular form of 'gain versus loss'. The person may stand to gain or lose with regard to many characteristics simultaneously (though not, of course, in the same degree for each) if she adopts a different activity. But to consider more than two dimensions at once is a rather complex task for the boundedly rational decision maker. In recognition of this, the characteristic filtering choice model we wish to propose suggests that at any moment choice takes place only with reference to two dimensions, the degree of potential surprise and a particular characteristic possessed by the competing schemes. The decision maker is assumed to possess a priority ranking over characteristics. If Figure 4.4 refers to the top priority attribute, then only schemes *II* and *JJ* are considered against the number two attribute, with one of the two schemes forming the neutral scheme or reference point for that attribute. So long as more than one scheme remains, the person continues to consider lower and lower priority characteristics in order of preference.

A problem arises if the person runs out of conceivably relevant

ttributes before eliminating all but one scheme of action. Evidently,
n choices over expenditure schemes, the cheapness attribute (which
nay have affected the performance of products earlier on in the
iltering process if quality is judged by price) will often be decisive;
ut not always and most choices do not, in any case, concern
ransactions. The following choice criterion is proposed as the means
f conflict resolution in situations where the cheapness dimension is
rrelevant.

> A person will select that scheme of action whose imagined
> possible outcomes permeate to the lowest level characteristic of
> her priority ranking permeable to any of the schemes, and
> which forms, at that level in her priority ranking, the neutral
> scheme amongst those schemes which are able to satisfy in
> prospect both the loss avoidance and gain aspirations for that
> characteristic. If no scheme satisfies both of these aspirations,
> the person selects the neutral scheme in respect of this
> characteristic, providing that she does not discover, as a result
> of the search process that this otherwise unsatisfactory
> outcome may provoke, a scheme hitherto not on her agenda
> which permeates to the same level and then acquires at that
> level the role of neutral scheme.

We apologise for making what may seem an unduly convoluted
tatement and urge our readers to examine it slowly several times till
hey have grasped the essentially simple idea it contains. It is
robably helpful if we state that the word 'permeable' receives a more
letailed discussion in section 5.7, but it can, for the present, be taken
simply as a shorthand for the phrase 'in terms of which the person can
lescribe the activity with a potential surprise curve'. For example, a
car is not usually considered for its nutritional properties. Defini-
tionally, the suggested choice criterion must apply even when there is
only one scheme remaining possibly to permeate, or 'filter down to',
the next characteristic scale on the person's priority ranking. If
Figure 4.4 were a depiction of the hypothetical outcomes a person
had in mind for the lowest priority characteristic to which any of the
schemes on her agenda were permeable, she would select scheme I
unless search revealed a hypothetically superior scheme; superior,
that is, in the sense of having a best-conceivable outcome $\geq A_G$ and a
worst-conceivable outcome superior to the worst one conjectured
possibly to be associated with scheme I. If scheme I actually is the
choice, the person recognises that she may not meet her aspirations in
respect of this characteristic, but is nonetheless lucky enough to face
an acceptable gamble. If she only had the choice between schemes K
and L on Figure 4.4 she would select K but not satisfied with the
gamble.

4.7 Two Variations on the Characteristic Filtering Model

In the model just proposed, choosers take seriously anything, whether good or bad, that seems *possible*. However, they seem to have a rather extreme attitude towards hazardous decisions. On the one hand, they wish completely to avoid relatively poor outcomes that seem to them to be at all possible, while, if they expect to achieve this (though it must be stressed there is no guarantee whatever that they will not in the event be astonished by something hitherto thought impossible), they are quite willing to gamble so long as there is the slightest possibility they might attain a particular, relatively good outcome. In respect of excessively poor outcomes they are intolerant of surprise to an extreme degree, yet in respect of adequately good gambling outcomes they are quite ready to be practically astonished every time they cross their gambler response thresholds and take chances. This would only seem obviously plausible if we were dealing with, say, potential surprise curves for profit or loss making schemes imagined by an extreme kind of entrepreneur, where A_L referred to the size of loss conjectured to be of sufficient magnitude to provide bankruptcy.

Having raised this possible objection we must provide a solution. The obvious behavioural remedy is to think of aspiration levels for potential surprise in respect of gains and losses. Assume the chooser prefers to avoid the prospect of losses beyond a tolerable size A_L unless, if they actually occurred, they would cause surprise *in excess of* a threshold level S_{AL} . Assume she also prefers to avoid hazardous schemes that pass this revised loss avoidance filter unless they also offer the prospect of gains of at least A_G which, if they actually occurred, would cause surprise *below* a threshold level S_{AG} . Different people may have different attitudes towards the prospect of surprise, just as, in probabilistic treatments, they are assumed not necessarily to have the same degree of risk aversion.

The remedy thus involves turning the filter system for each characteristic under consideration into a system of two sets of paired filters, rather than a pair of separate filters, in situations where the gambler response threshold has been crossed. However, it seems that there is no reason why the surprise aspirations, S_{AL} and S_{AG} , should necessarily be prevented from being the same for each characteristic. The surprise aspirations exist independently of the characteristic gain/loss aspirations A_G and A_L . This enables experience to affect the gain/loss aspirations without necessarily affecting the chooser's tolerance of surprise, and vice versa.

A diagrammatic representation for the modified model is shown,

or a single characteristic filter, in Figure 4.5. Potential surprise
curves for two schemes, *A* and *B*, are shown. Curve *AA* passes both
tests. Curve *BB* fails both tests. Failure entails the curve not passing
to the south east of the S_{AG} , A_G boundary, and/or passing to the
south west of the S_{AL} , A_L boundary.

To guarantee a single choice at the end of the multi characteristic
filtering process, our earlier criterion at the end of section 4.6 is
adequate. However, it might be argued that it is desirable to redefine
the term 'neutral scheme' in a way that reflects the assumed existence
of the S_{AL} aspiration. In this case, the neutral scheme for the
characteristic in question becomes the scheme on the agenda of

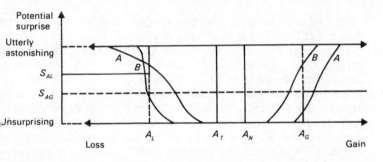

Figure 4.5

possibles which has the least undesirable possible outcome amongst
those conjectured to cause, should they actually occur, a degree of
surprise equal to S_{AL} .

This revised 'two point test' model is clearly behavioural in nature,
yet it is in some senses quite close to Shackle's own conception of how
people think about choices, for this too has a pair of outcomes upon
which the decision maker is assumed to focus her attention in respect
of any given scheme. In Shackle's theory there is an ascendency
function, depicted graphically as sets of indifference curves that
represent outcomes equally able to attract the chooser's imagination.
The chooser is prepared to trade potential surprise against possible
gain, and potential surprise against possible loss. 'Impossible'
outcomes, and outcomes involving no departure from the neutral
position, do not attract the chooser's attention. The most attention-
attracting outcomes are those where potential surprise curves are
tangential to these 'ascendency' indifference curves, and Shackle calls
them focus outcomes. Figure 4.6 shows a pair of focus outcomes in
respect of a single scheme's potential surprise curve, as well as giving
an impression of how Shackle thinks the indifference surface might

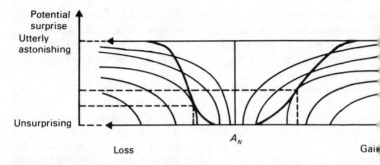

Figure 4.6

look. The attention-attracting power of an outcome increases as w
move to the south east or the south west.

In the present context there is no need to explain how Shackl
proposes that choosers move from examining focus outcomes t
make a final choice. But what is interesting (especially when it is see
in the light of our later dialogue, in section 4.9, on the relative meri
and ease of confusing compensatory and priority models of choice) i
that Shackle on one occasion unwittingly came literally thre
quarters of the way towards proposing the behavioural model w
depicted in Figure 4.5. This was in his (1958) discussion, where he ha
mentioned that in the Theory of Games the common solution to th
problem of choice is to choose the scheme which minimises th
maximum harm that an opponent can inflict. He objected to this a
follows:

Rather than *minimax* our losses, is it not more reasonable to fix for them som
maximum tolerable numerical size, to avoid any action-scheme which woul
bring losses larger than this within the range of possible or 'too possibl
outcomes, and *subject to this constraint* to choose that action scheme whic
brings within the range of possible or 'sufficiently possible' outcomes as hig
a positive success as we can find (Shackle, 1958, p. 66, emphasis in th
original).

This is as close to writing in the normal language of behavioura
theory that Shackle has come in his own publications, but his (198
reaction on seeing the first sketch of our modified characterist
filtering model is most interesting. He writes

I am keenly sympathetic to a discontinuous, step-variation treatment o
psychic matters: judgments, assessments, desires and counter-desires. I a
sure in these thoughts and emotions we often *change gear* rather than press
little harder or more gently on the accelerator. Thus when you explain th

he action-chooser must be supposedly able to shift his potential surprise
spiration levels *independently* of his gain-loss aspiration levels, I have some
nderstanding of this. The stepping-stone scheme would in some respects
uit my basic notions better than continuous curves, but we are all tempted to
;o in for continuity because of the 'instant solutions' we can get.

Ie then proposes a second variation on the model in section 4.6,
vhich allows more continuity than our own first variation model
vithout violating its basic idea:

have wondered whether there might not be, over some range of supposable
osses, a trade-off between tolerable supposable losses and associated
)otential surprise, and again between minimum supposable gain and
ssociated potential surprise. Might there not be, in fact, a *tolerable loss-gain
>otential surprise curve*? Any action-scheme whose descriptive potential
urprise curve, on the loss side, lay to the south and west of the 'tolerable'
urve, would be rejected and so would be one whose descriptive curve on the
;ain side lay to the north and west of the 'tolerable' curve (emphasis in the
>riginal).

This alternative variation on the basic model sounds a much more
rational' form of filtering with respect to a particular dimension, for
t is a stricter test than our own variation. Instead of a 'two point test',
he image of any scheme permeable to the characteristic in question
las to conform with a particular 'mould' of acceptability. It should
)e stressed that, in requiring a scheme to fit a particular conjectural
nould, the chooser does not 'add together possibilities' to arrive at its
:xpected value in respect of the dimension, in a manner akin to the
probabilistic theory of choice. She is simply saying that if an activity
represents a gamble, it is an acceptable one if, and only if, it meets a
set of conditions.

We are now faced with the dilemma of which model to select.
Although none of the arguments in the rest of this book is affected by
the choice of one of these models rather than the other, it would be to
dodge the issue if we were to provide no comment at all on which one
we favour. In the absence of detailed psychological investigations,
our initial inclination was to favour our own variation on grounds of
simplicity. Our case was that the market researcher, like her
respondents, must simplify the way she looks at the world in order
to see anything at all. However, to discover, in the context of a
practical use of the theory, the shape of Shackle's tolerable loss/gain
surprise curves would require the use of very detailed questionnaires.
Shackle (1982) agreed with this case in favour of our 'two point test'
model, saying that 'The argument from simplicity, from the need
to make questionnaire procedures practicable, is decisive. Your

model's ascendent claim is its efficiency as a practical marketing tool.'

Further reflection, however, has driven us to a somewhat different conclusion. In respect of characteristic dimensions which can be associated with obvious cardinal scales (such as profit/loss), we would stand by our arguments in favour of the 'two point test' model. But we now believe that Shackle's variation may well be an accurate depiction of how people think with respect to characteristic dimensions where mutually exclusive permeable outcomes lend themselves only to an ordinal ranking. With this kind of ranking we have, in effect, a chain of yes/no conjectures about the results of adopting particular schemes.

Recall the case of the person thinking about the possible implications of a climbing holiday for her state of health. It seems entirely reasonable to suppose that a person could find the prospects for her *desired* outcomes quite adequate (because they would not surprise her beyond certain measures if any one of them came about), be willing to suffer the counter possibility of a sprained ankle (because she regards it as likely to cause her more than a small, tolerable, amount of surprise if it happens), and yet reject the scheme because she finds the possibility of an outcome involving, say, a broken leg no less implausible than one involving a sprained ankle (i.e. she has a greater aspiration (is 'keener') to avoid a broken leg; she will only regard a scheme as satisfactory in this respect if she expects to be considerably surprised if she adopts it and *does* break her leg). For each yes/no question, then, the aspiration level is defined with respect to the potential surprise axis, and the set of such aspiration levels, laid together in an ordinal ranking, gives us Shackle's tolerable loss/gain surprise curve for the characteristic in question.

4.8 Policy Implications of Lexicographic Choice

An important theme in this chapter has been the conflict between various theories of how people process information when they choose, in particular whether they calculate and compare expected values by weighted averaging, or whether they avoid trade-offs between characteristics and attempt to pursue all of their goals subject to a priority ordering. It is an issue with strong policy implications for firms. These implications are not concerned with whether or not a higher price would, in the absence of oligopolistic complications, cause consumers to buy more or less of a product. Both types of theory turn out to be consistent with the Law of Demand, and with violations of it due to quality being judged by

ice. The policy importance of this controversy is not to do so much
ith the slope of a demand curve as with its position. But, before we
onsider policy, it is helpful to redefine the conventional neoclassical
eas of income and substitution effects.

In behavioural terms, an income effect may be said to have
ccurred if a relative price change affects the number of people within
hose satisfactory price ranges (budget sets) a particular product
lls. In either compensatory or lexicographic models people use
ese price ranges as agenda-restricting devices to simplify decision
king, and if a product is on more consumers' agendas we would
xpect more people to end up buying it. If price ranges have both
pper and lower bounds, a reduction in price *may* lead to the product
ppearing on fewer agendas, since the number of people to whom it
ow becomes too cheap to be given serious attention may outweigh
e number who now consider it affordable.

The analysis of substitution effects differs between compensatory
nd lexicographic models. In the former, a substitution effect arises if
wness of price *within* a budget range is a desired attribute, a 'good
ing'. In this case a price reduction will, unless quality is judged by
rice, necessarily increase a product's total score and make it more
kely that consumers will buy it. So long as cheapness remains a
esired attribute, substitution effects will be greater the fewer the
umber of desired attributes, because the size of its weighting will
end to rise. But if the cheapness criterion is not used in forming
xpected values, the substitution effect will be zero; any response to a
rice change will be an income effect.

In lexicographic models, by contrast, a substitution effect arises
nly if there are rival goods within the chooser's price range which
em to be at least satisfactory in all non-price dimensions felt to be
elevant. Price is used only as an ultimate tie-breaker. The more a
onsumer is a connoisseur of a particular type of product, the more
imensions she will have in mind when choosing. Hence she is less
kely actually to need to use price as a tie-breaker. If she does not use
rice as a tie-breaker, changes in relative price within her price range
ill not affect her choice; there will be no substitution effect for her,
ven though there might be for less knowledgeable or less interested
onsumers. Where most consumers are only interested in a few
haracteristics, and several products are reputed to be adequate in all
f these respects, substitution effects will be very powerful indeed
etween this group of products.

Lexicographic and compensatory models part company even more
ramatically in their implications for advertising and product design.
he lexicographic model implies that advertising should be aimed at
ringing about a change in consumer priority rankings in favour of

one's product if that product is discovered to be weak in terms of
conventionally high priority attributes and strong for less important
ones. Simply to emphasise strong points without trying to change
priority rankings may be absolutely futile as a way of increasing one's
market share, for such an advertising strategy amounts to little more
than reinforcing the opinions of the converted. If priorities cannot be
affected, attempts should be made to reduce aspirations or enhance
the image of one's product in respect of high level priorities. Failing
this, products must be redesigned so that they are adequate with
regard to potential customers' priority and aspirational structure
with no high level failings at all.

The case of the car market illustrates this very well. Reliability,
economy and rust resistance aspirations may commonly be accorded
high priorities. If a car is absolutely excellent on all other dimensions
but gets screened out at the first or second filters, that is the end of its
struggle for consideration. No matter how exciting and stylish a
Lancia or Alfa Romeo may be, it will be doomed to sell in small
quantities in the UK and US despite a seemingly 'competitive' price:
it cannot meet high priority rust resistance aspirations because it has
been designed for warmer climates where roads are not salted.
Likewise, unless the Citroen company can succeed with their sales
campaigns in persuading people to raise both their safety aspirations
and priorities, they would do better to devote their resources to
simplifying their cars to make them cheaper to service instead of
designing ultra safe but exceedingly complex suspension systems.
From the lexicographic perspective, the consistent success of the
Ford company in the UK, or the invasion of western car markets by
Datsun and Toyota, is not at all hard to explain. These firms have
been expert at designing cars which are 'good all rounders' in respect
of the high priority dimensions of the bulk of the new car market.
They may be so functional that they are bland, but excitement is the
sort of characteristic not ranked highly by mature family motorists
and fleet purchasers who constitute the main purchasers of new
cars.

As obvious lexicographic policy implication for the firm with a
'good all rounder' to sell, and which is trying to do battle with
another 'good all rounder', is that it should try to introduce new
product dimensions ahead of its rival. Since it will pay the rival to
attempt to do the same, victory goes to the firm which manages to
offer the highest ranking new product characteristic not offered by
its rival. This is an obvious policy but it is less obvious how to
discover priority rankings in situations where consumers have no
experience of the new attribute. This point is very much on the mind
of Lamberton (1971, p. 10), who uses the term 'hierarchy of wants'

without realising how unconventional he is being, and goes on to criticise the notion of perfect competition as follows:

In the real world, fraught with uncertainty, firms attempt to increase profits by searching for those things which satisfy the want which is just emerging. . . . For when wants are known and either stable or controllable, uncertainty disappears and monopoly power is possible. . . . Competition then only exists in a world of incomplete information.

The view that competition is a process of search, with implications for the relationship between Lancaster's characteristics theory, advertising, and the process of product differentiation, has begun to spawn quite a sizeable literature in the work of the minority of mainstream economists who have adopted the characteristics idea—see, for example, Lipsey and Rosenbluth (1971), Auld (1974), Lancaster (1975) and Archibald and Rosenbluth (1975). But all of this work is set within the standard compensatory framework and misses entirely the lexicographic implication we have proposed.

The key thing to understand when thinking about the relationship between choice models and policy may be summed up as follows. The possibility that consumers do not do attribute trade-offs in the manner of the expectancy value compensatory models in no way means that companies should not be aware of opportunity costs amongst attributes when designing products. In fact the reverse is true: a product only needs to be adequate to pass a particular characteristic filter test, and if a superior performance at one filter is achieved at the expense of attribute inadequacy elsewhere, particularly in respect of high priority attributes, all hope of a viable market share may unnecessarily be sacrificed. Designers attempting to grapple with this requirement do not, of course, have to compute an expected value for the bundle of attributes comprising the planned product as they examine attribute trade-offs. What they have is a linear programming problem, how to make their product in the image held in their potential customers' minds or, failing this, how to design a sales campaign most effectively to play on their potential customers' imaginations.

A final implication of lexicographic models which, unlike compensatory models, assume that information is processed by attribute rather than brand, is the only policy point raised in the brief discussion in Engel *et al*. They point out that

Given the current incidence of consumer overload . . . ads and other types of promotional stimuli may be screened out by the consumer if they do not prominently feature the preferred attribute and use that has the lead appeal. The tendency *all too often is to talk about the product first and to stress the benefit second* (Engel *et al.* (1978), p. 393, emphasis in original).

4.9 Lexicographic versus Compensatory Models: A Dialogue

THE CRITIC: I find your enthusiasm for lexicographic models quite astonishing, particularly now that I've had time to think about how I act in your favourite market example, i.e. when I'm buying a car.

THE PROPONENT: I was about to voice a similar concern for your faith in compensatory models. Don't think me rude, but I was about to explain that I don't think even you, as a first class neoclassical theorist, are smart enough rapidly to perform multiple weighted averaging calculations before you take a decision. You do realise that this is what compensatory models imply you are, in effect, doing, and in seven, plus or minus two, dimensions at that.

THE CRITIC: I take your point, but let me counter with an example. Suppose when I buy a car I don't care in the least about style, prestige, comfort and so on, and that all I want is cheap motoring. To find out what the cheapest car is I get a piece of paper and note down the relevant costs: initial price, depreciation rate, maintenance costs, petrol and insurance. Different models will be cheapest in some respects but not in others. I do a simple totting up of values with a bit of discounting thrown in for good measure and then choose the car with the lowest overall cost. The more cars have to choose between the more chance I have, in effect, to make marginal substitutions between the various characteristics. For example, I can trade, say, cheap running costs against a high depreciation rate. What I'm doing is precisely the same as a fleet purchaser will do when buying cars, and it's really just a simple form of project appraisal.

THE PROPONENT: That's quite an effective defence on the surface, but I can spot some rather important flaws in what you've just said. Suppose I took away your pencil and paper?

THE CRITIC: I'd use my pocket calculator instead; it's got ten memories!

THE PROPONENT: If I took that away as well . . . ?

THE CRITIC: I'd do it in my head, though I can see what you're driving at: it's going to be difficult to avoid losing my place or forgetting my total costings for the brands I considered first.

THE PROPONENT: Yes, and I don't usually notice you resorting to either pencil and paper or your calculator when you buy something.

THE CRITIC: That's probably because I don't perform the calculations in a conscious manner.

THE PROPONENT: I see. You want me to think of you as a black box and, because I can't examine your unconscious processes, accept that you use the compensatory method until I can provide an example which refutes your claim.

THE CRITIC: That's right, be a positivist for a change!

THE PROPONENT: All this is beginning rather to lead us away from a more important flaw I was going to expose in the example you gave, but before I do so I'll give my reason for doubting your supposed unconscious powers. I simply don't believe you can work out complex weighted averages unconsciously since, if I give you sets of numbers rather than products to evaluate you will get the answers wrong unless I give you a calculator or unlimited amounts of time.

My other point is related to this question of complexity too. In the sample you gave everything was expressed in a nice uniform unit—money costs—just like we attempt to do in a cost benefit analysis. But even a firm is going to run into trouble when it has to consider dimensions of its company cars which cannot be converted into money terms; comfort, style and prestige in a rep.'s car can affect the rep.'s success as a salesman. Not only does the 'cheap motoring' construct subsume a variety of subordinate characteristics but there may be other, relevant, non-commensurable dimensions of equal underlying complexity. I suggest that a firm, even if it has hired some operations researchers to do its 'cheap motoring' calculations in the manner you suggest, will find out which cars are cheap enough and then see, according to its other priorities, which ones offer enough style and so on until a single choice emerges. I believe this is what happens even if the factors all affect the profits of the company, though I'm assuming that the choice is taken by a single person or that all people voting on the decision have identical perceptions of what the competing cars offer, how they affect corporate performance, and that all have the same goals. If they don't then I suggest their votes will be arrived at by the same lexicographic approach but they will probably not be unanimous.

THE CRITIC: Could I get a word in here, based on a bit of introspection? I remember how I decided on my present car—I think I told you at the time, long before you tried to sell me this crazy theory.

THE PROPONENT: You said you bought the Ford instead of a Fiat because it was more economical despite being rather slower.

THE CRITIC: Precisely! I was doing a compensatory calculation by a sort of expectancy value method, despite your view that it's much easier to process information lexicographically, taking attributes one at a time.

THE PROPONENT: Precisely? I doubt it. Look at Figure 4.7, in which point *A* represents your Ford and point *B* the Fiat you didn't buy. The horizontal dotted line represents my view of your economy aspiration and the vertical dotted line your performance aspiration. Lines I_o and I_1 are indifference curves of the usual kind for a Lancaster model which, I think, represent your view of your preferences. Your justification for your choice is consistent with both theories. Both *A* and *B* offer adequate performance, but *B* is insufficiently economical.

THE CRITIC: I agree that both theories are consistent with what I said but in that case I think it will be safe to continue to use a compensatory model—especially since I've now seen that survey article by Fishburn (1974) you told me to read. The mathematics of lexicographic orderings really are rather beyond me.

THE PROPONENT: I won't ask if mathematical tractability is your first priority requirement in an economic theory as you might

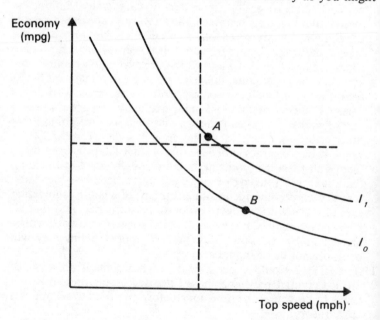

Figure 4.7

think I'm being facetious! I'll willingly admit that assumptive plausibility (so long as my high aspirations can be met) is, in the context for which I need it, my first requirement in a theory of choice. Your inability to cope with the mathematics of lexicographic orderings suggests that an assumptively realistic theory is one which makes no great demands on human information processing powers. My theory is adequate for my requirements in this respect, and yours is not. I note that my theory also seems to fit the facts in cases where your one does not (cf. Reilly *et al.*, 1976, and Whan Park, 1978) and is consistent with the evidence you offer in support of your theory.

4.10 Conclusion

In this chapter we have presented a critical examination of those theories of choice which have seemed likely contenders for a place in the core of behavioural economics. Ultimately, we have chosen a lexicographic approach as seeming the most suitable for, we believe, a lexicographic reason: the relatively small demands the theory makes on the information processing capabilities of the people to whom it is supposed to apply render the theory acceptable, and compensatory theories unacceptable, according to our first priority choice criterion of *a priori* plausibility. Compensatory models which assume that our brains function like multimemory pocket calculators, or the computers professional economists use for project appraisal work, seem vastly over-optimistic in their view of what most of us can achieve in our heads. The fact that boundedly rational people can design things as complicated as computers does not imply they are as clever as computers. If they were they would have much less use for them and, in any case, it must not be forgotten that such things are the result of teamwork by specialists talented in their particular fields.

To economists trained always to think of convex utility functions lexicographic choice models naturally seem irrational: if top priority aspirations are exceedingly high, outsiders, with different priority rankings, will frequently observe choices being made that seem to involve grossly suboptimal outcomes. But the everyday person frequently expresses a desire to achieve a particular goal 'at all costs' and, as with the case of Shakespeare's Richard III who offered his kingdom for a horse because his life depended on it (Steinbruner, 1974, p. 105), often seriously means to be *single minded* in respect of a particular target. Furthermore, we have the evidence before our eyes every day that priority-based choice systems *do* often lead to what we believe to be grossly suboptimal outcomes if schemes are chosen in

5 Images, Motivations, and Lifestyles

5.1 Introduction

Any decision is, as Boulding (1971, p. 28) has observed, 'a choice among alternative perceived images of the future'. An image may be thought of as if it is a set of potential surprise curves with which a person has conceptualised a particular feature of the world or sequel to a choice. But where do these images come from and what are decision makers trying to do when they choose one scheme of action in preference to another? It is conventional for economists to assume that people have *given* preferences and perceptions and leave to psychologists the task of answering these questions. In this chapter we shall break with this convention and integrate economists' and psychologists' ideas to develop an 'economic theory' of motivation and perception. It is necessary to do this in order that firms can make practical use of our lexicographic theory of decision making and public policy makers can begin to assess to what extent firms can shape choices in a way which threatens customer welfare. An analysis which covers only choices between given images, subject to given preferences, provides few clues as to how malleable choices might be in any particular context. Furthermore, since it is only possible to ask a limited range of questions of any sample of prospective customers, it may be impossible even to discover *given* preferences (should they exist in any meaningful sense) without some detailed understanding of consumer motivation. Only with such an understanding may it be possible to ask fruitful market research questions and judge whether or not there is scope for influencing aspiration levels, priority rankings and perceptions.

The theory of motivation which we shall outline is not, strictly speaking, new. It is in large part an adaptation of George Kelly's (1955, 1963) theory of personality, which, as we shall see, has many close antecedents, in many disciplines, ranging back, literally, as far as Adam Smith. Kelly's work is, furthermore, not unfamiliar to consumer behaviour researchers in marketing departments: they have already begun to use the 'repertory grid' questionnaire technique, that he developed for use in a clinical context, in their attempts to analyse market segmentation in terms of common lifestyles. Despite this, we believe that in this chapter we are offering a novel contribution to the analysis of motivation. Kelly's works, and the related contributions of other authors, have not hitherto been properly articulated within an economics context. Marketing theorists make very little use of Kelly's conception of what people are trying to do as they choose. This is not really surprising, since, on the surface, it is far from obvious that many everyday choices can be made to fit in with what Kelly is proposing. However, once it is demonstrated how this can be done, the implications for the design of sales strategies, consumer protection policies, and incentive systems can be seen to be far reaching. Discussions of these aspects will spill over into the last two chapters of this book.

Although Kelly's theory of motivation lies behind everything we shall have to say in this chapter, and, indeed, the rest of the book, we shall not state it formally till section 5.7, the last section before our conclusion. This may sound odd, but it is quite deliberate. It is easy for the formal terminology, which Kelly uses to give precision to his idea, to make it seem daunting to newcomers. We propose to introduce it in a fairly informal way first of all, with our discussion centred on how Kelly's basic idea relates to choice, rather than on how it conceptualises the ways in which people arrange their thoughts. In section 5.2 we introduce Kelly's main idea and compare it with the work of other authors who have come to somewhat similar conclusions. Section 5.3 then shows in broad terms how Kelly's view of how people think about objects and events relates to Lancaster's type of analysis of choice in terms of bundles of characteristics. Section 5.4 brings the discussions thus far together to show how normal consumer choices can be interpreted from the Kellian perspective. Section 5.5 relates the concept of personality to ideas concerning scientific research programmes, business strategies and lifestyles, in order to draw attention to the significance of complementarities. Before we at last state Kelly's theory in formal terms, we consider in section 5.6 how people cope with dilemmas and ambiguities. This section develops further the previous chapter's analysis of lexicographic decision making processes and it is one of the most important in the book, for its arguments concern the processes whereby images are actually formed prior to choice.

5.2 The Inquiring Person

Kelly's central idea is very simple, yet it is one which many people are prone to dismiss on first hearing as likely to apply only to academics or an intellectual élite. Kelly suggests that it may be fruitful to view people as if they are *scientists* in a very general sense. That is to say, we should substitute for the utility seeker the notion of the inquiring person, who is attempting to come to grips with the world by an empirical process. The inquiring person seeks to discern patterns in, or impose order upon, the complex world in which she finds herself.

In principle, a person can imagine any pattern whatsoever to exist, providing she has a mental 'menu' of components from which she can construct it. She can then attempt to test her theory by acting in a manner which may lead to evidence appearing which seems to support or refute it, either clarifying or shattering her image. If each day people imagined and attempted to test many entirely new ideas, their behaviour would seem to others to be very chaotic. In practice, such kaleidoscopic shifts of the imagination and behaviour are constrained by the relatively limited 'menus' that people possess, and by the fact that it often takes a long time to accumulate enough evidence to sustain or destroy an image to a person's satisfaction (see further section 6.6).

The types of theories that people form, and the patterns of evidence that they see, depend on their inbuilt predispositions; their experiences amongst people who have formed their own distinctive world views; and the environments in which they happen to find themselves. When people disagree about which activities are appropriate in particular circumstances, or which views are acceptable and which are rubbish, they should really be seen as arguing over who has the appropriate theory, or sees the appropriate image of reality. (This view of clashes of values is central also to Thompson's (1979) *Rubbish Theory*, which is often very close in spirit to Kelly's work, yet which nowhere refers to it.)

Kelly's suggested way of viewing human behaviour would not make sense if the world were characterised either by the extreme of perfect knowledge, or by a total absence of discernible patterns. Scientific activity of any kind requires the perceived existence of seemingly soluble puzzles. By considering the two extreme situations where inquisitive activity is ruled out, we shall try to show why Kelly's assumption may be a better way of describing motivation than the conventional notion of utility maximisation.

First we shall consider a world of perfect economic knowledge, such as Debreu's (1959) contingent commodity economy. In this economy traders are assumed to be fully informed about prices and the properties of all goods. They do not know for sure which environmental states will actually come about at any time, but they can arrange to buy and sell precisely specified commodities whose delivery is contingent on particular states actually occurring. Markets are costless to operate and there is no unexpected technical progress. Hence decision makers have no need to postpone making commitments for the future while waiting to acquire information. They can insure against every eventuality in the present and, as a result, markets only have to open once. No one makes any mistakes and there is no need to change any of the contingent commodity contracts at a later date.

In Debreu's imaginary economy differences between imagined and actual experiences can only result from incorrect assessments of which environmental states will actually occur at any moment. But Debreu's is a probabilistic world, a world of repeatability (cf. section 3.8), so, on average, actual and imagined experiences always correspond perfectly. Furthermore, people never forget anything and always know precisely which properties commodities are going to comprise. Scientific activity is unnecessary in this world, but it is also hard to see what pleasures such a world can offer. The perfectly informed trader can experience everything with total accuracy in her imagination. It is therefore difficult to see why she should ever need to experience anything in reality. When she listens to a piece of music, for example, she knows what is coming next at every point, she understands the thematic and harmonic structure, the dynamics and the orchestral textures. There is nothing that is unexpected, nothing which cannot quite be grasped.

A world of complete information seems more akin to a state of complete boredom rather than, constraining endowments aside, a state of bliss. In such a world there is no real outlet for choice in Shackle's (1979) sense, i.e. choice that is creative and *anticipatory*.

If we now consider the opposite extreme, a world where nothing can be taken for granted, we find that, though things are far from boring, pleasure-seeking activity does not seem possible. It would be a world of complete chaos and terror. Life in it would rather resemble a never-ending series of examinations on subjects in which one had never been schooled, or the experience of being arrested and interrogated by officials who speak a different language whilst one is travelling in a foreign land—only much worse. Hutchison (1977, p. 10) suggests that in a world where all human behaviour, both individually and in aggregates, was completely unpredictable, almost all economic or social life and cooperation would be impossible to manage. Any random action would seem to be as good as the next for people who could only perceive a raging sea of kaleidoscopic changes. If people could not conceive of *any* potential surprise curves for any characteristic scale, the characteristic filtering method of taking decisions, which we proposed in the previous chapter, would break down completely.

It seems that an existence that is neither boring nor uncomfortable is one where the events with which we are confronted are mysterious, but mysterious only within, literally, *reasonable* bounds. Usually people are able to control their lives to avoid extreme boredom or terror; gradually they explore more and more and expand their understandings of the ways of the world. When they are young, they are, to some extent, protected by their families from incomprehensible situations and reassured that basic regularities exist. When they are older, laws and social conventions perform much the same function. People who fail to form an understanding of the world around them, or of themselves, are not usually 'happy': in common parlance, they are people who 'can't cope'; in Kellian terms, they should be seen as having so far failed as scientists in the laboratory of life.

It is remarkable how many scholars, in diverse disciplines, have independently arrived at similar conclusions to Kelly on the nature of the human predicament. Already we have mentioned recent work by Shackle and by the social anthropologist Thompson. In the 1920s the philosopher John Dewey was writing that

We live in a world which is an impressive and irresistable mixture of sufficiencies, tight completeness, order, recurrences which make possible prediction and control; and singularities, ambiguities, uncertain possibilities, processes going on to consequences as yet indeterminate.

A world that was wholly risky would be a world in which adventure was impossible . . . (Dewey (1929), p. 43).

For Dewey, the essence of human fulfilment and delight consisted in outcomes being in question, of the discovery of regularities amid indifferent and divergent things. If there were nothing potentially blocking an outcome 'fulfilment would be at once, and in so being would fulfil nothing' (Dewey (1929), p. 54). Half a century later, we find Scitovsky listing various exciting activities and noting that

the challenge or threat is an important precondition in all of them, and so is the uncertainty: the prospect of failure and the less than certain expectation of being able to cope. . . . In general people dislike uncertainty and go out of their way to remove it. Only when either one's stake in the outcome or its futurity is strictly limited and under control is it actively sought (as in gambling) or accepted as pleasant (Scitovsky (1981), pp. 3–4).

The philosopher of science, Sir Karl Popper, and the great child psychologist, the late Jean Piaget, were both fundamentally influenced in their work by their observations of how children sought regular patterns and would not proceed to explore new areas or acquire new skills without returning frequently to familiar territory for reassurance (see Popper (1976), p. 48, and Boden (1979), p. 33). Children wish to explore but they can tolerate only so much uncertainty as they do so. The return to the familiar seems to imply an unwillingness to assume that because things have happened in a particular way in the past they will continue to do so in the future. There is little point in expanding inquisitive activities into peripheral areas if one's core tenets are wrong. Unease that they might be is what lures us back to check, at the cost of the lesser terror of not knowing more about what are presently believed to be 'peripheral' matters.

Kellian themes also crop up in the work of the ethnomethodological sociologists, whose lineage runs from Weber and Schutz to the more recent work of Garfinkel (1967). For this group of theorists, the topics of concern are the means by which people strive to achieve what Schutz (1943, p. 136) quotes Weber as calling the *Entzauberung der Welt* (disenchantment of the world); how such attempts are affected by social interactions; and how shared expectations affect behaviour in a social setting. Clearly, the search for understanding is a self destructive activity: while we fail to achieve it we remain enchanted by our problem, but when we succeed we become disenchanted (in common parlance: bored). We then move on to investigate other puzzles.

Of all the antecedents of Kelly's work, perhaps the most fascinating to economists will be Adam Smith's little-known study of the history of astronomy (discussed in Skinner, 1979). In seeking to understand how astronomers evolved new ideas Smith began by considering how people in general behave. He argued that people desire to avoid sources of pain and acquire those of pleasure. But, unlike later utility theorists, he saw pleasure as relating to a state of the *imagination*, corresponding to tranquillity and composure. The discovery of a break in a pattern causes surprise, and this rapidly leads to *wonder*, which Smith saw as a source of pain, of discomfort, of anxious curiosity. As Skinner observes, Smith argued that

The *response* to this situation involves the pursuit of some explanation, with a view to relieving the mind from a state of disequilibrium (i.e. lack of 'composure'); a natural reaction, given Smith's assumptions, designed to eliminate the sense of wonder by providing an appropriate ordering of the phenomena in question, or some plausible account of the links between different objects (Skinner (1979), p. 113, emphasis in original).

Thus it is wonder, and a desire to remove it by discovering patterns, that drives people into action. In the last stage of Smith's account of mental stimulus the concept of *admiration* is introduced. To quote from Skinner (1979, p. 113) once more: 'Smith suggested that once we have succeeded in providing an acceptable and coherent account of a problem, the very existence of that explanation may "heighten" our appreciation of the "appearances" in question.' Smith's arguments about the nature of human behaviour fitted in well with the course of events in the history of astronomy. New theories emerged here only after observations revealed problems with existing modes of explanation, which had once seemed *satisfactory* (cf. section 3.9). Initially, the astronomers attempted to modify their existing frameworks. But their *ad hoc* modifications eventually became so complicated as no longer to appeal to their imaginations. This drove them to give up the process of modification and develop something radically different: a simple alternative means of explaining the same phenomena. Copernicus' notion that the earth revolved on its axis and span round the sun at high speed seemed a startling novelty, but it was one which enabled the removal of anomalies concerning the positions of other heavenly bodies, which accumulations of observation had begun to reveal. However, in removing one kind of wonder, the Copernican theory revealed another, namely the puzzle as to why people were not thrown off the spinning earth.

Kelly's work, then, is not without its antecedents. But it is Kelly who gives the notion of the pattern-seeking, inquiring person its most general and formal structure. In anticipation of an obvious riposte from utility theorists, we note that Kelly himself was quick to recognise that conventional hedonistic terms (as well as the nonsubjectivist, behaviourist psychologist's notion of reinforcement) could be redefined in the language of prediction and validation; but he could see little point in doing so if he was correct to believe that the primary concern of the human race is with the anticipation of events (see Kelly (1963), p. 158).

5.3 The Nature of Things and Events

To analyse how the inquiring person attempts to cope with the universe in which she finds herself, it is necessary to have some prior conviction as to the nature of the universe. Kelly (1963, p. 6) begins by arguing that the universe is an *integral* structure, which 'functions as a single unit with all its imaginable parts having an exact relationship to each other'. These relationships may be far from obvious in the present, but '*time provides the ultimate bond in all relationships*' (1963,

p. 6, emphasis in original). A view of the universe which is very similar to Kelly's, and which usefully illustrates his point about long run universal complementarity, is central to Ray Bradbury's (1953) science fiction short story 'A Sound of Thunder'. This tale is concerned with the difficulties involved in arranging dinosaur-hunting holidays for time-travellers without affecting the subsequent course of events. The arrangement is that the only dinosaurs to be killed are those which would have died anyway, shortly afterwards, from natural causes. They are then left to decay where naturally they would have done so. However, one hunter falls from the antigravity pathway and accidentally treads on a butterfly. When they return to the future they find that this minute ecological disturbance has been multiplied dramatically and much has changed.

The universe is not merely an integral structure, it is also a structure whose form is continually changing: as Kelly (1963, p. 7) observes, the universe 'exists by happening'. So the inquiring person not only has a complex entity about which to theorise, she is forced also to deal with a moving target which may keep causing her theories to predict very poorly. Kelly argues that the way a person attempts to face up to this is by building partial models: 'When one limits the realm of facts, it is possible to develop a detailed system without worrying about the inconsistencies in the system which certain peripheral facts would reveal' (Kelly (1963), pp. 9–10). Thus he argues that a person treats the universe *as if* it is composed of separable features, even though everything is really linked together in the long run.

In an ever-changing universe a person can only theorise about those 'things' which stand out as distinctive and *relatively durable patterns* against their more formless and fleeting backgrounds. Kelly argues that people think about 'things', or, more generally, 'events', with the aid of a system of construct scales—metaphorical axes of reference which they use in a 'compare and contrast' manner to form multidimensional templets. These templets are then examined to see how well they seem to fit in with reality. An event is envisaged as a particular temporal and spatial configuration of constructs. Kelly's view is obviously rather similar to that of Lancaster or modern marketing theorists, who describe events as bundles of characteristics or attributes. His perspective is even closer to that of Shackle (1943), who writes of people thinking about the world in terms of *limited* numbers of symbols, dependent on upbringing and experience, which they combine to form theories. In choosing the word 'construct', however, Kelly's intention is to emphasise that any property with which an event is credited is merely a theoretical impression, tentatively accepted until a case for revision becomes apparent.

Furthermore, since interpretations of reality are interpretations in the light of theories, formed by people with different construct systems, there can be no unique, objective universe, only varieties of subjective, personalised reality.

How robust any person's theories about the universe will be seems, in the light of the work of Simon (1962), to depend on the nature of the linkages between her constructs and between the events about which she attempts to theorise. Simon suggests that the more *decomposable* a structure is, the more likely it is to survive in a turbulent environment. 'Things' will not be very durable in the long run if they are closely coupled with other things which are prone to change, or if the parts of which they are themselves composed are changing and impinge upon each other as they do so. In the long run Simon, like Kelly, sees the universe as an integral structure, but in the short run he finds it useful to see it as a decomposable hierarchy. This is how Kelly suggests the inquiring person approaches it too, and such a person separates out events with the aid of a construct system which is, itself, partially separable. If the universe changes too fast for a person's system of theories to be able to continue to fit it, she must either discard some of her theories and obtain new ones, or limit their realm to those events with which they can cope. If she cannot change her system of thought in the long run, her ability to understand the changing pattern of events will crumble away.

5.4 Motives and Choice

A motive may be defined as an enduring predisposition to strive to attain a particular goal. Unlike most personality theorists, Kelly avoids characterising people as if their behaviour is underlain by many complex motivating forces. Kelly (1963, p. 12) simply assumes that a person wishes to be able to predict and control the world in which she finds herself. Since maximisation is prevented by uncertainty and bounded rationality, we must express the inquiring person's goal in terms of an aspiration to add to her ability to cope with the world at a particular rate.

In attempting to predict and control the world in which she finds herself the inquiring person has to face up to the existence of opportunity costs. The limitations of her endowment mean that she cannot explore one new area without foregoing the chance to explore something else. Similarly, she cannot use her resources to explore without foregoing the ability to control things. The only qualification to such constraints on her behaviour arises in situations where there is the possibility of complementarity; for example, where an activity she chooses to impose a particular form of order on the world she sees also enables her to test hypotheses about aspects of the world which she understands less well. But even an activity which offers complementarity has to be chosen at the expense of other activities.

The inquiring person also needs to bear in mind that the consequences of certain choices may put her in situations where she is forced to form theories about events which she is poorly equipped to analyse. She will avoid making such choices unless they seem to be necessary in order that she may obtain answers to questions that she finds particularly fascinating, or in order to keep still more incomprehensible situations and events at bay. Generally she will attempt to choose that bundle of activities which places her in the best position of which she can conceive for coping with the world. Like a student, she will not willingly choose to investigate subjects if she expects to 'fail in her examinations'. Her theory of her own ability to cope with unexpected or partially surprising outcomes will determine whether or not she decides to cocoon herself in the midst of familiar things (to isolate herself from the prospect of being unable to understand what is happening) or sacrifice the chance of imposing a familiar image before her senses in order to explore interesting new situations. If she is confident enough to try the latter she may ultimately emerge with either a more comprehensive view of the world or, if she is unlucky, with even her earlier and confidently held images shattered.

In general, we suggest that the choice of an activity by a person may enable her to meet her aspirations to predict and control the world in the following ways, which may occur separately or together according to the nature of the activity.

(i)   It may help her ensure that she is not faced with unfamiliar situations which she cannot comprehend. By constructing images around her which conform with her theory of how the world should/does look she can exclude incomprehensible happenings and thus control her interface with the world.

(ii)   It may directly facilitate the testing of an interesting hypothesis about a feature or relationship between features of the world, by providing evidence of the presence of particular patterns. These patterns may concern new features which she has not previously attempted to explore (she 'elaborates' her world view, to use Kelly's shorthand) or finer dimensions of things of which she has some prior experience (she adds 'definition' to her world view, in Kelly's terminology, or, in normal parlance, becomes a connoisseur).

(iii)   It may enable her to present an image of herself to others which she thinks conforms with her 'self-image'—her theory of herself. If other people interpret her image as she thinks they will she will find it easier to cope with the world: they will not ask her questions which she cannot be expected to answer (cf. sections 7.2 and 7.3) and may themselves behave in a way which provides evidence to answer her questions or conform with her theories.

(iv)   The activity may indirectly enable her to obtain answers to her questions about the world by serving as a kind of investment good. Basic food and shelter obviously come into this category. It could also be seen as a more general case of (iii) above. An activity may be felt necessary as a tool for obtaining answers to a variety of different questions: e.g. a sports car might be construed by a young man as likely to attract women or enable him to experience what it is like to drive fast and test his skills as a driver, as well as being interesting to him because he wants to see how it compares with other cars.

(v)   It may, as in the case of a job, generate the wherewithal for imposing a controlled environment which conforms with expectations, or for asking further questions.

(vi)   It may serve an escapist role for a person who is dissatisfied with the way she is coming to perceive events, or whose cherished theories have been shown to be incorrect. This is a variant of (i) and rather resembles what one might call an attempt at 'data mining', as with the case of a person who finds life too mundane and turns to drink because it offers the possibility of a different view of things, or of no view at all.

To illustrate how this view of behaviour differs from conventional simplifying notions of utility maximisation, consider the case of a person who watches a television serialisation of a novel. Kelly would probably see the interest in this activity as consisting in its ability to provide viewers with an unfolding scheme of events (tightly specified, or merely themes) which they can attempt to anticipate. The fascination with the lives of the artificial characters lies in their close correspondence with the real world the viewers encounter day by day or wish better to understand. If people can anticipate successfully how fictional characters behave in environments similar to their own, they will find it easier to cope with their own everyday problems and will perhaps see them in a new light. Similarly, they can form impressions of other parts of society that they have not yet encountered. When events become harder to comprehend, or increasingly fail to correspond with a viewer's image of reality, she will switch off. Either the picture portrays an unrealistic, unhelpful image, or her own construction of events may be wrong and she may fear that to continue watching 'this rubbish' may undermine her confidence in her ability to cope with similar situations. When things become excessively predictable she will also switch off, unless, that is, an ability to converse about the programme is an essential prerequisite for entry into a social environment that she seeks to comprehend. This is probably only *part* of a Kellian perspective on the reasons why people may be attracted to watch a particular television programme. But it may at least help to show that by using Kellian ideas we may gain insights of use to policy makers (e.g. television executives), which could not be obtained from utility theory.

However, it must be emphasised that, although we may often guess reasonably accurately how behaviour may be construed in Kellian terms, we have no *a priori* way of knowing precisely how people are construing events: the opportunity costs they have in mind are as personalised as the reality they see (cf. Buchanan and Thirlby (eds) (1973)). Past observations of *behaviour* are not necessarily a good guide to subsequent choices; what is necessary to predict choice is an understanding of how people *think*. For this reason, psychologists of the personal construct school take the following as a practical maxim: 'If you want to find out why someone does something, ask her'. (See Bannister and Mair (1968), Bannister and Fransella (1971).) But they are only too aware of the need to analyse with great care the data they obtain from using Kelly's repertory grid technique. Factor analysis helps to minimise the possibility of results being confused by the reactions of people to the researcher and to inconsistencies between images.

5.5 Personality, Synergy and Lifestyles

Kelly (1955, p. 526) reports that the patients he encountered who kept 'getting into trouble' with exotic adventures tended to have construct systems which almost anything *seemed* to fit. They confidently plunged themselves into all sorts of activities thinking that they would be able to cope with them. The typical person, however, feels that her ability to anticipate events is rather more limited. Consequently she does not engage in a 'buckshot' search for answers and instead confines her attention to particular areas about which she believes she can theorise adequately. When she finds evidence at odds with her theories she will attempt as far as possible not to make major revisions in her view of the world. This resistance to changes in her view of the world also helps to ensure that, outwardly, her behaviour seems to conform to a fairly regular broad pattern. This pattern of choices and activities we call the person's lifestyle. It is a pattern determined by her personality, by the way she thinks about the world. That is to say, patterns of choice are determined by patterns of thought.

Now, the fact these patterns hold together for substantial periods of time is a vital factor in enabling firms to make sales projections. To the extent that individuals' personalities and lifestyles are reasonably durable features, firms can use sample applications of Kelly's repertory grid questionnaire technique to map their markets in terms of the broad world views held by groups of potential customers. This activity of drawing cognitive maps is known as psychographics and helps to make it possible to work out to whom a particular product will appeal when sold in a particular way at its 'normal cost' price. Figure 5.1 is a summary psychographic segmentation of the US market. More detailed studies of much narrower lifestyle groups are to be found in the writings of the 'New Journalists', such as Tom Wolfe (1969, 1977), which, although not written explicitly from a Kellian perspective, are serious attempts to uncover how certain types of people think, and how this affects what they choose to do. Let us explore in more detail why these patterns persist.

Figure 5.1. Eight Male Psychographic Segments

Group I   *'The quiet family man'* (8 per cent of total males).

He is a self-sufficient man who wants to be left alone and is basically shy. Tries to be as little involved with community life as possible. His life revolves around the family, simple work, and television viewing. Has a marked fantasy life. As a shopper he is practical, less drawn to consumer goods and pleasures than other men.

Low education and low economic status, he tends to be older than average.

Group II   *'The traditionalist'* (16 per cent of total males).

A man who feels secure, has self esteem, follows conventional rules. He is proper and respectable, regards himself as altruistic and interested in the welfare of others. As a shopper he is conservative, likes popular brands and well-known manufacturers.

Low education and low or middle socioeconomic status; the oldest age group.

Group III   *'The discontented man'* (13 per cent of total males).

He is a man who is likely to be dissatisfied with his work. He feels bypassed by life, dreams of better jobs, more money and more security. He tends to be distrustful and socially aloof. As a buyer, he is quite price conscious.

Lowest education and lowest socioeconomic group, mostly older than average.

Group IV   *'The ethical highbrow'* (14 per cent of total males).

This is a very concerned man, sensitive to people's needs. Basically a puritan, content with family life, friends, and work. Interested in culture, religion, and social reform. As a consumer he is interested in quality, which may at times justify greater expenditure.

Well educated, middle or upper socioeconomic status, mainly middle aged or older.

Group V   *'The pleasure oriented man'* (9 per cent of total males).

He tends to emphasise his masculinity and rejects whatever appears to be soft or feminine. He views himself as a leader among men. Self-centred, dislikes his work or job. Seeks immediate gratification for his needs. He is an impulsive buyer, likely to buy products with a masculine image.

Low education, lower socioeconomic class, middle aged or younger.

Group VI   *'The achiever'* (11 per cent of total males).

This is likely to be a hardworking man, dedicated to success and all that it implies, social prestige, power and money. Is in favour of diversity, is adventurous about leisure time pursuits. Is stylish, likes good food, music, etc. As a consumer he is status conscious, a thoughtful and discriminating buyer.

Good education, high socioeconomic status, young.

Group VII   *'The he-man'* (19 per cent of total males).

He is gregarious, likes action, seeks an exciting and dramatic life. Thinks of himslf as capable and dominant. Tends to be more of a bachelor than a family man, even after marriage. Products he buys and brands preferred are likely to have 'self-expressive' value, especially a 'man of action' dimension.

Well educated, mainly middle socioeconomic status, the youngest of the male groups.

Group VIII   '*The sophisticated man*' (10 per cent of total males).

He is likely to be an intellectual, concerned with social issues, admires men with artistic and intellectual achievements. Socially cosmopolitan, broad interests. Wants to be dominant, and a leader. As a consumer he is attracted to the unique and fashionable.

Best educated and highest economic status of all groups, younger than average.

Source: W. D. Wells (1975) 'Psychographics: A Critical Review', *Journal of Marketing Research 12*, May, pp. 196–213, p. 201. (Reprinted from the *Journal of Marketing Research* published by the American Marketing Association.)

From a structuralist standpoint the key to understanding any overall image is an understanding of how the parts are *linked* together. The essence of pattern is complementarity, something which conventional economists are most unwilling to discuss as a result of their reductionist outlook (but which is an important factor explaining the persistence of this outlook). It is the interlinked nature of the theories that a person holds about the world that makes her attempt to remove inconsistencies with the minimum possible adjustment to her world view. The linkages between the theories that comprise a person's world view arise naturally as a result of her attempt to make the most out of her limited menu of perspectives for viewing the world.

A useful parallel may be drawn at this point between the Kellian view of personality and Ansoff's (1968) contribution to the behavioural theory of the firm. In his work on corporate strategies Ansoff suggests that to survive and prosper firms must confine their attention to those areas which their resources equip them to handle in a relatively advantageous way in the pursuit of profits or growth. They should then restrict their attention still further, to those activities which seem to enable them to combine their skills in a *synergistic* way (Ansoff (1968), pp. 72–5). That is to say, firms should look out for those things they are particularly good at and exploit linkages between them when diversifying their activities (1968, pp. 94–7). Thus firms will not be interested in prospects in all markets and will specialise in those areas where past experience suggests that failure will be least likely. Such strategies, if adopted, help the process of market coordination, for they enable firms in a market to have a good idea of whom their main rivals are likely to be and what they might be attempting to do (cf. section 2.3 and Richardson (1960)). We would suggest that much individual behaviour, as it is exhibited in the lifestyles that people adopt, can be seen as a manifestation of a similar search for synergy, at both physical and mental levels.

If a person can see a means of exploiting complementarities when building up a protective screen against unpredictable happenings, she will release resources that she can use to explore peripheral areas. Similarly, when she is attempting to elaborate her perceptual field, she can exploit linkages between activities and theories, or choose activities that enable her to explore several things at once. But the problem with linked activities is that, if one of the components fails, the whole structure may be threatened unless the component can be repaired, or the structure itself is decomposable into small sub-structures. Since commitment to ideas comes before choice of physical activities, it seems appropriate firstly to consider difficulties caused by mental linkages. Here, it is useful to bring the work of Lakatos (1970), on the behaviour of academic scientists, to bear on our discussion.

Lakatos is concerned with the consequences of the fact that it is never possible for a scientist to test a single theory in isolation. Assumptions *may* be theory-laden, test techniques and interpretations of results certainly are. So, when a scientist discovers an inconsistency or an empirical anomaly, it will be far from obvious whether the trouble really lies with 'the theory' ostensibly being tested. But if she keeps returning to first principles to start afresh she will not get very far. Lakatos (1970, pp. 132–7) argues that the scientist gets round this problem by making a methodological decision to accept as given, in her 'scientific research programme', certain 'hard core' propositions. Where difficulties are encountered the evidence is questioned or the auxiliary theories ostensibly being challenged are modified in an *ad hoc* manner (if the research programme is 'degenerating' (Lakatos (1970), p. 118)) until the problems seem to be solved. Some theoretical propositions thus have higher status than others—i.e. a higher priority for maintenance—and are allowed to go unquestioned so that the process of scientific inquiry is not held up unnecessarily. The academic scientist assumes that it is safe to act as if her theories are not interlinked, and that her theory is not rotten to its 'hard core' if something appears not to be quite right. Only in extreme circumstances will she abandon one research programme in favour of another and, when she does so, her whole approach to her science may change.

Unless a new scientific research programme is available which seems to overcome existing difficulties, without leaving vast open gaps of knowledge that an old but seemingly rather shaky programme can say something about, the scientist will feel she has a strong case for arguing in favour of her established approach. It has served her well hitherto and may be repaired in the future. More importantly, her experience in using it means she will be better equipped to see how it might be repaired than how the new alternative might be developed. She will have developed a set of procedures to apply in particular sorts of situations, which seem to work (cf. sections 6.4 and 6.5); she will not yet have such a set to apply to the alternative new hard core of ideas.

The 'hard core' precepts of the academic scientist are, we suggest, entirely analogous with what Kelly calls the inquiring person's 'core constructs' and what Thompson (1979) in his Kelly-like 'rubbish theory' labels more conventionally as 'values'. Academic scientists try to obtain new data or modify fringe theories in order to carry on their inquiries without sacrificing their 'hard core' and all the understandings that have been built up on top of it. Kelly sees the inquiring person as behaving in the same way when things go wrong, by means which we shall discuss in detail in subsequent sections and to which Thompson's own treatment is a useful introduction. Thompson argues that people attempt *physically* to remove from sight those items which conflict with their views of the world—i.e. which are at odds with their values—or, if this is simply not possible, *ignore* them. 'Rubbish', in his analysis, is anything which is seen by a person as out of place, and is something to be swept out of sight or 'tidied up' so that it fits into a preconceived mould. Thus we may argue for the demolition of a decaying mansion that we see as a blot on the landscape; we may move to a new neighbourhood if the behaviour of people living nearby does not conform with our theories of 'reasonable conduct' and cannot be made to do so; we rebuke our children when their opinions and styles of dress are at odds with our visions of how they ought to be; we turn to another television channel to avoid being made uneasy by what we see. The more an inquiring person has expanded her research programme, her personality, into wider and wider areas, the more is at stake if a core idea is challenged, so the more concerted her attempts 'to clean things up' will be. It should now be obvious why the behaviour of older people is often very hard to change: their views of the world have become very highly integrated.

Commitments to particular, linked, mental constructs lead to commitments to particular lifestyle choices. These choices should be seen, in the light of section 5.4, as investment inputs for the inquiring person's 'research programme'. If activities are linked, the unexpected need to forego one component may be very disruptive. If a car is essential to get to work and the cost of motoring rises unexpectedly, a person who has committed herself to, say, a rural lifestyle may thus be quite prepared to make what seem to others to be extraordinary sacrifices of things that comprise the 'normal stuff of everyday life', in order to avoid the even greater disruption of a move back to the city. When complementarities are being exploited, we should not be at all surprised to find, at the industry level, the kind of high price inelasticities of demand that have been emphasised by Pasinetti (1981) (cf. section 2.2).

Where consumers recognise that they live in a turbulent environment, and that there are linkages between their activities, they will, as Richardson (1960, p. 178) has observed,

have motives similar to those of entrepreneurs for deliberately introducing adaptability into their expenditure programmes and can adopt similar ways of doing so. The greater the uncertainty of their future income, the less willing they will normally be to purchase expensive indivisible articles which are durable or which require the consumption of various complementary goods in order to yield utility; like entrepreneurs, they will discriminate against programmes of a highly capitalistic nature.

Richardson's little-known work on consumption complementarities leads us to a new perspective on the discussions of section 3.6, where we mentioned that expenditure on durable goods may dry up suddenly if changes in the 'state of the news' lead to increased uncertainty about income flows. Even if total spending does not fall in such a situation, there may be a sudden shift in the *pattern* of sales in the direction of more flexible bundles of commodities. For example, instead of committing herself to regular payments by purchasing a new car now, a person may bring forward plans to upgrade her electrical appliances, *in stages*, until her future position has become clearer. In the interim she lessens the possibility of an unnecessary disruption of her overall lifestyle. Whenever disruption costs are high due to complementarities, and the 'state of the news' prone to erratic shifts, stable sales patterns may rest on very flimsy foundations even if long term world views are relatively durable.

The central notion of Kelly's theory, that people attempt to impose *patterns* of order on the complex world surrounding them, is of its essence concerned with relationships between objects, with complementarities. It is a notion that firms ignore at their peril, particularly if they are in the business of producing cosmetics, clothing, or home furnishings. Potential customers may have been brought up to believe that, say, 'things should match' or that 'anyone who mixes antique and modern furniture, or blue carpets and yellow curtains, has got no understanding of taste'. If so, the firm which ignores the scope for creating a product range which *fits* in with the colours, shapes and general appearance of items in the range produced by other firms may needlessly forego profits and sales even if its products are entirely adequate in measurable, engineering terms. The reasons why common expectations can play a very powerful role in shaping the patterns with which people attempt to surround themselves are examined in detail in Chapter 7.)

5.6 Dilemmas

In the previous section we explained how people tend to avoid making adjustments to core ideas when they encounter anomalies and inconsistencies. Usually, by choosing particular amendments to fringe ideas or attempts to manage the environment confronting them, they can preserve their overall world views. But, despite our earlier emphasis on the impact of uncertainty and bounded rationality on choice, we discussed such world view-preserving choices as if they were clear cut. We did not consider the situation which Bateson (1973) calls the 'double bind', where the person faces a choice but no matter what she does she feels she 'can't win'. It is not uncommon for people to complain that they are in 'two minds' or 'caught on the horns of a dilemma' when they are taking a decision. Unless they choose at random, they must eventually be in only one 'mind' even if there is no scheme which obviously dominates in all dimensions.

Most decision makers do not find themselves hesitating indefinitely like Buridan's ass—which starved to death because it could not decide which of two identical and equally close bales of straw to eat—nor do they choose at random, but they *do* frequently find choice much more difficult than economists typically recognise. An economist would normally suggest that if a person perceives several *different* courses of action they must comprise different bundles of characteristics. Hence a double bind problem can always be reduced to an analysis of the relative opportunity costs of the proposed, yet imperfect, solutions. The chooser cannot win a perfect victory, but one imperfect scheme may dominate over another in some dimensions, depending on the structure of her preferences. We have argued that people cope with opportunity costs by the characteristic filtering lexicographic method of choice, rather than by weighing up relative attribute trade-offs and calculating expected values. If people have priority rankings over characteristics, choice should be relatively straightforward, even in the double bind case and, in our lexicographic model, even when there is uncertainty. How, then, is our model to be reconciled with the fact that people do often have trouble making up their minds in situations where something has to be sacrificed?

There seem to be three factors that are responsible for the surfac inconsistency between our model and the perceived existence o dilemmas. First, decisions makers are often only partially able to articulate what their priorities are. This is particularly likely to be th case in new situations where they recognise that several conflictin dimensions are pertinent yet have little idea where, or in which orde these should be fitted into their pre-existing priority ranking Second, a decision maker may have difficulty in actually admitting to herself what her priorities are, because to do so would seem t compromise her ability to sustain images with even higher prioritie (e.g. her self-image as a particular kind of person). Third, a decisio maker may be well aware that a particular dimension is importan and is affected by the activities she is considering, but be very unsur as to precisely how it might be affected—i.e. she may have grea difficulty in defining potential surprise curves for the activities i question in respect of a particular dimension which she does not wan to ignore.

The activity of making up one's mind consists in constructin images of the future, at least one of which *seems* to involve les important sacrifices than the alternatives. Now, although we can b conscious of using our senses to gather information for constructin images, 'the processes of image formation are unconscious' (Bateso (1980) p. 39). Choice is concerned with alternative images of th future, but, since the future cannot be known before its time, thes images are inherently conjectural. As such, they are prone to shapin by unconscious cognitive processes, until that which is seen as th appropriate course of action no longer appears to involve inconsisten behaviour.

To obtain insights on the processes of image formation i situations of complexity and uncertainty, we have to move, fron using Kelly's personal construct theory, to consider the experimenta research of cognitive psychologists, such as Ames (vividly describe by Bateson (1980), pp. 40–5) and Rosenberg *et al.* (1960). Kelly tend only to write as if people have already formed their construct concerning the possible outcomes of choice, or to discuss ho outcomes affect subsequent constructions of events. We shall dra heavily on Steinbruner's (1974, Chapter 4) integration of th implications of this 'cognitive' work, subject to the followin qualification. We believe he goes too far when he concludes that

[The mind] does not match the uncertain structure of the environment i which events might take a number of alternative courses. Rather, it impose an image and works to preserve that image. A single course of events i projected; evidence for alternative outcomes is manipulated to preserve th expectations. We might call this, then, the *assumption of a single outcome calculation* (Steinbruner (1974), p. 123, emphasis in original).

Steinbruner rejects the probabilistic theory of choice in hazardous situations, advancing similar reasons to those offered by Shackle. However, because he is not familiar with Shackle's alternative way of conceptualising how people envisage *ranges* of possible outcomes, he appears to have been driven to a viewpoint which seemingly denies the everyday observation that people often feel uncertain of what is going on, or will happen, even when they have made up their minds what to do. Steinbruner's 'single outcome' approach to choice seems to be very much a special case of our own analysis.

Steinbruner (1974, pp. 103–9) argues that the cognitive experiments on perception indicate that when decision makers encounter trade-offs between values, they examine values separately in respect of their perceived options; they do not actually perform trade-offs. They use the following means to ensure that the course of action they decide upon fits in with their values (1974, pp. 114–22):

(a) the use of images and arguments from analogy;
(b) inferences of transformation (wishful thinking);
(c) inferences of impossibility;
(d) negative images (exaggerating the disadvantages of rejected activities—a 'sour grapes' approach, one might say);
(e) attempts to obtain social corroborations.

In making up their minds, decision makers attempt, in effect, to 'have their cake *and* eat it'. But what determines how their perceptions are shaped in the face of opportunity costs? It is natural for us to suggest that the chooser's *priority* system is responsible, and to note that Steinbruner's discussions of the implications of experimental work on perception add weight to our earlier (section 4.9), *a priori* arguments for rejecting compensatory models (which, incidentally, included the model discussed in section 4.4, that was developed, before his work on perception (1960), by Rosenberg himself). Steinbruner makes no reference to lexicographic theories of individual choice that pre-date his work, but he *seems* to share the priority idea (without mentioning the word 'priority') when he observes (1974, pp. 108–9) that

by its own internal logic, the mind severs under uncertainty the lateral relationship between separate values and sets up separate decision problems, each governed by a single value or a set of values hierarchically arranged.

In terms of our own model, we would suggest that the perceptual shaping process operates at three points. First it can involve what amounts to a fudging of the shapes of potential surprise curves

and/or aspiration levels for (unconsciously) lower priority dimensions if their attainment levels stand to be threatened, *when
previously they were not*, by the adoption of an activity that wi
enable higher priority aspirations to be met. Second, where th
importance of a particular dimension is more ambiguous than th
ways in which events may be construed in terms of it, this dimensio
will be accorded a place in the chooser's priority ranking whic
involves no compromises being necessary. That is to say, it is made t
matter only if schemes which perform well in respect of it are als
rated favourably in respect of pre-existing priorities. Third, the min
constructs potential surprise curves in respect of high priorit
dimensions, where previously there were none, that are favourable t
the selection of the activity which would otherwise obviously surviv
the maximum number of stages in the filtering process, in order c
priority, with no gaps except for the hitherto theory-deficier
dimensions.

These processes do not operate instantaneously and, while they a
taking place, the chooser may feel that she faces an agonisin
dilemma. Eventually, however, the chooser's mind will cobbl
together a strong enough case for it to appear to her that the activit
she chooses is the best available in respect of the 'probler
dimensions' and does not compromise anything important else
where: i.e. the excessive ambiguities and the opportunity costs tha
were the causes of the dilemma vanish. In some situations th
person's subconscious theory fudging activities may involve her i
ignoring lower priority considerations altogether. Her mind wi
dismiss them as unimportant if further search seems unlikely t
uncover a way of meeting them that does not compromise highe
level goals.

Clearly, if a person is not fully aware of her own priority syste
and has such an inflexible construct system that the image-shapin
process fails to take place, the decision making method that we hav
proposed breaks down. The person remains in several minds an
cannot choose. But this will not usually be the case. Ultimately, mos
people are pulled in one direction rather than another by th
combined forces of their partially unconscious priority rankings an
their cognitive processes.

If our lexicographic idea is correct, people will not trade distan
and near manifestations of a particular characteristic against eac
other. Instead they will consider, consciously or otherwise, near an
distant manifestations of a characteristic as separate features, whic
they will rank in order of priority. That is to say, the distant futur
will not be traded against the near future by some discount factor bu
will have a lower priority. Cognitive fudging is easier for huma

inds to perform the further into the future it is necessary to look. However, if cognitive processes do not succeed perfectly in resolving n inconsistency that is looming on the horizon, there will be a endency to brush it aside—the person who cannot presume that she vill be able to 'cross that bridge when she comes to it' must ompromise any higher priority image she has of *herself* as someone vho is able to cope with the world.

.7 The Formal Content of Kelly's Theory of Personality

o far in this chapter we have considered how the notion of the person as a scientist' can be adapted to explain economic events, and ow events come to be envisaged, in fairly informal terms, in order to nake this unfamiliar idea easier to grasp. We should now be ready to xamine the formal content of Kelly's theory. In its original xposition it is set out as twelve statements—a fundamental postulate elaborated with the aid of eleven corollaries—in which each word is lefined with great precision. This takes up a great deal of space, so in his section we shall reproduce the elements of the theory and explain vhat they mean with the aid of brief examples instead of an in-depth, vord by word, breakdown.

FUNDAMENTAL POSTULATE: *A person's processes are sychologically channelled by the ways in which she anticipates vents*. People attempt to test how much sense they have made of the world by discovering how far they can predict and control what will happen. The ways in which people anticipate events depend on the blinkers through which people view the world. These blinkers, or, as Kelly prefers to call them, personal constructs, structure and restrict a person's behaviour. However, they do not rigidly determine what a person does; they merely channellise it, leaving scope for creativity. To illustrate this we note how Kelly's vision of channellised thinking can easily be married with Koestler's (1975a) theory of creativity via 'bisociation'.

Koestler argues that creative activity involves the sifting together of different sets of blinkers—frames of reference that would usually be ordered differently and be seen as incompatible—until something clicks into place as a new way of looking at how things fit together. This comes out nicely in Kelly's (1969, pp. 60–1) own recollection of how he got the idea for his theory of the inquiring person. He had been spending an afternoon alternating between advising post-graduate students and seeing patients. From one perspective he saw the students as young scientists attempting to cope with the complexities of their subject; from another, he saw his patients as people attempting to cope with the complexities of everyday life Suddenly, a click of 'bisociation' caused him to see his patients as they were scientists who were attempting to cope with everyday life by formulating theories about events and avoiding situations which they found uninteresting or impossible to analyse.

Kelly would have been much less likely to have stumbled across his idea had he not been working as a clinical psychologist. Even though his invention of the theory of the inquiring person was no predetermined by the fact that he was working in this context, the context had a great bearing on the constructs he selected to use to cope with his busy afternoon. The greater a person's repertoire of constructs and ability to handle information, the more creative she is likely to be and, as a result, the more difficult it is going to be even for someone who knows her repertoire to predict which new ideas she will have and what she will decide to do. This factor is always going to be the fundamental barrier which prevents a complete pinning down and manipulation of a person's economic imagination via attempts to control her expectational environment.

The Kellian analysis of human behaviour contrasts sharply with that of mainstream behaviourist psychologists. Kelly sees it as the asking of questions in the light of *forward-looking* appraisals of the possible sequels to actions. Behaviourists see it as a mechanical *response* to given stimuli. The inquiring person's expectations of what will happen *may* be related to what she has previously experienced but, as is clear in the individuality corollary of Kelly's theory, there is no presumption that people placed in the same situation will enjoy the same experience. There are striking paired parallels between behaviourist psychology and neoclassical economics, and between Kelly's 'personal constructs' approach to psychology and behavioural theories of the firm. As Latsis (1972) points out, in neoclassical economics the decisions of agents are seen, in effect, to be 'situationally determined' by objective data. Differences in behaviour are thus discussed as if they arise from different endowments and market environments, not because of different interpretations of the past and anticipations of the future.

CONSTRUCTION COROLLARY: *A person anticipates events by construing their replications.* People attempt to cope with the world by constructing, in their minds, templets of features of the world and then seeing whether or not these templets actually fit. As we explained in section 5.3, everything has to be seen in metaphorical terms: if someone asks us to describe something we explain what it is *like*, how it shares characteristics with other events.

INDIVIDUALITY COROLLARY: *Persons differ from each other in their construction of events*. People may be attempting to do

ie same things yet act in different ways. When confronted with a
iven set of circumstances they may expect different things to happen
they take a particular course of action. In academic science there
re frequent disagreements over theoretical and empirical appraisals
f events. Kelly is asking for us also to see disputes in everyday life as
heoretical and empirical disagreements. Thus, there is a scientific
ngle to be seen in, court cases where two sides are trying to establish
notives and what really happened (cf. Bennett and Feldman (1981),
r in arguments between football fans over which teams are worthy of
pecial interest, whether or not a player was offside, or who will win
he League Cup. Theories about the nature of the world are at stake
n *any* dispute.

The individuality corollary represents a barrier which a firm must
overcome if it is to have any hope of obtaining production and
marketing economies. It needs somehow to persuade potential
customers to form the same impressions of what it is selling, and to
ind the same characteristics worthy of high priority attention.

ORGANISATION COROLLARY: *Each person characteristically
evolves, for her convenience in anticipating events, a construction
system embracing ordinal relationships between constructs.* We have
earlier argued that people think in hierarchical terms in order to cope
with complexity and handle inconsistencies. Kelly is proposing the
same sort of idea. A person's construction system should not be
thought of as a simple ladder of priority relationships but as a
sometimes tangled, tree-like structure, in which some constructs may
appear in several subsystems and occupy different levels in them
according to the context in which they are used.

Consider how a person might see, for example, a particular piece of
music by Beethoven. At a low level it might be seen as fitting into a
highly specific construct 'is/is not Beethoven's Fifth', which might be
subordinate to the construct 'Beethoven's versus other composers'
symphonies'. This might in turn be construed as a subordinate
implication of the construct 'concerto versus symphony', or
'orchestral versus chamber music', and so on up to the level 'good
music versus bad music' or, ultimately, 'music versus noise'. In order
to meet the requirements for good music the composition would have
to be construed to comprise a particular arrangement of characteristics. Beethoven might be thought better than, say, Wagner or
Stravinsky because it moves at a pace that enables the listener to
discern evolving patterns, being neither so slow as to be boring, or
so wild as to be incomprehensible. In deciding whether something is music or noise different people may well use different
criteria, different systems of decomposition. Someone may require a
piece to contain themes which she can whistle; someone else may

merely require it to be sound produced on musical instruments

People may rank constructs in entirely different ways. For example, 'good versus bad music' might subsume 'classical versus popular music' for some people but be subordinated by it for others. In the subsuming case the person does not judge the goodness or badness of music according to whether it is classical or popular, but according to some other criterion. In the subordinate case the test for whether music is good or bad is the extent to which it resembles classical music (or, for some other people, popular music).

A knowledge of how potential customers' construct systems are ordered can be a great help to firms designing sales campaigns or choosing which commodity to produce. If potential customers' constructs are presently ordered in a way which will lead them to reject a particular product, the firm must either produce something else or engineer a reordering of constructs until they comprise an appropriate system. So long as a firm can keep its potential customers' attention for long enough to present a reasoned case for thinking differently, it may be able to bring about the necessary reordering. The firm has to be able to demonstrate that an existing ordering is inconsistent; that it is, literally, *unreasonable*. The potential customer then has to accept the firm's suggested 'consistent' ordering unless she can quickly think of something even better, for otherwise she has a gap in her world view. Having generated the right mould of thought via its sales pitch, the firm can then go on to show that it has a product which fits this mould. If its sales logic *appears* to be unarguable, a person who has been taken through the argument cannot refuse to buy the product without beginning to suffer doubt about her own ability to make sense of the world. The consumer wants to be a rational chooser. However, in obtaining a seemingly rational view of the world, she unwittingly is made to sacrifice her sovereignty.

DICHOTOMY COROLLARY: *A person's construction system is composed of a finite series of dichotomous constructs.* The blinkers through which people see things, or, in Kelly's terms, the constructs they use to categorise them, are bi-polar characteristic dimensions like the axes of the potential surprise diagrams of the previous chapter. To describe something in terms of a particular dimension it is necessary to say what it is like and what it is not like—one cannot speak of a car as 'fast' without implying that it shares properties with other things characterised as 'fast' and is different from things characterised as 'slow'. Likewise, one cannot describe a particular car as a 'Ford' without implying similarities to other cars called 'Fords' and a distinctiveness against 'non-Ford' cars.

People do not possess infinite numbers of constructs with which they can form theories of how to categorise particular events; e.g. the person who is not greatly interested in cars may appraise them as 'fast versus slow' but not 'Ford versus other makes'. Often they will not even have time to see events in all the dimensions they have available, a point which acquires a crucial importance in sections 6.4 and 6.5, where we discuss 'cybernetic' decision making. The number of constructs in terms of which a person attempts to construe a particular event may be related to her intelligence, education, upbringing, past interests, and so on.

CHOICE COROLLARY: *A person chooses for herself that alternative in a dichotomised construct through which she anticipates the greater possibility for the elaboration of her system.* A person chooses, in whatever dimension she is appraising possible courses in action, the activity which enables her to obtain the best prospect of improving her ability to cope with the world, or, at least, prevent the world from becoming less predictable. The inquiring person's choice of behaviour is thus a choice of which question to ask, the choice of which hypothesis to test. When a person attempts to surround herself with reassuring patterns she is asking, in effect, 'can I keep unpredictable and incomprehensible events out of my sight?' When she is more adventurous she is asking 'is my theory about this event an adequate representation of what is really there?'

In order to be able to ask particular questions of the world the inquiring person will construe certain environmental features to be necessary. The properties of commodities are not sought for 'their own sakes' but as means to an end, or because they *symbolise* the presence of necessary prerequisites for obtaining answers to those questions which are most able to attract the chooser's attention. Which property can be symbolised by something else will depend on the way a person's construct system is ordered.

Given a person's requirements for her inquisitive activities, we suggest she will choose between competing schemes of action according to the lexicographic method of decision making outlined in the previous chapter. Kelly himself does not discuss precisely *how* choices are made, nor does he explain how the inquiring person thinks about uncertainty when her theory of an event is rather loose with respect to some constructs. This is an important gap in Kelly's work, but we believe we have filled it with our behavioural adaptation of Shackle's potential surprise analysis and the discussions in section 5.6.

RANGE COROLLARY: *A construct is convenient for the anticipation of a finite range of events only.* The construct axis 'sweet versus sour' is not usually very relevant in theorising about the nature of a house. Similarly the construct axis 'open fired versus centrally heated' is not one in terms of which a potential surprise curve concerned with a food product can be defined. Those features which a construct cannot subsume under its heading may be said to lie outside that construct's 'range of convenience'. The higher the level a construct occupies in a person's system of thought, the wider its range of convenience is likely to be. For example, the construct 'warm versus cool' may be relevant for thinking about food as well as houses.

EXPERIENCE COROLLARY: *A person's construction system varies as she successively construes the replications of events.* People will revise their theories about the precise nature of the intersects of characteristics that comprise particular events in the light of experience, as part of a continuing attempt to form more accurate representations of the nature of events. This process of revision, which other psychologists would call learning, takes three main forms. First, a person may alter her assessment of where a particular event stands in respect of some construct axes. In the light of Shackle's potential surprise analysis, we would note that, where the person had a somewhat loose theory, her inquisitive activities might have helped her to narrow down, for some dimensions, the *range* of possible outcomes she construes for a particular event. Second, the ordering of constructs may be altered; e.g. in the light of experience, popular music might be seen in a different way so that 'classical versus popular' becomes subordinate to, rather than subsuming, 'good versus bad music'. Third, increasing connoisseurship causes new constructs to be added to the person's system, either at the bottom of a particular subsystem or slotted in at higher levels. That is to say, the person puts new items on her agenda of things to look for when appraising a situation.

MODULATION COROLLARY: *The variation in a person's construction system is limited by the permeability of the construct within whose range of convenience the variants lie.* How much a person can experience depends on how many perspectives she has from which to anticipate events and how constricting they are. For example, a neoclassical economist's constructs restrict her to analysing equilibrium situations and force her to exclude any study of dynamic processes evolving through historical time. Similarly, a person who has not been explained the rules of football, and whose constructs are somehow not conducive to inferring the appropriate patterns when she observes the game in action, may come to construe it as 'twenty-two men kicking a round piece of leather around a large field'. Constructs which are highly specific and act as powerful 'blinkers' Kelly labels as 'impermeable'. A person with an imperme-able construction system must, if she is not frequently to be bewildered, confine her attention to those events which can permeate her system and, if she is forced to encounter other events, she will have to force them into conformity with her world view, however bad the fit—a fudged interpretation of what is going on may be better than no interpretation at all.

FRAGMENTATION COROLLARY: *A person may successively employ a variety of construction subsystems which are inferentially incompatible with each other.* When an onlooker observes someone performing seemingly incompatible acts her observations may have either of two explanations. Either the person has some blind spots and contradictions that she is unaware of in her construction system, or there is no real incompatibility and it is just that some constructs are superordinate to others. An obvious example is that on occasions it may be necessary to be 'cruel to be kind'. Similarly, a person may drive in a manner that others see as dangerous, yet profess to have a fear of flying. An explanation of this apparent inconsistency *may* be that when the person is driving fast she feels she is less likely to have an accident than most drivers because she is more skilled than average, whereas if she is in an aeroplane other people control her destiny. In order to uncover the truth behind such patterns of behaviour it will often be necessary to make a very careful questionnaire investigation of the subjects involved.

COMMONALITY COROLLARY: *To the extent that one person employs a construction of experience which is similar to that of another, her processes are psychologically similar to those of the other person.* Although people often see the world from differing perspectives, this does not mean they will *always* come to different conclusions about appropriate images of the future. Sometimes they will use similar sets of constructs and identical bodies of 'common-sense' knowledge, while exposed to the same phenomena. But at other times, they *may* experience the same things despite being exposed to different phenomena, precisely because they see the world from different standpoints.

SOCIALITY COROLLARY: *To the extent that one person construes the construction processes of another, she may play a role in a social process involving the other person.* Unless we can understand how other people think we will function very ineffectively in a social situation. A lecturer who overestimates her students' information handling skills, for example, may succeed in teaching them very little. Similarly, a salesperson who cannot understand how her potential customers perceive her product and its rivals may fail to achieve many sales. The present book owes its format to its author's awareness of the need to make its contents accessible to economists who view the world with different sets of blinkers from his own. If it successfully anticipates the ways in which they will construe it, and the objections that they will raise against it, it is less likely to be condemned as rubbish. Just as a marketing manager must pay heed to the perceptions of her customers, so the academic who proposes a new scientific theory cannot afford to neglect the blinkers through which those who are attached to existing frameworks view the world.

We end this illustrated guide to the formal content of Kelly's theory by pointing out that it is a theory hallmarked by its reflexivity. We are using it as a device for coping with thinking about how economic agents cope with the real world. If economists generally can come to see how the theory can function as a set of blinkers, as a construction subsystem, which sheds light on their cloudy images of the relationships underlying economic occurrences, Kelly's experience corollary may apply with *their* psychological processes. His experience corollary also serves as a warning that we should take note of the dangers of insisting on a fixed world view, and recognise that the theory we are proposing may have to be revised in the light of experience.

5.8 Conclusion

In this chapter we have attempted to suggest that it may be fruitful for economists to devote rather more attention to decision maker's motivations than it is conventional to do, and that human behaviour can usefully be seen not as evidence of hedonistic, 'utility seeking' activities but as the manifestation of attempts by people to reduce the mysterious nature of the world surrounding them. Choices are seen from this perspective to be concerned with which theories a person should attempt to test, which puzzles she should try to solve. In integrating this analysis of motivation with the lexicographic theory of decision making developed in Chapter 4 we gave particular emphasis to the possibility that people may fudge the shapes of their potential surprise curves as they evaluate rival schemes, so that what they foresee appears to conform with their views of the world.

Critics may attempt to argue that the proposed theory of motivation is unscientific, because 'confirming instances' can be rationalised everywhere, and not practically applicable because of its complexity and concern with thoughts inside people's heads. We have attempted to rebut such suggestions in advance by referring to Kelly's 'repertory grid' technique for discovering how people think, which reduces a researcher's need to make external rationalisations of observed behaviour. All of the examples offered in the chapter were, it must be stressed, hypothetical illustrations of the ways in which people might see the world around them. They were chosen only to help the reader understand the theory, not as generally applicable cases for application. The theory itself suggests that *any* way of viewing the world to which a person subscribes will enable her to 'see' confirming instances everywhere, since inconsistencies will eventually be filtered out or twisted so that they are not seen.

The theory that has been articulated denies the preordained and immutable nature of preferences usually assumed by neoclassical economists. Inquisitive activity and the concept of equilibrium are incompatible. Experience modifies the inquiring person's world view continually unless she asks such vague questions of the world around her that she experiences nothing. However, it is conceded that sometimes the notion of given preferences may be a useful approximation since it is rare for experience *fundamentally* to cause a person to revise the way she views the world.

6 Budgets, Habits and Behaviour Dynamics

6.1 Introduction

This chapter, as its title suggests, is concerned with dynamic aspects of consumer choice. We shall attempt to fill three important gaps in the analysis of decision making and motivation in the previous two chapters. The three areas of concern are as follows.

First, in Chapter 4 the discussion usually proceeded as if choices were being made between rival activities that were fairly similar in nature, selected as being within an acceptable budget range. But we did not discuss in detail how such budget ranges might be determined, or how consumers might decide on the order in which they would devote their attention to rival budget categories. The latter was a rather important omission given that the whole point of budgeting is to break up an otherwise complex problem of resource allocation into a series of manageable subproblems to be investigated sequentially. In section 6.2 we attempt to provide solutions to both of these puzzles. Section 6.3 then considers the policy implications of this analysis.

Second, it could be argued that although the lexicographic theory of decision making proposed in Chapter 4 makes a brave attempt to face up to the fact of bounded rationality, it portrays an approach to choice which is still far more complex than the real life techniques for making decisions that people use in situations where their choices are not of crucial importance. For example, a person shopping in a supermarket may not buy an identical bundle of goods each week but she does not seem to spend much time worrying about individual items when she finds that prices have changed, new brands have appeared, or some products are out of stock. Sections 6.4 and 6.5 of this chapter will therefore attempt to analyse, respectively, the ways in which the choice process is simplified in such situations, and the ways in which brand managers may attempt to generate or break brand loyalty if they have a knowledge of how such decisions are taken.

Third, the inertia associated with the concept of brand loyalty naturally leads us to the question of how habitual behaviour in general can be reconciled with the notion of the inquiring person, that was proposed in Chapter 5. Section 6.6, which is followed by a brief conclusion, attempts to resolve the apparent inconsistency between the inertia that can frequently be observed, and our suggestion that people wish to improve their abilities to cope with the world and attempt to do this by a process of exploration and hypothesis testing.

To set these discussions in context it is helpful first briefly to consider a central behavioural concept in the study of dynamics, which has been left a somewhat implicit feature in previous chapters. This is the *decision cycle*, originally proposed by Dewey (1910, p. 72). Dewey's idea that decision making is a lengthy, multistage process is at odds with the essentially timeless neoclassical view of choice. A neoclassical theorist usually makes no mention of the time horizon over which substitutions are made at diminishing marginal rates, and depicts choice as a discrete act, not as a continuous process. We would wish to propose the following six stage decision cycle, which incorporates elements from Dewey's original five stage model, the circumspection-pre-emption-control cycle of construction used by Kelly (1955, p. 551), and the three and five stage cycles of, respectively, Simon and Clarke, which have been discussed critically by Loasby (1976a, pp. 88–94).

(1)   *Problem Recognition.* A problem may be perceived as a result of a failure of attainments to match up to aspirations, or as a result of routine scanning to avoid oversights, which suggests that targets are unlikely to be met. Information picked up purely by chance may signal the existence of a problem, but, for the signal to register, the decision maker must have a prior disposition to fit the information into the appropriate context.

(2)   *Search.* The full set of relevant alternatives may not be given, and may even be impossible to define. The decision maker therefore has to search for courses of action between which to choose, unless she believes she already has some potentially satisfactory options at hand.

(3)   *Evaluation.* This is the stage in which the decision maker formulates her theories about the possible sequels to particular choices. It is, of course, entirely possible that this activity will reveal further problems and push her back to stage 1.

(4)   *Choice.*

(5)   *Implementation*. This is often difficult and only partially accomplished.

(6)   *Assessment*. Here the decision maker examines whether what has been decided has been achieved, whether or not her theory was correct and the problem thereby solved. If the evidence is in some sense unsatisfactory, and if her cognitive processes cannot rapidly shape it to seem otherwise, she is driven back to stage 1.

Within any particular decision cycle, the six stages may themselves be broken up into substages involving subcycles. Budgeting, to which we now turn, may be thought of as part of the search stage of the decision cycle, but it involves the need to theorise, choose, and so on.

6.2 Budgeting and Choice

Budgets are devices that people use to enable themselves to cope with bounded rationality and uncertainty. A consumer lacks the computational skills which would be necessary for making choices between all-embracing bundles of diverse, well-specified commodities. In a complex and ever-changing environment she cannot know even which options will be available, at which prices, during her planning period. A set of budget ranges, and a plan concerning the order in which she will attend to them, enables her both to confine her area of search and the need to process information at any one time, and to leave her options open in respect of particular contingencies.

A budget range, or a set of budget ranges, then, is a means to an end, just as any commodity selected from within a budget range is a means to an end. When a consumer selects her budgets she may be thought of as choosing them by applying a characteristic filtering test to rival budgeting schemes, just as she does when choosing between ultimate market transactions. It is easy enough to suggest that the choice of budgeting schemes should be treated as if it is a choice between less abstract commodities, but it is less obvious which characteristics an acceptable budget range, or set of budget ranges, will have to possess if it is to survive more stages than its rivals in a priority-based filtering process.

To shed more light on the process whereby budgets come to be selected, let us simplify matters first of all by considering the hypothetical case of a person who is choosing in a static environment, and whose priority system has the following form. Her top five priorities can only be satisfied by expenditure on one distinct category of commodities. Her sixth to tenth priorities can only be satisfied by expenditure on a second distinct category of commodities;

and so on. We are thus assuming someone with an unrealistic but very convenient hierarchy, for there are no horizontal or vertical linkages between the activities.

Such a person can construct a budget range for a *single* category at a time, without worrying about other expenditure categories at all, so long as she looks at categories in the correct order. Her first task is to discover how much she needs to spend on the first category of activities in order to meet her first five priorities. But she does not know about all the properties and prices of commodities included in the first expenditure category. Her budget range, she hopes, will enable her to avoid unnecessary search. However, because uncertainty exists, there is a possibility that whichever budget range she selects will be inappropriate. If she chooses one with a relatively high lower bound she may fail to discover a cheap but adequate way of meeting her priorities, and thus end up spending more than is necessary. This sort of mistake would leave her with a smaller residual to budget in respect of other expenditure categories, so she might needlessly fail to meet some lower priority aspirations. To choose a budget range with a low upper bound could also be a mistake: she might fail to discover a satisfactory activity and be forced to start searching again.

For each budget range the consumer has in mind, she has to ask herself which kinds of activities it is likely to lead her to discover. What she needs to discover is at least one expenditure strategy which, itself, will pass a characteristic filtering test in respect of priorities one to five. If she believes that several possible budget ranges would lead her to discover such a strategy she has a tie to break between the relevant budget ranges. To break the tie, we suggest that she will compare the budget ranges in respect of other dimensions to which they are permeable, in order of priority. These dimensions could include: a) narrowness—since a narrow range may save search time; b) lowness of the lower bound—since a low bottom limit reduces the possibility of unnecessarily high expenditures; and c) degree of 'up-marketness'—since an expensive price range might permit a superior search environment, with better sales assistance from staff in better-appointed shops. If no budget range seems likely to lead to the discovery of an activity which will meet her first five priorities with no gaps, she must choose the one which seems likely to bring her as close as possible to meeting these priorities, unless, of course, she can expand her set of possible budget ranges (e.g. by borrowing). Thus, failing a budget range which meets her 'first-best' requirement, the next-best budget range is the one which seems likely to lead to the discovery of an activity which would dominate as neutral scheme in respect of the fifth priority after passing filter tests for the first four priorities.

Having chosen her budget range by this procedure, the consumer then uses it as intended. She chooses between the schemes which are in the relevant price range, and of which she is aware, by the usual lexicographic method. She is left with a residual sum to spend on satisfying her lower priority aspirations. She then begins the budgeting process again, this time in respect of the second expenditure category and priorities six to ten. She continues to form budgets and make expenditures in this way until she has no more resources left.

Let us now consider the more complex case of a person who has to choose in a turbulent environment and whose priorities bear a relationship to activities which is complicated in two significant respects. The first is that she may be aware that several activities can affect her attainments in respect of a single goal. For example, the kinds of food a person eats, the sort of house in which she lives, and the car she drives, may all in some way serve towards creating an image which she regards to be sufficiently consistent with her self-image. Particular activities may be either synergistic or positively antagonistic in respect of an aspiration level. An example of a synergistic mix would be where a person is convinced that if she spends nothing on a car she will fail to create a satisfactory image, whereas if she cuts back on, say, housing expenditure and uses the money to buy a car she will be able to meet her image aspiration (cf. section 5.5). However, if she cuts back too far on her housing expenditure and buys a very expensive car she may once more fail to generate a satisfactory image – e.g. people may think she is rather peculiar if she has an exotic car but very poor accommodation.

Where activities are positively antagonistic it gets more expensive to meet an aspiration the more they are mixed together. For example, suppose a person has an aspiration to avoid spending her time repairing things. If she rents a house and has a relatively new car she may meet this aspiration. She may do even better, for the same monthly expenditure, in respect of this goal if she buys a brand new house and does not run a car. But, if she tries to finance buying a house *and* running a car from this level of budget, she may only be able to afford an old car and a decaying property, and, consequently, may find herself spending too much time repairing them.

A second complication is that a given activity may affect attainments in respect of several goals, but there may be gaps between the goals. For example, a consumer's priorities might be as follows. First: a nutritional goal, met only by the consumption of food (a goal whose satisfactory attainment is likely to be thought of in conjunctive terms – see section 4.3). Second: a shelter goal, met only by the consumption of housing. Third and fourth, and sixth to ninth: goals whose attainments are affected by motoring *and* other forms of consumption. Fifth, tenth and twelfth: goals whose attainments are only affected by motoring consumption. Eleventh: a goal whose attainment is affected by activities other than motoring.

These complications mean that activities are not properly separable. But the consumer *has* to treat them as separable in order to be able to cope with her bounded rationality and the uncertainties of her environment. When she works out her budgets, then, she tries to select a form of separation which will lead her to make a sequence of transactions which, *ex post*, will sum together in such a way as to leave her in a position where she has met a greater number of her priorities, without leaving any gaps between them, than she would have been likely to meet by using an alternative separation strategy. We thus suggest that, when priorities and activities are related in this complex way, budgeting should be seen as the activity of choosing between alternative, mutually exclusive, *programmes* for action in respect of the overall set of goal priorities. Each programme comprises a *set* of budget ranges and an intention concerning the *order* in which attention will be devoted to them. We suggest that choice between these programmes will be made by subjecting them to a normal characteristic filtering test, just as in the earlier example of the choice of a single budget range, where the decision was less complicated.

Given her system of priorities, the consumer's budgeting choice will be dependent on: (a) the volume of resources she has left over from the previous planning period; and (b) the outcomes she imagines to be possible in the light of a mass of snippets of information about the environment and how it is changing. Let us illustrate the second point by considering a few hypothetical examples of the thoughts that might rush through someone's head as she evaluates alternative strategies: 'That strange noise the car is making may turn out to be very expensive if I delay getting it serviced till the end of the month'; 'Isn't this the time of the year that Scottish Opera send out their priority booking forms to subscribers?—Still, I suppose I could pay in instalments by banker's order this time'; 'That royalty cheque from the publisher should have arrived by the middle of the month'; 'If I am going to lose my no claims discount as a result of that crash, I had better start putting money aside for a large motor insurance bill at the end of the year'; 'If I end up going out to restaurants for evening entertainment as much as last month, it will be a waste to continue buying so much food in the supermarket'; 'Doesn't that hi-fi sale end on the fifteenth?'; and so on. In situations where activities are linked in respect of different sets of priorities, the importance for the consumer of choosing a particular sequence of expenditures will be greater the more turbulent the environment and the more 'lumpy' expenditure items that are involved in particular budget categories. And the more uncertain the consumer is about the environment she faces, the more her choice of budget plan will be contingent on the state of 'the news' (cf. sections 3.6 and 5.5), as she tries desperately to avoid choosing a plan that will leave her with important targets imperfectly attained.

Whichever budgeting strategy the consumer chooses, she will continue to try to implement it during the relevant planning period, *unless* it becomes sufficiently obvious that events are not unfolding as expected and that a better plan of action might be conceived. That is to say, her behaviour during the plan implementation period should be thought of as if it is *programmed* to lead to particular broad choices of ultimate expenditure activities.

We end this discussion of the theory of budgeting choices by considering the role that price changes have to play in determining the pattern of consumption across budget categories. This discussion is important because it helps to make clear why we felt it necessary to support Pasinetti's critique of the importance neoclassical theorists assign to 'substitution effects' (section 2.2) and to propose a new behavioural view of income and substitution effects (section 4.8).

When proposing the analysis in section 4.8, we were considering income and substitution effects at the level of the individual item of purchase. The conventional route to defining these effects—the marginal rate of substitution—was ignored because we were speaking of consumers making purchases of 'lumpy' products; we were not prepared to theorise as if consumers chose 'a bit of everything' (cf. section 3.4). Thus we conceptualised income effects of price changes in terms of whether or not they would make a product appear within the budget ranges of more consumers; i.e. whether or not more people would be able to *afford* a product or would view it as an inferior good. A substitution effect was only said to occur if, having arrived within a budget range (or having already been there prior to a price change), a product sold in different amounts, when a different price was charged, as a result of price being used as a tie-breaker between products which were otherwise equally satisfactory. Clearly, this new view of income and substitution effects cannot make sense in the context of budgeting. A neoclassical reader, however, might, not unnaturally, wish to point out that our concern with indivisibilities would not be justified in the context of budgeting. Such a reader might suggest that our theory of budgeting is simply a fancy way of describing the process of separation which conventional utility tree analyses depict as involving marginal substitutions between rival budget categories. This is a viewpoint which we shall attempt to challenge during the rest of this section.

Our first objection to the notion that budgeting involves *marginal* substitutions between categories of commodities, in the light of relative prices, is based on our bounded rationality assumption. Consumers will be prevented, by a lack of information handling capacities, from considering vast lists of possible budget plans, each slightly differentiated by its mix of budget ranges or proposed sequence of expenditures. To simplify their budgeting efforts, consumers will look at a relatively small number of sets of 'conventional' *rounded* figures. Changes of allocation between categories in response to price changes will thus be discontinuous. Continuity will only be observed in the aggregate, and only if people using similar sets of rounded numbers do not all change their allocations at the same time. Structural stability in the economy as a whole seems to depend on people having different thresholds of response (cf. Richardson (1960) and Hirschman (1970)).

Secondly, we wish to raise a fundamental problem concerning what it means to argue, in the context of budgeting, that a rise in the cost of, say, 'transport' or 'food' leads consumers to substitute in favour of other kinds of commodity. The problem centres on the question of providing indices of price and quantity for groups of heterogeneous commodities. We seem to be encountering, in the context of consumer behaviour theory, a problem similar to the one which provoked the Cambridge Capital Controversy (Harcourt, 1972). The problem in capital theory is that different types of machines can only be added in value terms, yet wage changes will affect their reproduction prices. It is therefore not meaningful to say that rises in wages cause substitution in favour of more capital-intensive methods of production. One can say that rises in wages lead to more expenditure on machinery (if they do), but one cannot say that there is more machinery in existence than otherwise would have been the case—there may be more of some machines but less of others.

In our depiction of the budgeting process the consumer is trying, like a firm, to 'produce' various priority outcomes by mixing together expenditures on various budget categories. If the price of, say, electricity falls, a consumer may change her electricity budget, planning to consume rather more electricity in various loosely construed contexts. We can add together units of, say, electricity, if not different types of uses of it, in a simple way. But how do we meaningfully say that a fall in 'the price of food' which leads to a change in a consumer's food budget and her pattern of food consumption, has led to any particular price, substitution or income effects in terms of changes in the 'amount of food' consumed? If the consumer reduces her consumption of some kinds of food in response to relative price changes between food *subbudgets* (meat/fish/vegetables/dairy produce) that have lowered the overall food price index, we cannot be sure that she is consuming more food *generally* even if she has increased her consumption of other types of food. And the same problem arises at successive subbudget levels, until we eventually come down to the level of the individual commodity, where indivisibilities will often once again render inappropriate the neoclassical view of marginal substitutions in response to price changes.

But suppose we ignore the index number problem, perhaps recognising that it is inherent in the budgeting process that price indices for categories of commodities are, in any case, going to be highly conjectural constructs. If we do this, we can then move on to note that, where there are changes in relative index levels, their significance for quantities transacted in particular budgeting categories depends critically on the structure of priorities and linkages between activities. Substitution effects of the neoclassical kind will be at their least significant for commodity groupings when: (a) a consumer's budget is predetermined in large measure by past budgeting decisions which involved regular commitments to fixed activities (cf. section 5.5); and (b) a consumer's priority system bears the sort of simple relationship to activities suggested in the example at the start of this section. In such a system a cheapening of the first class of activities results in a proportionate contraction in the budget range and no change in the 'volume' of this class of goods consumed. There is simply a larger residual from which lower budget ranges will, in sequence, be selected. The volume of goods to be consumed in this class will only rise if previously the real value of the person's resources was insufficient to enable her to meet her first group of priorities in its entirety. This is purely an income effect, not substitution effect, and, as Pasinetti's analysis reminds us, it is an effect which rising affluence would have produced in time anyway, regardless of price changes. By similar arguments we can see that a cheapening of the second class of activities, if the second and first groups of priorities were both already being met, would not lead to changes in the volumes of consumption of either kinds of activity by the consumer; and so on, for other activity categories.

With linked activities, where budget coefficients are not largely fixed by prior commitments, there is much more scope for changes in group price indices to lead to quantity substitutions between groups, despite the chooser having a priority system of aspirations. Cheaper ways of meeting particular aspirations may become available. For example, if the price of clothing falls relative to motoring, a person may plan to buy more clothing and do less motoring, thereby hoping to meet her image aspiration for a lower cost. However, the constraint she faces in doing this is her ability to do less motoring without compromising her motoring-specific priorities. If these priorities prevent her from doing less motoring, and if all of her priorities whose attainments are affected by clothing seem likely to be met, she will not buy any more clothing. She will transfer the money she saves to other budget categories. Priorities which can only be met by one kind of activity thus hinder substitution effects in response to price index changes between budget categories, even if most priorities can be met by a variety of types of expenditure.

6.3 Consumer Budgets and Corporate Policies

Once they have chosen particular budget ranges, consumers will not undertake detailed examinations of products outside them unless given good reason to do so. It is therefore important that firms wishing to engage in volume production should attempt to discover which budget ranges their potential customers commonly have in mind. In the previous section we argued that people will tend to think in terms of 'conventional' rounded numbers when working out their budgets. It is not just bounded rationality that will make a consumer think of possible car budget limits of, say, £5000, £5500, or £6000, rather than £4986, £5487, or £6009. Consumers are also encouraged to do this by consumer magazines which group products within such 'neat' price ranges in order to facilitate detailed comparisons, and by the tendency of firms to cluster their products in groups slightly below the upper ends of conventional price ranges because they are aware of the fact that consumers think in such terms (cf. Andrews (1950), p. 154). Conventions have a tendency to be upheld for somewhat circular reasons. Popular products in particular categories will, in turn, be used as image-forming reference points when budget programmes are being selected.

Now, if there is a tendency for consumers' budget ranges to be clustered in particular markets, these markets should effectively be regarded as segmented and largely immune from price wars. The outlet for corporate aggression will be through new designs of products/marketing packages. If products are priced according to normal costs, the key investment planning question concerns which product/marketing package should be offered just within the *upper* end of the popular price range. For example, it may be the case that most buyers of family cars have in mind a price range of £5000 to

£6000. To get them to spend to the limit of their budgets, a firm should offer a model crammed with appropriate 'extras', so that it survives more priority filters than rival products and price does not have to be used as a tie-breaking characteristic. If a basic design sells for less than £5000, a well-trimmed variant may sell in much greater quantities than its spartan counterpart, even if priced nearer to £6000, because it will arrive more frequently on customers' agendas. This 'luxury' model will probably have to compete with 'basic' models of larger, executive cars from another segment of the market. However, so long as it is adequate in respect of high level goals that these larger basic cars can enable purchasers easily to attain (e.g. spaciousness), its superiority in terms of minor matters should enable it more frequently to survive more stages in the filtering processes of customers in this part of the market. The limit on the small car's ability to do this is the extent to which an illusory image of luxuriousness rubs on to the rival 'basic' models from their more expensive counterparts.

In the market example in question, it would be foolish to keep adding compulsory 'extras' to a basic product if, as a result, its 'normal cost' price exceeded the typical maximum budget, unless such budgets were to some extent malleable. The extras might mean that if the upper budget limit were, say, £6200, a car would dominate in most characteristic filtering tests if it sold at £6195. However, if the upper budget limit were only £6000, it would not even be given the chance to take the test. If the budget ranges of buyers of executive cars cluster on, say, £7000 to £9000, a firm which offers a range of cars at between £5800 and £6800 may be engaged in a disastrous strategy. To produce a car that is bigger but less well-equipped than 'top of the range' models in the £5000 to £6000 price band, yet which is not in the executive league, is to fall surely between two stalls and to win needlessly thin sales. One might do reasonably well in the £6000 to £7000 price band with the upper range variants, though sell hardly any of the basic models. However, twenty per cent of sales in the £5000 to £6000 market segment could be much more profitable than fifty per cent of the poorly populated £6000 to £7000 segment, particularly if a firm has tooled up for large scale production without properly understanding how the market is segmented.

It may sound as if these arguments about product positioning to take account of the budgeting phenomenon entail a rejection of the principle of normal cost pricing. They do not. Consumer preferences shape the budget range within which it will be profitable for a firm to confine its attention, unless a marketing strategy can be designed to produce a reordering of what is regarded as an acceptable budget range. But within this range the firm has the task of designing a product that will survive consumer filtering processes better than the offerings of rivals. In the early stages of product development the firm will have several broad designs in mind. But it will be aware that, no matter which one it ultimately opts to produce, it is constrained to set a price so that it only earns a normal rate of return over the product lifecycle as a whole. The firm therefore makes sales projections at normal cost prices. The product then chosen is the one which best suits the long run interests of the majority of those involved in taking the decision. If they discover that this form of pricing would leave them unable to make satisfactory returns on any of the schemes, they will set in motion search for ways of reducing unit costs. That is to say, the *position* of the firm's cost function will not be invariant with sales projections and the cost positions of rivals. We have a 'price-minus theory of cost' (cf. Smyth (1967)) but one which does not violate the normal cost theory of price. Consumer preferences focus the firm's attention, but the firm does not equate marginal costs and revenues simultaneously to arrive at a price.

The greater the number of consumers that can be persuaded to think in terms of a given budget range, the more a firm can enjoy economies of scale. But how can potential customers be persuaded to change their budgets? We shall try to provide some answers to this question by taking the case of the car market once again, addressing first the task of pushing people into spending more.

If a firm offers a poorly trimmed 'base' model outside the lower end of the 'conventional' budget range, it will attract the attention of the target group of customers; i.e. the group which is looking for cars in a lower budget range. A large amount of the image of the more luxuriously trimmed models rubs off on to the base model, while it can also be shown to be in a different technological league from other models in the price range. It may, therefore, be given serious investigation. There are then two main means by which a salesperson can attempt favourably to affect the size of a potential customer's upper budget limit. First, she can try to demonstrate that the customer can only refuse to buy a more expensive model on the basis of an unreasonable set of priorities. For example, she may point out that 'the deluxe version has a radio, so it's much *safer* on long journeys—you won't fall asleep at the wheel. I know that better trimmed rival products at the same price as our base model have radios, but this doesn't mean *they* are safer. Their steering and braking systems are years out of date.' Second, she may attempt to show that although the deluxe model is more expensive it is well worth the extra cost because it has greater synergy potential. Hence the customer can spend less on other activities without apparently jeopardising higher priorities. *A priori*, we would expect appeals to the car's ability to bolster the customer's image to be particularly successful in creating this impression. However, the success of any means aimed at expanding budgets will be constrained by the extent of crucial commitments the consumer has already made in respect of higher level budgeting activities which entail regular financial commitments.

Similar techniques can be used to move customers 'down-market', away from other companies' products. Firms can suggest that it is unnecessary (i.e. it would be *foolish*) to spend more than a particular sum to satisfy reasonable needs, and attempt to show that goals which could be met from residual expenditure should be worthy of higher priority than some of those met by 'up-market' examples of the activity in question.

6.4 Cybernetic Choices

The decision makers that we have been considering do not think through all the possible implications of the problems they are attempting to solve or of the solutions they choose to adopt. Frequently, inexperience and a lack of suitably permeable constructs will mean that they choose after making only a very partial examination of possible options. A consequence of such behaviour may be that problems keep arising; decision takers are continually propelled around the decision cycle. The more problems there are crying out for solutions, the less it will seem possible for a decision maker to step back and make a cool, detached and detailed appraisal of any one of them. Such an investigation might prevent more problems from arising in future, but it might simply have the effect of overloading the decision maker with information, with the result that she is even less confident that the solution she selects will be adequate.

Where decisions have to be taken at speed, the sort of theory forming and filtering activity central to our lexicographic choice model may be precluded. Instead the chooser will resort to using rule-of-thumb, programmed 'recipes' from a menu of possible solutions. She will be on the lookout for particular configurations of a few select variables, and when she sees one of these patterns she will automatically select a particular recipe and perform its repertory of operations. She will not consider alternative courses of action, nor conceptualise in detail the outcome that ensues. She will perform the operation and then carry on monitoring what happens to the group of variables, drawing other recipes into operation if she observes appropriate 'trigger' sets of signals. This form of behaviour, where simple feedback mechanisms displace deliberative thought, has been labelled *cybernetic* decision making by Steinbruner (1974, Chapter 3) (see also, Simon (1962)). Behavioural theorists, unlike Baumol and Quandt (1964), do not claim that people use such methods of decision making because they are 'optimal', merely because they seem satisfactory (cf. Loasby (1976a), p. 213).

An obvious example of the cybernetic model in operation is the person driving to and from work in her car. Her use of the accelerator, brakes and gear box is determined by the signals she receives concerning the proximity of other vehicles, from traffic signs, and from the noise of her engine. She does not have time to evaluate in any detail the possible consequences of alternative rates of acceleration and braking, or choice of route. So long as the journey is completed at a satisfactory rate, and the movements of the fuel gauge do not trigger too many trips to the filling station, she will not question her choice of activity. Only a persistent failure to meet her priorities will force her into a detailed search (possibly using other cybernetic decision recipes) for a new recipe book, a new travel lifestyle (e.g. she may consider the possibility of buying a smaller car, using public transport, or using a less direct but less congested route). If she asked herself each day whether her recipe for getting to work could be improved upon in each of its many dimensions, she could well find herself paralysed in a state of 'hyper-reflexivity'. She might become like the centipede that was called upon to explain how it coped with coordinating so many pairs of legs simultaneously and was never able to walk again, because, on thinking about the puzzle, it realised it did not know the answer.

Life is impossible to handle if we question everything and keep returning to first principles: we have to presume that, in some areas at least, we have recipes for success. It is only by making frequent use of the cybernetic decision process that we can release time for deliberative thought about puzzles that we presently cannot deal with by using our existing set of recipes.

In section 4.3 we mentioned the disjunctive method of taking decisions, in which a single attribute is used as the criterion for choice. We argued that in situations of genuinely fanatical behaviour it seemed to suffer from a logical contradiction, since a connoisseur would be able to break one attribute up into a variety of subordinate constructs. However, in situations of ignorance or unconcern, the disjunctive approach to choice may seem, in the light of experience, to be an adequate cybernetic choice technique, particularly if the price dimension is used, or if a certain attribute (e.g. a brand name) has been found to serve as a proxy for many others. Two examples may help to illustrate the disjunctive method of choice performing this role. First, a person may not be a connoisseur of margarine and may have as a rule that she will purchase the cheapest 500g tub she can see on her weekly shopping trip, if, and only if, she has no unopened tubs in her refrigerator when she goes out shopping. Second, after selecting her budget for the purchase of a new piece of hi-fi equipment, she may, not being a connoisseur, judge quality by price and purchase the most expensive unit she can afford from the display in a particular (cybernetically chosen) shop.

Let us consider briefly, before moving on to look at the policy implications of cybernetic decision making, whether or not it is applicable in the context of budgeting. In the 'characteristic filtering' analysis of budgeting in section 6.2, we emphasised the effects of environmental turbulence. Our decision maker was worrying about possible car repair bills, lost insurance discounts, the chances of making one-off savings when buying expensive durables, and, perhaps implicitly, changes in her social life. In this environment of partially-predictable discontinuities, it is likely that she will think carefully about what she is going to allocate to each budget category. The same can obviously be said of a person who is deciding what sort of home she can set up as a result of marriage or moving to a new job, even if the environment is relatively stable in other respects: here, the budgeting choice is a lifestyle choice. But in gradually evolving environments, and where the chooser is sufficiently well-endowed as to have room for manoeuvre if she makes budgeting mistakes, it would seem plausible to argue that budgeting decisions are cybernetic rather than deliberative. Kay (1979) sees the budgeting of resources in large, multiproduct firms in these terms, and it appears not unreasonable to apply his idea more generally.

6.5 Policy Implications of Cybernetic Decision Making

If the rule of thumb procedures that people use for choice lead them not to purchase the products of a particular firm, then that firm must attempt to demonstrate that a superior decision procedure exists, which happens to involve purchasing its product instead of one produced by a rival. Suppose, for example, that a firm wishes to sell a luxury margarine to consumers who normally insist on buying the cheapest brand and who usually ignore quality signals. This firm must demonstrate that the application of this rule is inconsistent with the chooser's underlying priority system. It might thus be appropriate to emphasise that cheap margarines, unlike 'Brand X', are high in cholesterol, which can be harmful to health (cf. section 7.3), and to suggest that the correct purchasing rule is 'buy the cheapest cholesterol-free margarine'. For a second example, suppose that people choose between different brands of washing-up liquid on the basis of the cheapest product per unit volume, and find this rule works satisfactorily. A firm which has developed a more effective, concentrated product must focus its advertising emphasis entirely on the fact that the *form* of the decision rule is irrational and should be broken. It must demonstrate, without overloading potential customers with information, that its product is the cheapest to use despite its higher price per unit volume. If it can do this successfully it would be a complete waste of advertising resources to emphasise that it is also, say, 'kinder to the user's hands'. Such a characteristic is only worth publicising if there is some doubt that consumers can be convinced that the concentrated product is the cheapest to use.

The purchasing contexts in which cybernetic rules are likely to be used are those where the consumer is too busy to think in terms of many dimensions. Thus, if one programmed decision rule is to replace another, the advertising strategy should concentrate almost wholly upon a dominant dimension, apart from suggesting that other brands are all *nearly enough the same* in respect of other properties. With such a strategy, the consumer is told that a *particular* simple criterion is appropriate, that if she *did* carry out a detailed appraisal of all the brands she could afford (in either lexicographic or compensatory terms) she would come to the same conclusion. The implication is that it is a waste of time—a mistake—to consider other brands if the impression given by the advertisement is correct. The inquiring person wants to be able to predict and control the world; she therefore wishes to avoid making unnecessary mistakes. Hence, if the advertisement seems credible and she cannot provide a reason why the dominating characteristic should be dismissed, she can only reject the brand on the basis of *un*reason. If she has no strong presumption as to which properties a particular kind of product should offer—no image of the 'ideal'—she needs a basis for choice if problem-solution requires that one brand or another must be bought, and the advertisement is providing just such a basis.

But the extent of any individual firm's ability to engender the choice of a particular purchasing rule, in situations where consumers do not undertake detailed evaluations of rival brands, is constrained by the marketing activities of its rivals. A mass of conflicting claims may lead the consumer to find that no brand has a more credible case in favour of it; that there is no disjunctive choice criterion which is obviously the best. Even if she has the time available, the consumer cannot apply a detailed lexicographic evaluation procedure if the contradictory suggestions made in different advertisements leave her unable to theorise and form potential surprise curves concerning the various characteristics offered by rival brands. She can only form theories *after* some experimentation and comparison, or if she has time to read consumer magazines. If she already has a recipe that seems to be adequate for solving the problem in question, she will have no reason to experiment unless she wishes to become a connoisseur of the solutions to the problem. The resources that firms have used in creating what adds up to a confused image of their rival brands can hardly be said to have been employed to the benefit of the consumer. If she has paid attention to the advertisements she has had her time wasted. Furthermore, the costs of advertising will figure in the rival firms' calculations of entry-forestalling, 'normal cost' prices, so the consumer ends up paying to be bombarded with information that she cannot handle.

6.6 Inertia and the Inquiring Person

In situations where cybernetic decision methods are used, the chooser is often taking action directly to *control* the environment in which she seeks, by other means, to attain a greater ability to *anticipate* events. Control, as Kelly (1955, p. 525) observes, 'permits one to elaborate his prediction system while maintaining its essential features.' A person who purchases, by some cybernetic rule, a particular brand of 'Aspirin' is usually only interested in the product for its ability to remove symptoms of colds and headaches. Unless she is a doctor or works for a drugs company she will not be terribly concerned with how Aspirin tablets of any particular brand work. Her inquisitive activities proper will concern more interesting or urgent mysteries of the world. Her reluctance to break with her established cybernetic procedures is thus easy to understand. In other contexts, however, the sources of inertia are rather more complicated. It is the aim of this section to provide an analysis of this aspect of behaviour dynamics.

We start by noting that an unchanging pattern of action should not necessarily be seen to imply an absence of inquisitive activity. Any scientist will often have to repeat experiments in order to be convinced that she has not observed purely a chance confirmation or refutation of her theories. Empirical evidence is a pattern which is seen to repeat itself. This point is relevant even where an activity has been selected as a kind of investment good because it is construed as likely to present a particular image of the chooser to other people, the aim being to elicit from them a response which clarifies other images. The audience will not always be convinced immediately by the image that has been projected. The person (or firm) attempting to project an image must do so for long enough for a *reputation* to be acquired. If a person attempts to project different images to several groups of people in quick succession, each group may end up seeing several different images. As a result, she will either lose all credibility (see further Goffman (1971)) or simply confuse them by presenting an overall image of enigmatic or unstable behaviour. Such an image will hardly be conducive to obtaining a positive response, unless the aim is to make the observers suffer from anxiety and behave defensively.

An example may help to clarify the point that apparent inertia and inquisitive activity are entirely compatible. (Of course, if people could be guaranteed to see patterns immediately there would be no need to offer such an example!). Consider the case of a person at a party who has to decide how fast to circulate amongst the other guests. If she circulates rapidly she can meet a lot of new people (i.e. she can engage in elaboration). However, if she mixes only with people she already knows, she may improve her ability to anticipate their behaviour by getting to know them better. (Kelly would call this activity 'construct definition'.) But party conversation with people she knows may also enable her to elaborate her perceptual field if she comes during the course of it to hear about hitherto unfamiliar facets of the world. Thus she may find it most interesting to carry on mixing with people she knows, getting to know them better simultaneously with discussing new areas of interest. The payoff from getting to know people she has not met before may be very low if she is unlikely to meet them again.

The explanation of inertia just given may be the sort of explanation that a person would use to justify not talking with unfamiliar party guests. Kelly's theory of personality, however, leads us to suspect that it is only part of the story, and may not even be the real explanation. A new perspective may be gained by considering the role played by emotions. We note first that Kelly (1955, p. 508) defines *aggression* as 'the active elaboration of one's perceptual field'. An aggressive person is not afraid to find out what happens if she attempts to adopt a particular course of action. She is willing to meet and make challenges and encounter new situations. To mix with unfamiliar people at a party, or to try *any* new commodity or activity, is to act in an aggressive manner.

An attempt to mix with unfamiliar people is certainly a test of a person's ability to cope with the world. There is the possibility of embarrassment and confusion. Any attempt immediately to start a specialised conversation will be prone to result in blank faces. It is necessary first to build up a pattern of shared expectations by asking a series of hierarchically-related questions and answers until a fruitful form of discourse comes into focus. To break into an existing conversation between unfamiliar people may be more difficult still. As Garfinkel (1967, p. 40) shows, by comparing transcripts of conversations with reports of what the participants understood them to be about, many conversational expressions are absolutely meaningless unless an auditor knows the previous course of the conversation, and either knows or can assume something about the biographies and intentions of the speakers. A person may be aware that if she mishandles her attempt to be aggressive she may come out of the situation with her self-image shattered. She may be unable to cope with the prospect of appearing to be a fool in everyday situations. If this is the case, it is likely that, by the mechanisms discussed in section 5.6, her cognitive processes will make her existing conversation with people she already knows seem worth pursuing. It will appear to seem less boring than it might otherwise have done.

Kelly would argue that, in the example given, the main barrier to aggressive behaviour is *anxiety*. He defines this (1955, p. 495) as 'the recognition that the events with which one is confronted lie mostly outside the range of convenience of one's construct system'. As Bannister and Fransella (1971, p. 35) put it,

We become anxious when we can only partly construe the events which we encounter and too many of their implications are obscure. Sex for the chaste, adulthood for the adolescent, books for the illiterate, power for the humble and death for nearly all of us tend to provoke anxiety. It is the *unknown* aspects of things that go bump in the night that give them their potency.

People will thus attempt to avoid situations about which they cannot theorise, or which threaten severely to damage their views of the world and themselves. However, unless they adopt reclusive and cabbage-like existences, they will have to place themselves in *some* situations that have the potential to damage their world views. A major part of the activity of budgeting time and money between competing pursuits will be concerned with discovering mixes of activities that keep anxiety within tolerable bounds.

Kelly's view of anxiety makes it possible to see our earlier discussions of consumer lifestyles (section 5.5) in a new light. Anxious people, whose construct systems are not very permeable, will only ask vague questions of the world and make vague commitments to the future. In return for their 'cowardice', they will only receive vague evidence, of an incidental and fragmentary nature. They may take a long time to experience anything at all, but the vague questions they ask will not usually entail the need to ask even stronger ones in consequence. They may exhibit such extreme inertia that it seems to others that their personalities are not developing at all. Impermeable construct systems, it must be added, seem also to be responsible in cases where a lack of personality development takes the opposite extreme of form, i.e. where people drift, dissatisfied, from one brief commitment to another in a relatively patternless manner, trying to discover things of which they can make sense, and to find their niche in life. An observation by Kelly (1955, p. 524–5) on marriage, and the sort of person who avoids it, makes the point rather vividly:

The uncertainties and vicissitudes of married life require a breadth of viewpoint and an open mindedness toward certain kinds of things. Without this kind of permeability in one's construction system, one's tolerance of incompatibility will be so limited that he will not attempt marriage, or if he does acquiesce, may soon seek to dissolve it in divorce.

The types of question which someone will think she can ask of the world, just like the types of question which a pupil might expect to be able to ask a teacher in a classroom without seeming impertinent, or foolish, will depend very much on what she has experienced (willingly or otherwise) in the past. She is not born with a given repertoire of questions to ask. To form theories a person needs to have points of reference against which likenesses and differences may be construed. Children with affluent parents will have less to be afraid of than children from poor backgrounds, for they are more likely to have been subjected to wider experiences at an early age (e.g. they will be more likely to have been to the opera, restaurants, and on foreign holidays). Their education may have been better and in the course of it they will have encountered people from a wide variety of backgrounds. Middle and upper class children will also tend to use a much more refined language structure than those from working class backgrounds, a point which is significant insofar as their construction processes are dependent on how they speak. They will thus be able to order their thoughts in more complex and individualistic ways and be more adventurous (see further Bannister and Fransella (1971), pp. 106–8). It should now be clear why education and social class are such important factors in the determination of market segmentation into lifestyle groups, as in Figure 5.1.

Even people who are adept at formulating theories about diverse aspects of the world are deterred from aggressive behaviour by the human tendency towards forgetfulness and the consequent fleeting nature of much experience. The typical person does not have the novelist Marcel Proust's astonishing ability to conjure up in minute detail images of times long since past. Fading images require us to repeat our experiments, and the payoff from a 'refresher course' in a particular area may be much higher than that to aggressive behaviour in new areas. Following the discussions of cognitive processes in section 5.6, however, it is as well to recognise that attempts to recreate past experiences may really be ways of avoiding facing up to the fact that the world has changed in ways that we cannot comprehend, rather than ways of recapturing something we have genuinely forgotten.

Forgetfulness and information overload are usually hard to separate. A piece of music, for example, may remain fascinating because, each time we listen to it, we do not attempt to get to grips with just a single element: we attempt to experience the whole and the orchestral brilliance, say, is so overwhelming that we fail to recall the themes. If we fail to decompose things in the appropriate way, we experience very little each time we confront ourselves with a particular feature of the world (cf. section 3.4).

We end this discussion of the reasons for repetitive behaviour by considering briefly a source of inertia with more of an economic than a psychological basis. In a world of complexity and uncertainty markets are not costless to use. People who switch between alternative 'interesting' durable goods necessarily have to bear transactions costs and trade-in losses. For example, a person will not be able to experience very many cars or items of hi-fi equipment in any depth greater than that provided by a salesperson's demonstration unless she has a very large budget. This is one reason why, at any moment, people will attempt to choose the nearest thing they can find to their 'ideal' means to an end, and avoid experiencing the 'rubbish' events which they can construe in terms of the same dimensions.

6.7 Conclusion

In this chapter we have been considering how the dynamics of consumer behaviour are affected by bounded rationality. Budgeting and cybernetic, programmed, decision methods enable consumers to avoid unnecessary search and reduce the need to process information. This leaves them with more time for deliberative thought and genuine inquisitive activity. However, even in this context, bounded rationality is still a major barrier affecting the sorts of activities a consumer will choose and her willingness to switch between activities. She cannot think about or remember everything of interest and she cannot perceive patterns instantaneously.

Anxiety is the emotional side of bounded rationality—the chooser's feeling that if she puts herself in a particular situation she will be unable adequately to understand what is going on. Anxiety is something that the inquiring person tries to bring within tolerable bounds. If she fails to do so, either by restricting herself to predictable situations or by lowering her aspirations and facing up to the implication that she is less able to cope with the world than she had hoped, she will be in need of clinical attention. In the developed world, rising affluence and the development of the Welfare State have removed many sources of anxiety. As a result, some people can be more adventurous and voluntarily adopt challenging activities without compromising their anxiety-avoidance aspirations (cf. Scitovsky (1981)). But there are still many people who, despite economic growth, can seem remarkably unadventurous; people who seem to wish to experience little more than what is to be seen on television, or what it is like to own a bigger house or this year's model of a conventional car; people who never do anything different from others or out of the ordinary. To help understand why this may be the case we shall turn, in the final chapter, to consider the social context in which the inquisitive, but anxious, person acts out her life.

7 Choice in a Social Setting

7.1 Introduction

In previous chapters we have emphasised repeatedly that the images decision makers see, the tools of thought they have for viewing the world, and their aspirations and priorities, result more from social experience than innate predispositions. Policy makers have to recognise that it is only possible to define objects and activities, and know what counts in a particular categorisation (e.g. food, drink, clothing, unreasonable behaviour, and so on), in the light of a knowledge of the cultural context in which the categorisation is taking place. An obvious example is that, for very different reasons, beef does not count as 'food' for practising Hindus or vegetarians. Preferences and beliefs are, as Steedman (1980) puts it, 'intrinsically non autonomous'. Very many activities are also social activities in the more obvious sense that they involve the participation of several people and some attempt at *communication*. Under the latter heading we include not merely those activities which involve direct contact (e.g. by letter or telephone, or meeting in a public gathering of some kind). Following Goffman (1971) and Douglas and Isherwood (1980), we also recognise the communicative dimension of the self-images that people try to project, the acts they put on and the games they play—even if their intended audiences do not notice what they are doing (cf. also sections 5.4 and 6.6).

Behaviour is intrinsically social and so, therefore, is choice. Even a hermit, and we are all hermits in some degree, cannot isolate herself entirely from society—she only survives into adulthood with the aid of society's guidance and protection; her property rights are defined by an institutional framework. In short, there are social bounds on one's ability 'to do one's own thing'.

In this chapter we are going to take for granted the intrinsically social nature of beliefs and the communicative aspect of many choices (detailed analyses of the latter topic are provided by Douglas and Isherwood (1980) and Goffman (1971)). This leaves us free to concentrate our analysis of choice in a social setting on 'social pressures' to conform with normal patterns of consumption and workplace behaviour. Post Keynesian economists commonly assume that such pressures exist and are important, but they rarely attempt to analyse them in any depth. Experience in a particular social environment affects the way we think and the kind of images we may need to present to others to elicit particular responses, but it does not completely remove our ability to think creatively or our desire to experiment with unusual activities. Why, then, do we conform quite as much as we do; what are the social pressures that restrain our aggressive, elaborative tendencies?

In attempting to answer this question we shall divide the analysis into four sections, which are followed by some concluding thoughts. Section 7.2 is an attempt to look at the barriers to deviant behaviour in cold, rationalistic terms, developing further some of the ideas from Chapter 5 and section 6.6. In section 7.3 we then consider how firms may attempt to overcome these barriers. Section 7.4 is concerned with competition in the workplace and labour markets. It adds an oligopolistic perspective to our analysis of barriers to deviance as well as suggesting a generalisation of the 'normal cost' analysis of product market pricing to cover factor markets. Lastly, in section 7.5, we consider bargaining processes and attempt to explain the restraints on making aggressive opening gambits as well as the reasons why negotiations may sometimes be broken off even if this seems presently to inconvenience both parties. Throughout the chapter the emphasis will be on choice as a reasoned, anticipatory activity. We do *not* wish to give the impression that the person choosing behaves as if she is unthinking and is, in some sense, a complete social and cultural 'dope' (cf. Garfinkel (1967), p. 68).

7.2 The Benefits and Costs of Social Interaction

People with different lifestyles are willing to interact socially in different degrees. Some are very outgoing, while others reduce to a minimum the number of social encounters in which they engage. But even some of the former are conspicuous in their willingness to accept the conventions of the groups in whose circles they mix, instead of attempting to be deviants and establish individual images of themselves. Some insight on these different behaviour tendencies may be gained from considering, from our inquiring person perspective, the benefits and costs of social interaction.

We suggest that there are six main reasons why a person may wish to interact with other members of society:

(1)   Whether she likes it or not, decisions taken by others will affect her ability to predict and control her life. By attempting to get as near as possible to where such decisions are taken she may be able to reduce her anxiety levels and enhance her possibilities for aggressive behaviour. If she can wrest control of information flows from other people she can have power over them.

(2)   Other people can help her form theories about the nature of things by offering advice and information.

(3)   Other people can help her test theories, either directly (e.g. 'What do you think of . . . ?'), or indirectly (e.g. where she can observe how they fare in particular circumstances).

(4)   She finds some people particularly interesting and wishes to clarify her images of them.

(5)   In industrial societies, social interaction in the workplace is essential if she wants to obtain income with which to predict and control events, or if she wishes to test certain of her skills.

(6)   If she can find out what are the 'commonsense things which everyone knows', and take them on trust, she will be able to take a lot for granted and proceed more rapidly to adventurous activities. Social codes and customs, as well as the legal framework and the reputations of people and products, help greatly to reduce anxiety.

Membership of a particular social group may thus enable a person to improve her ability to anticipate events. But the cost of joining and continuing as a member of a social group is that other members of the group may require that a person presents an image which is neither at odds with the group's views as to how private a lifestyle may be enjoyed, nor at odds with its conventions with regard to consumption behaviour or beliefs that may be held. Deviant behaviour, even over seemingly minor matters of detail, will occasion demands for *justification*—demands not unlike a mild version of the Spanish Inquisition. These demands result not only from curiosity but also anxiety. By doing something at odds with the expectational norms of the people with whom she mixes, the deviant is, knowingly or otherwise, making a challenge to their world views.

Anxious demands for justifications of 'unusual' behaviour are the mild first stage in a *hostile* reaction which can, in *some* cases, culminate in the ostracisation of the deviant. In personal construct theory, hostility is defined as 'the continued effort to extort validational evidence in favour of a type of social prediction which has already proved itself a failure' (Kelly 1955), p. 510). Hostility generally manifests itself in attempts by people to persuade others, by argument or brute force, to conform with their expectations in order to prevent their previously constructed images from being destroyed. Kelly (1955, p. 510) observes that hostility, as a method of coping with the unexpected, 'is the method of Procrustes, who was always stretching his guests or cutting them down to a size to fit his bed'.

It is important to note that an action which shatters only a seemingly minor everyday expectation may provoke an exceedingly explosive hostile response. This is evident in the experiments reported by Garfinkel (1967, pp. 42–4). He arranged for 'victims' to be asked everyday questions, such as 'How are you?', which were immediately followed by unconventional supplementary queries, such as 'In what sense do you mean "fine"?'. The effect of the supplementary question was to shatter the image of a normal passing exchange, thereby making it uncertain what was going to happen next. The 'victims' typically panicked and became exasperated and abusive, or tried simply to *ignore* the questions (cf. sections 5.5 and 5.6).

Justification demands become all the more acute the more mundane the activity in which the deviant has failed to indulge. To the person who, say, drinks neither tea nor coffee nor alcohol, it may easily seem that society is virtually uninterested in any of her other differentiating characteristics. Everywhere she goes, the inquisition will begin the moment she shatters the conventional expectation (and, as often as not, leaves her host *embarrassingly* unprepared to offer a substitute beverage). Furthermore, so long as she continues to deviate from the norm, conversation will continue to return to the topic and she will be encouraged to behave in the normal way.

The 'justification problem' may cause three kinds of difficulties for someone who deviates from the behaviour patterns of her reference group. First, the time spent in self-justification may eat into the total interaction time to such an extent that the deviant obtains few benefits from mixing with the group. Second, there is the risk that she will be ostracised if she breaks *too many* of her reference group's expectational norms, or acts against particular *core* constructs, and cannot offer *socially acceptable* reasons (which need not be her real reasons) for what she is doing. Finally, there is the risk that other people will demonstrate publicly that the justifications she has offered for her behaviour are, in some sense, inadequate. In the last case, the price is not the loss of the benefits of being a member of the social group, but the possible destruction of her own self-image. If a person offers demonstrably inadequate justifications for her behaviour she will look rather stupid. Worse still, if she cannot provide any justification at all for the views she holds or the decisions she makes, she demonstrates that she does not understand how the world works, and that her choices have not been based on any well-conceived choice criteria. The person who cannot justify what she does—or, to put it somewhat differently, who cannot clarify or preserve her images—cannot be acting rationally, for rational choices are based upon reasoning.

The upshot of these arguments about the justification problem is that if people do not wish to be ostracised or condemned as irrational by those with whom they mix, their ranges of choice are necessarily restricted. A person who cannot provide a socially acceptable reason for *not* selecting an activity must select it if its consumption takes place in public. Similarly, she will not feel it safe to buy a particular product unless she can justify her decision to purchase it, or, if she cannot do so, unless it seems sufficiently likely that she will not be called upon to make a justification (either because the product is an approved subject of 'commonsense' knowledge as a means to a particular end, or because it will be kept away from the public eye). The extent to which someone will find it necessary to justify a given purchase will depend upon her reference group and the relationship of this group with other social groupings, for this will determine how private a lifestyle she can normally expect to enjoy, and whether or not the purchase in question is 'unusual'.

A decision maker often has to act in the presence of several social groups simultaneously. She may thus succeed in justifying her choice to her reference group, only at the cost of incurring the hostility of other people. Since she is challenging the world views of the latter, they will be keen observers of her subsequent fortunes. They will be hoping to point out that, *ex post*, the decision is not justifiable to anyone, precisely as they had been asserting *ex ante*. This means that if a person makes public statements committing herself to, and 'justifying' particular choices of activity, she will have a reason for remaining committed to them at a later date: if her past promises of results are not justified by events, her credibility as a decision maker—and hence her self-image—will be undermined.

As Wolf (1970, p. 788; 1973, pp. 666–7) has pointed out, once we take account of the possibility that choosers are concerned with the effects that particular outcomes can have on their credibility as decision makers, it becomes easy to see why people frequently persist in activities—much to the consternation of neoclassical economists

—seemingly because of, rather than despite, sunk costs. If sunk costs are not seen to be 'sunk' so much as 'in need of justification', we can well expect people to behave as if the past has a present value. This is a perspective which becomes particularly credible if developed in the light of our earlier (section 5.6) discussions about the management of inconsistencies and dilemmas.

A person will obviously reveal herself to be a fool by persisting in an activity if the return to devoting marginal resources to that activity is *unambiguously* lower than that to using them elsewhere. However, so long as there is some uncertainty, the returns a person perceives to be possible will depend on the workings of her cognitive processes. If *she* had not been the person previously to commit the resources in question, her present opinion of the plausibility of a particular marginal return, on promise of which she now stakes her future credibility as a decision maker, might be the same as that held by critical onlookers. However, if the rosy future her cognitive processes cause her to see *does* come about, the marginal commitment she makes may generate a net return so high as fully to justify her past commitment, leaving her credibility intact. Thus, even if events presently seem to others to be pointing towards failure, a person may 'see' that it is worth chancing further resources on the possibility that things will come out right in the end. So long as she continues an experiment which would not have been possible had particular costs not been sunk, her critics must suspend judgment on whether these costs were 'justifiably sunk'. They cannot say 'I told you so'. And, while the experiment continues, the critics may turn their attention elsewhere, or it will become possible to see the past differently. As Wolf (1970, p. 784) remarks, reminding readers of Orwell's *1984*, 'In general the past is more supple, malleable and reinterpretable than we are comfortable to admit'. In the long run, of course, the person *may* be forced to admit that she has been 'pouring good money after bad', but in the short run her expenditure buys her the right to delay someone else's judgment of her behaviour.

7.3 Images, Emotions, and Policy

A person will be most anxious about not being able to justify her behaviour to her peers, or with the prospect of embarrassing interchanges at the point of purchase, when she has to make choices outside her usual frames of reference. Additional information may be available if she asks a friend or sales person for it, but she may be unwilling to do so in case her questions are construed as inane, or lead to her being talked into spending more than she had planned and thus to her losing control of the situation (even to the extent of being 'taken for a ride' by a salesperson who exploits the state of information impactedness). But if she is afraid to seek 'ammunition' for rational choice, she may be alarmed that her stock of information and criteria for making a decision would, taken together, constitute a very poor justification of any particular choice. Her strategy may therefore be to pick a product which is commonly known to be an 'acceptable performer', even if she has little idea why this is so or whether the label is actually justifiable in the mind of an expert. Having purchased the product, she gradually becomes able to justify her choice with the benefit of hindsight. In effect, then, her actions are the reverse of those in conventional choice models. She decides *after* the event, not before, why her choice *is* appropriate (cf. Garfinkel (1967), pp. 113–4).

Clearly, such 'retrospective decision making', and, more generally, *any* social influence on choice which leads to people copying the behaviour of others, can make things very difficult for firms which do not already produce leading products, or products which meet with the approval of opinion leaders. Matters are even more problematical for a firm whose product has acquired something of a *stigma*. The person who purchases a stigmatised product will be more than usually prone to be confronted with demands that she justifies her purchase. People who wish to establish their self-images of relative superiority will attempt to ridicule her by asserting that the purchase is not justifiable (e.g. 'You mean that you've bought a —— ? But everyone knows that no one in their right mind would buy a —— ; haven't you heard from the papers about how they . . . ?'). In this section we shall attempt to show how firms may be able to break such socially-influenced patterns of behaviour, and consumer inertia generally, by using marketing techniques to affect consumer emotions. However, before we do this, we think it is appropriate to note how the social dimension of choice gives an added twist to out earlier arguments about the potential for instability in the demand for durable goods (sections 3.6 and 5.5). This sort of instability can be ruinous for leading and stigmatised producers alike. The twist concerns *conspicuous* consumption.

Our Kellian perspective naturally leads us to see conspicuous consumption as a means whereby an inquiring person attempts to establish what position she occupies in the scheme of things, and hence whether or not her self-image is justified. But one person cannot change her relative position in (or join) a group without threatening its other members. As Kelly (1955, pp. 509–10) observes,

The very fact that [the social pusher] insists on construing himself as belonging to [a] social group is threatening to those who are already identified with the group. They see, in their impending reciprocal identification with him, *a major shift coming up in their core role structures*. That is *threat* (emphasis added).

The response of anyone who feels threatened in Kelly's sense of the word will be to take action to preserve her image of where she stands in society. In this case, such action involves an increase in her own conspicuous consumption. The consequence of this is not only that the initial 'social pusher' is threatened, but that the person who initially felt threatened casts herself in the role of social pusher in the eyes of other people. Under threat, then, people may be driven to spend on consumer durables regardless of whether their existing ones have become excessively boring or worn out.

It may only take a withdrawal of expenditure by a minority of individuals concerned more with the embarrassment that an inability to keep up payments (e.g. as a result of redundancy) would cause, than with being insufficiently able to 'keep up with the Joneses', to spark off a kaleidoscopic contraction in sales. Neither 'the Joneses' nor third ranking consumers, who constitute 'the Joneses' for even lower levels, will feel such a pressing need to spend. The shift in spending will therefore spread along the chain of reference groups. In a social world, complementarity is strong and the marginal *private* return (cf. Hirsch, 1976) to marketing expenditures designed to stop an initial breakaway by a minority (or start one in an upward direction) may be very high indeed.

Anxiety is the most obvious emotion for firms to try to exploit as they design marketing campaigns to expand or maintain their sales. Our analysis suggests that a firm should try to show that people who refrain from (or cease) purchasing its products will find their self-images, and their abilities to anticipate events, undermined. This is a technique which is central to the sales campaigns of, for example, the American Express Company. The person who purchases an American Express card is buying a status symbol and the right to obtain particular kinds of service without having to answer certain questions. American Express 'will do nicely'; the cardholder will not be embarrassed if she has insufficient cash to meet unexpected expenditures.

A firm needs also to ensure that *its* products will not cause potential purchasers to feel they might be stepping out of their depths. It must therefore attempt to make its products easy for inarticulate and inexperienced members of society to use without an undue risk that they might throw up evidence at odds with their (often over-optimistic) self-images. Advertisements can reduce uncertainty and provide ammunition with which purchasers can justify what they are doing.

Consider how participants in the UK property market have, in recent years, attempted to change the behaviour of affluent workers by shaping their feelings of anxiety. Building Societies have tried to attract deposits on the one hand by creating anxiety about future needs for finance, and, on the other, by attempting to remove 'us and them' fears about staff/customer interactions. To do the latter, they have used images of smiling, 'girl next door', counter staff and slogans suggestive of a club-like atmosphere ('We're with the Woolwich'; 'I've got the Abbey Habit'). Such slogans, it must be added, are designed also to make consumers think of a *particular*, barely-differentiated society when setting out to open accounts. Despite the informal images which Building Societies have attempted to foster, some workers may still feel anxious about going on eventually to buy their homes, because they do not feel well-placed for dealing with middle class building society managers, solicitors and estate agents. Their position will have been made much easier by 'friendly' property companies (e.g. Barratt Developments) which offer to find mortgages for them and generally make the process of purchase as simple as possible. It is also noteworthy that such companies have also attempted to attract these first generation buyers to their sales offices and showhouses with advertisements emphasising that it is *irrational* to rent in times of inflation; that there are, however, tremendous *uncertainties* involved in purchasing homes secondhand; and that, for example, 'You know where you are with Wimpey.'

As an alternative to attempting to shape a customer's image of whether or not she will be able to cope with future events if she does/does not purchase their products, firms can attempt to demonstrate that a customer will be acting in a way that is at variance with her self-image if she fails to purchase their products. Here, the emotion to be exploited is *guilt*. This is closely related to anxiety in Kelly's theory of personality, and is defined (1955, p. 502) as 'the awareness of dislodgement of the self from one's core role structure'. A person feels guilty if she finds herself doing the sort of things she would not have expected to do if she is the sort of person she has always thought herself to be. As Bannister and Fransella (1971, p. 36) observe, 'To live in a world where you cannot understand and predict others can be terrifying—how much more terrifying it is to find that one cannot understand or predict oneself.' Even if a person can escape the need to make public justifications of particular actions, she may still decline to purchase a particular commodity, even a well known one, in order to avoid an excessive feeling of guilt. The obverse of this point is that a person will be prepared even to buy a hitherto stigmatised product if a failure to purchase it would make her feel excessively guilty.

It must be emphasised that attempts to shape feelings of guilt and anxiety in order to affect sales patterns will often require considerable guile. It would be very easy for a firm to end up producing hostility instead if it went as far as to show that the customer was foolish to have sunk resources into trying other products in the past. It is simply no use, in terms of our lexicographic analysis of choice, to design a product which could be shown to dominate at lower priority levels but which someone cannot choose without making an excessive self-confession of foolishness. If a person's number one priority is to preserve a satisfactory self-image (cf. the quotation from Bannister and Fransella in the previous paragraph), she will simply filter such a product from her attention unless she is already trapped face to face with a salesperson.

In the latter case, there is the possibility of success, despite hostility, due to the consumer's cognitive processes managing her perceptions (e.g. concerning whether or not she can afford the product) to avoid the destruction of a vital image. For example, a person may be unable to conceive of a way of saying 'no' which is not at odds with her self-image, having unwisely allowed a doorstep salesperson into her home and having been taken through the 'sales logic'. She may, therefore, end up buying something simply to save face. With less captive customers, a firm is most likely to succeed in displacing its rivals if it can show potential purchasers how easy it is, even for people supposed to be experts, to make the kind of mistake it is implied they have been making by choosing rival brands. Advertisements which quote press reports expressing *surprise* at improvements to a stigmatised product may be one way of achieving this result, as well as providing ammunition for justifying deviant choices. This technique has been used extensively in British Leyland advertisements in the period 1980–2.

Very little academic research has been conducted into the significance and use, in sales campaigns, of images which relate to feelings of guilt and anxiety (Dash *et al.* (1979) is a rare example, and is entirely supportive of our arguments). This is unfortunate, not only from the standpoint of the corporate policy maker, but also for anyone concerned with consumer welfare. Our analysis leads us to believe that there is considerable scope for using such 'non-price', emotional images to shape consumer choices, and that modern corporations, as is evidenced by the nature of their marketing methods, also believe this is true. To the extent that their strategies reduce feelings of guilt and anxiety, without first creating them where otherwise they would not have existed, there is a social gain (unless demand is diverted overseas, causing unemployment). But, insofar as new anxieties are created, and consumers do not have budgets large enough to buy supposed remedies to all of them, there is a social loss (unless aggregate demand is kept at a higher level than policy makers would otherwise have been able to maintain).

7.4 Labour Mobility, Wages, and Productivity

The majority of social encounters in which a person participates will take place in her working environment. These encounters will inevitably have some effect on worker attitudes and productivity. This is a fact which is ignored in neoclassical economics, where the analysis typically proceeds as if employment contracts are fully specified on both the input and output sides. But, as was argued in section 3.7, in the real world employment contracts are, with good reason, left incompletely specified. In this section we shall consider some of the consequences of this contractual vagueness and the inherently social nature of work. One implication of what we shall have to say is that the neoclassical approach may be dangerously incomplete and potentially misleading, but our main aim is to be constructive rather than critical.

First let us consider the question of labour mobility. The neoclassical worker has no reluctance to move between jobs in response to changes in relative, perfectly specified, input and output conditions. She knows precisely what she is letting herself in for if she moves to a new job. In the real world, by contrast, contractual incompleteness means that new jobs are inherently associated with anxiety. As Andrews (1949a, p. 224) argues,

When he has settled down in a particular factory, a man will also have got used to it, developing an intimate knowledge of the habits and requirements of the management under which he works. (Just what a strange foreman means by a particular remark may be a mystery which causes a great deal of worry to a new man, until he gets to know the foreman and the way he sets about things.) All these consequences of familiarity combine in the end to make the work itself seem easier and make the performance of the daily duty become more of a routine. Working in a new business must bring enough preliminary trials and tribulations, but, however light these may prove in fact, there will be the added fears of the change, in prospect.

The upshot of all this is that an individual business cannot be supposed to draw on the whole labour supply in the occupations in which it is interested. It is much more near the truth to regard it as having its own supply of labour.

It is important to realise that Andrews' remark about the upshot of the effect of anxiety on labour mobility is not intended to suggest that a labour supply *function* exists at the level of the individual firm, any more than does a product demand function. Anxiety means there will at any time be a group of workers who wish to stay attached to a particular firm. The situation is analogous to that in product markets where 'preferring the devil you know' gives customers a reason for giving their existing suppliers repeat orders (i.e. goodwill) so long as no other supplier seems to be offering an obviously better way of enabling them to meet their aspirations. However, the labour market, like product markets, is in a state of constant disequilibrium. All firms, except those in a dire state of decline, will be needing to recruit new labour at some levels to fill job slots vacated by retiring workers or promotions. New workers can be recruited from the ranks of the unemployed—i.e. those involuntarily displaced from employment, and new recruits to the labour force—and the minority of employed workers who are not afraid to move in order to meet aspirations they are presently failing to attain. To recruit these workers firms must offer competitive remuneration packages, just as, in order to attract new or floating customers in their product markets, they must offer a competitive product. The 'normal cost' analysis of price determination generalises to wage determination. If a firm attempts to set a wage below what other firms are offering for a particular, broadly specified, job, it will be under pressure from its unions to bring its wage into line with the 'normal' level. In times of full employment it will need to do this anyway, in order to attract applicants, once word spreads about its poor terms of employment.

In product markets, firms facing a shortage of customers at their 'normal cost' prices do not usually lower their prices, because of the risk of starting a damaging price war. In labour markets, firms facing shortages of particular kinds of workers will not usually raise their wage rates. Rather, they will either automate or train and promote proven employees from lower levels in their internal labour markets, recruiting more easily-available unskilled workers to replace those they upgrade. This may involve difficulties in the interim, just as it will not always be easy to think of and develop a better product to sell to overcome a present shortage of customers for an inferior product at a 'normal cost' selling price. However, it pays off in the long run as the firm avoids bidding up wages against itself to no avail.

Attempts to raise wages to overcome a local shortage of skilled workers would tend to be fruitless for two, related, reasons. First, the barriers to mobility produced by worker anxiety will make it very difficult to attract skilled workers to a given locality from the rest of the country. This means that, second, the firm will only be able to expand its employment at the expense of its local rivals, who will be driven to retaliate. Similarly, attempts to cut wages when the labour market is slack may be precluded by the possibility that, even if there is not outright union resistance, individual workers, who have been offering effort outputs in excess of the minimum that their employers would find acceptable, will start to behave in a perfunctory manner. Job idiosyncracies prevent a worker's superiors from knowing precisely what she is doing. Hence she can begin, say, to offer only half-hearted assistance to new recruits and blame any falls in productivity on the quality of these inexperienced employees. Where employment contracts specify job inputs and outputs only in vague terms, money wage cuts may lead to reduced productivity and output, so wage stickiness in times of unemployment may well originate on the demand side of the labour market (for a more detailed analysis, see Earl and Glaister (1979)).

Workers within any given firm will themselves be aware of oligopolistic aspects of its processes of internal competition. If they do not offer at least the volume of output which new recruits could normally be expected to offer during their probationary periods of employment, they will be replaced. At a later stage, if they fail to offer similar outputs to workers in identical job slots, they will be excluded from consideration for promotion. It is up to the workers themselves to decide whether to work harder than is absolutely necessary. However, if voluntarily-offered contributions in excess of these normal levels of productivity cannot easily be quantified or identified, why should a worker offer them? Two reasons may be advanced: first, a worker may feel guilty about offering only the minimum acceptable contribution to the firm's output; second, she may conjecture that her chances in the promotion race will be enhanced if she gives the impression that she is 'keen and helpful', even though no one can quantify precisely what this means.

But the worker who is conspicuously keen and helpful is by definition a deviant and may be called upon by her peers to justify her behaviour. Deviant effort levels will be easier to justify where the rewards to extra zeal come by promotion, rather than by currently paid bonuses for quantifiable additions to output. In the (increasingly less common) bonus system, the 'rate-busting' worker who earns abnormal bonuses will be informed by her colleagues that her behaviour is antisocial and foolhardy since, in the long run, it will simply result in the standard output requirement being increased. Unless the deviant can justify her behaviour (e.g. by attempting to create feelings of guilt in the minds of her critics), she will have to conform with their image of normal conduct or be ostracised. If no bonus system operates there will be no well-specified rate which a zealous worker can be seen to be 'busting'; her promotion-seeking activity cannot, therefore, jeopardise the position of any workers except insofar as it makes their own efforts to obtain promotion less likely to succeed. However, even the modern system of reward by promotion is limited in its ability to engender output. For example, if a worker conjectures that there are more workers prepared to work for promotion than there are promotion slots to be filled, her own zeal may be attenuated. There is little point in starting an 'effort war' unless a worker is either confident that she can be one of the victors, or feels guilt at working below her capabilities.

Where a worker is performing a specialised task as a member of a team, the effectiveness of promotion as an incentive to greater effort is rather more open to question. Non-commensurable workers will be recommended for higher level jobs by managers of their respective teams. Promotion may therefore depend more on the strength of the recommendation than 'objective' qualities. But a team manager has a strong incentive to recommend *weak* performers for promotion since their replacements may turn out to be better and raise the productivity of the group. How damaging this perverse incentive will turn out to be depends on whether or not the team manager is concerned by the possibility of her superiors discovering what she does, and by the prospect of adverse reactions by the rest of the group if they feel the wrong person has been promoted. The restraining power is greater the more the team manager is afraid that other team members will make their discontent known directly to her superiors.

We may sum up our arguments as follows. Firms will have strong incentives to set wages for jobs open to external recruitment in line with those offered for similar jobs by their competitors, and to change them only when competitors' wages change. Workers who obtain employment at these 'normal' wage rates are constrained to offer levels of output which they conjecture to be *at least* the same as would be offered by a would-be incumbent of their present job, or of a job to which they aspire to be promoted. However, since employment contracts give only a limited guidance as to what output levels will be necessary to survive a period of probation or achieve promotion, workers are forced to use each other's behaviour patterns as reference standards when deciding what to do. In deciding whether or not to deviate from the normal patterns they observe, workers will have to decide whether they can cope best with performing guiltily, below their capabilities, or anxiously, above the productivity rates of their colleagues, who will be hostile to their behaviour. A worker who sees herself as superior to her colleagues will necessarily have more guilt about not working to what she sees as her full capabilities, and will be more impervious to criticism from those whose comfortable existences her zeal threatens to undermine. It thus appears that, if there is no collusion and no team interest in a particular level of productivity, solidarity is only possible among workers in similar job slots if they regard themselves as similar people. Since a promotion-based incentive system does not usually promote all participants, workers are encouraged not to see themselves as identical even if they presently occupy an identical level in a firm's hierarchy. Promotion pyramids may thus be better at engendering output than are bonus systems related to current productivity levels.

In the absence of firms and workers willing to be, respectively, wage leaders and effort leaders, changes in relative wages and productivity conditions must be agreed upon *collectively* following negotiations between representatives of industries and worker groups. Bearing this point in mind, we turn to our final theoretical section.

7.5 Bargaining Processes

Bargaining has always presented a problem for conventional, neoclassical economists. They see it generally as involving a one-shot confrontation between a monopolist and a monopsonist. This leads them to conclude that a deal will necessarily take place so long as the buyer values the object in question more highly than does the seller, but they cannot explain how a price ultimately comes to be chosen somewhere between these two valuations. In this section we shall present an alternative analysis of bargaining based largely on Shackle's (1949, Chapter VI) work. We have modified Shackle's theory slightly to make it consistent with our own characteristic filtering theory of choice. This alternative analysis overcomes the indeterminacy problem by recognising that it arises in the conventional treatment because no mention is made of how either participant decides how much ground to give. Bargaining is a sequential process, not a discrete act, and typically involves either or both parties lowering their demands in stages until an agreement becomes mutually acceptable or negotiations break down. A theory of bargaining requires a theory of what determines the rate of 'climb down' that the protagonists are prepared to tolerate. Once such a 'climb down' theory is available, a bargaining solution becomes very simple to grasp.

The novelty of Shackle's analysis of bargaining is that it centres on the fact that participants are usually not concerned only with the outcome they achieve at the end of their present negotiations. They also have in mind their credibility in subsequent bargaining rounds.

They are worried about the consequences of *losing face* by making an excessive 'climb down' in the present. If they give a lot of ground now they will find it harder to cope when next they bargain. Word will get around that they are easy game and their later opponents will be much more confident about standing firm.

At any stage in a bargaining process, when it is her turn to make a new offer or accept a suggested price, the seller has to think what will be her possible short run and long run gains and losses if she adopts a particular course of action. (We shall talk only about 'sellers' choices, to simplify the analysis, for a buyer can be thought of as a seller too: she is just selling something else (even if it is only money) in return for that which she buys!) In the case of a new offer, her course of action is a 'bargaining stance' comprising a particular offer *and* a particular plan of response to counter offers made in response to this offer. A plan of response involves a resolution about the maximum 'climb down' rate that the seller will tolerate in subsequent bargaining rounds without breaking off negotiations. Given the offer to be announced, and the plan of response attached to it, the seller will have an implied minimum acceptable price below which she cannot ultimately go without violating her resolution. This minimum acceptable price is likely to be somewhat above the reservation price she would require if there were so many other sources of supply that there was no prospect of bargaining and, consequently, no risk of losing face through an inappropriate choice of bargaining stance.

The higher the seller's initial asking price—her *gambit price*—the higher may be the price ultimately agreed upon. However, the higher the gambit price, the more it may be necessary to lower the asking price in subsequent rounds, and hence the less surprised she would be at having to lose face in order to reach an agreement of some sort. Having proposed a particular gambit price, she may find herself forced to break off negotiations if the rate of ascent of counter offers is so slow that she can see no way of reaching an agreement in the negotiating period without herself climbing down at a rate that involves an excessive loss of face.

The seller will have many possible combinations of gambit price/climb down strategy, but she can only try one of them. To choose she must form conjectures of her opponent's gambit price/ascent strategy. A given pair of seller/opponent gambit prices/strategies—i.e. a pair of bargaining stances—will imply a determinate solution with either a particular agreement or a breakdown of negotiations. If the seller thinks it in some degree possible that her opponent will make a particular choice of bargaining stance, then a particular determinate outcome will seem possible to that degree only if she herself adopts a particular bargaining stance.

The locus of 'determinate outcomes/potential surprise' associated with her expectations of her opponent's possible bargaining stances, and a particular stance of her own, is her theory, her potential surprise curve, in respect of her particular bargaining stance. If she knew for sure what her opponent's bargaining stance was going to be, her choice would be clear cut, but she can only guess how her opponent is thinking. Her conjectures will thus have to depend largely on her knowledge of her opponent's previous 'face' at the bargaining table: hence the importance of not losing face.

It is now necessary to consider how the bargaining outcomes are imagined by the seller for each bargaining stance she has in mind possibly to choose. Shackle (1949, p. 106) argues that the relevant form of imagined outcome is *net gain*, which is made up as follows. First, there is the *gross gain*, the difference between her reservation price (the absolute minimum price which just compensates for what she is having to give up) and the hypothetical agreed price. From this is subtracted the value she places on the loss of face she will have to suffer by climbing down (her *descent*, as Shackle puts it) from her gambit price, in keeping with her plan of response. Shackle argues that this negative value will depend on the seller's expectations about the scale, number, and time-distribution of her future negotiations with parties aware of her behaviour in the present negotiating context. If people do think in terms of the possible net gains that are associated with a given bargaining stance that they could adopt, then the potential surprise curves they construct for the strategies they have in mind can be subjected to the usual characteristic filtering test procedure, to see how well they may match up with aspirations. The seemingly most satisfactory bargaining stance will be chosen. 'Net gain' may not be the only dimension relevant here; other relevant characteristics may include the time it will take to complete the bargaining process, the possible atmosphere at the bargaining table, and so on. Whatever the other relevant characteristics, the bargaining process will only start if both parties can conceive of bargaining stances that, in prospect, seem to offer adequate positive net gains.

The net gain idea seems rather implausible in situations of complexity, where the present and possible future bargaining outcomes are to some extent non-commensurable. For example, a trade union leader may on one occasion be negotiating over a pay increase and, on another, be concerned with the scale of redundancy or a change in work practices and conditions. Here, it seems likely that gross gain in the present bargaining round and loss of face will be valued separately, then ranked according to the negotiator's priorities (cf. the end of section 5.6). Negotiators who are not direct beneficiaries in the terms of the present agreement seem likely, *a priori*, to rank 'avoiding an unacceptable loss of face' higher than 'achieving a settlement that gives greatest benefit to a present third party'. Given their conjectures about the possible bargaining stances of their opponents, such negotiators will be constrained to start with lower gambit prices than they would if they had the reverse priority ranking, and will be more likely to break off negotiations even if this is very inconvenient for the third party.

The idea that a separate, and higher, value is accorded to avoiding loss of face may help to explain why it is that politicians are often willing to break off negotiations and, if need be, use military hardware to fight to preserve particular images (e.g. that the UK is still a great power and cannot be pushed around by a country like Argentina over the question of sovereignty in the Falkland Islands) regardless of economic considerations. In a lexicographic model this is quite understandable, for there are no trade-offs between goals. A war may be economically ludicrous to undertake on any cost benefit analysis that refers to the *material* welfare of a country's population, but, if it is necessary to preserve 'national pride', and, more importantly, a leader's self-image, it is likely to be undertaken all the same. If the war persists longer than expected, and voters eventually wake up to the economic cost of it, then negotiations may be resumed: to the leader, the 'image damage' of a climb down may begin to seem less than that due to an unjustifiable use of resources. Ambiguities about either source of image damage will place the leader in a dilemma, which her cognitive processes will solve for her by making her see a course of action that enables her to meet the maximum number of her priorities in order, and with no gaps. In this sort of situation, the means to meeting her self-image priority are likely to be more ambiguous than those pertinent for lower priorities (such as the desire not to see other people being killed) and it is in respect of her self-image priority that her perceptions eventually have to be moulded. Similar comments could be made with respect to economic warfare between industrialists and trade unions.

It seems appropriate to close this discussion of bargaining by pointing out how it relates to our earlier analyses of competitive interdependence and information impactedness (cf., particularly, sections 2.5, 2.8, 3.7 and 7.4). Conventional, timeless, equilibrium theory uses monopolistic analysis to avoid oligopolistic indeterminacy in product and factor markets, but finds that if the customer is a monopsonist, and there is bargaining instead, a determinate solution is not possible. By introducing time into our analysis, and recognising that future possibilities are often constrained by present actions, we have been able to come to terms with both oligopoly and the problem of bargaining.

There is an obvious parallel between the bargaining process and oligopolistic competition. Actual and potential sources of alternative supply severely constrain the ability of any seller to set high prices (or low effort outputs) in the present without regard to the effects this will have on her long run position. If a supplier's time horizon is neither so short that alternative sources of supply, presently unavailable, are irrelevant to her choice, nor so long that entry considerations completely swamp the value of short run monopoly returns, a seller has a strategic decision to make about the 'gambit price' she will charge and the volume of entry she will risk encouraging. Her 'gross gain' is the short term investment funding she generates; her 'loss of face' is any reduced ability to cope in the future due to the subsequent appearance of competitive supply sources.

7.6 Concluding Thoughts

Running throughout this book is a theme against which the analysis we have proposed may appear justified or worthy only of dismissal. It is that the conventional economist's view of rationality is one which it is irrational to accept if the aim is to have a theory which is likely to be neither dangerously misleading nor impossible to operationalise. The world is a very complicated place, full of interdependencies between events in the past, the present and the future, and amongst events in the present. Furthermore, events themselves, if we dare to isolate them, are complex structures. Because of this, it is either impossible or irrational for people to choose what to buy and sell, or which prices to charge, in something approximating the manner suggested in marginalist equilibrium theory.

We have rejected neoclassical notions of rationality, but we have not rejected the idea that decision makers have reasons for their choices. We do not accept Kornai's (1971, pp. 108–9) suggestion that, if a set of eligible alternatives has been narrowed down sufficiently, choices are random. (Kornai seems to have in mind a conjunctive satisficing approach to choice, in which a random selection is made from amongst those schemes which perform satisfactorily in respect of an entire list of characteristics.) To suggest that, in a world of bounded rationality, choices are random within some boundary is to go too far in the opposite direction from conventional theory.

In order to understand why someone chooses something it is necessary to understand her reasons, i.e. how she thinks and what she imagines will happen as a result of making a particular choice. In order to make someone choose differently it is necessary to demonstrate that her reasons for selecting what she would otherwise do are inconsistent, or change the images of the future that she sees. In a world of bounded rationality and an unknowable future no one can be thought of as having 'given preferences' at any moment, which cannot be altered by a reasoned case presented as part of a marketing strategy. However, to be able to reason with someone effectively, it is necessary to wrest her attention from those who would like to shape her behaviour in a different way, and then understand her own, existing logic. It will be rare for such a concerted selling effort to be possible. To brainwash someone (in Kelly's terms, to engineer a reordering of her constructs) it is necessary to keep her away from alternative sources of ideas for a long while. Ultimately, then, there are limits to the extent to which a single firm can encroach upon consumer sovereignty. But these limits in no way detract from the need for a theory of choice which can be operationalised with the aid of questionnaire techniques: if firms cannot succeed in moulding consumer thoughts to favour their products, they must discover the structures of the moulds that they should make their products fit.

Bibliography

Akerlof, G. (1970) '"The Market for Lemons": Quality Uncertainty and the Market Mechanism', *Quarterly Journal of Economics 84*, August, pp. 488–500.

Andrews, P. W. S. (1949a) *Manufacturing Business*, London, Macmillan.

Andrews, P. W. S. (1949b) 'A Reconsideration of the Theory of the Individual Business', *Oxford Economic Papers 1* (New Series), pp. 54–89.

Andrews, P. W. S. (1950) Some Aspects of Competition in Retail Trade, *Oxford Economic Papers 2* (New Series), pp. 138–75.

Andrews, P. W. S. (1951) 'Industrial Analysis in Economics', in Wilson, T. and Andrews, P. W. S. (eds) (1951) *Oxford Studies in the Price Mechanism*, Oxford, Oxford University Press.

Andrews, P. W. S. (1958) 'Competition in the Modern Economy', Reprinted from Sell, G. (ed) (1958) *Competitive Aspects of Oil Operations*, London, Institute of Petroleum.

Andrews, P. W. S. (1964) *On Competition in Economic Theory*, London, Macmillan.

Andrews, P. W. S. and Brunner, E. (1952) *Capital Development in Steel*, Oxford, Basil Blackwell.

Andrews, P. W. S. and Brunner, E. (1975) *Studies in Pricing*, London, Macmillan.

Andrews, P. W. S. and Friday, F. A. (1960) *Fair Trade: Resale Price Maintenance Re-examined*, London, Macmillan.

Ansoff, H. I. (1968) *Corporate Strategy*, Harmondsworth, Penguin Books.

Archibald, G. C. and Rosenbluth, G. (1975) 'The "New" Theory of Consumer Demand and Monopolistic Competition', *Quarterly Journal of Economics 89*, November, pp. 567–90.

Armstrong, W. E. (1939) 'The Determinateness of the Utility Function', *Economic Journal 49*, September, pp. 453–67.

Auld, D. A. L. (1974) 'Advertising and the Theory of Consumer Choice', *Quarterly Journal of Economics 88*, August, pp. 480–7.

Bain, A. D. (1964) *The Growth of Television Ownership in the UK—A Lognormal Model*, Cambridge, Cambridge University Press.

Bannister, D. and Mair, J. M. M. (1968) *The Evaluation of Personal Constructs*, New York, Academic Press.

Bannister, D., and Fransella, F. (1971) *Inquiring Man* (2nd edn 1980), Harmondsworth, Penguin Books.

Bateson, G. (1973) *Steps to an Ecology of Mind*, St. Albans, Granada/Paladin Books.

Bateson, G. (1980) *Mind and Nature: A Necessary Unity*, London, Fontana/Collins.

Baumol, W. J. (1972) *Economic Theory and Operations Analysis* (3rd edn) London, Prentice-Hall International.

Baumol, W. J. and Quandt, R. E. (1964) 'Rules of Thumb and Optimally Imperfect Decisions', *American Economic Review 54*, March, pp. 23–46.

Bausor, R. (1981) 'The Rational Expectations Hypothesis and the Epistemics of Time', Paper presented at Cambridge Journal of Economics Conference on the New Orthodoxy in Economics, Sidney Sussex College, Cambridge, 22–5 June.

Beck, P. W. (1972) 'Technological Advances—Help or Hindrance? An Industry View', *Chemistry and Industry*, 1 April, pp. 285–7.

Bennett, W. L. and Feldman, M. S. (1981) *Reconstructing Reality in the Courtroom*, London, Tavistock.

Bither, S. W. and Miller, S. (1969) 'A Cognitive Theory of Brand Preference', in Macdonald, P. R. (ed) (1969) *Marketing Involvement in Society and the Economy*, Chicago, American Marketing Association.

Blaug, M. (1980) *The Methodology of Economics: Or How Economists Explain*, Cambridge, Cambridge University Press.

Boden, M. A. (1979) *Piaget*, London, Fontana/Collins.

Boulding, K. E. (1956) *The Image: Knowledge in Life and Society*, Ann Arbor, University of Michigan Press.

Boulding, K. E. (1971) 'The Economics of Knowledge and the Knowledge of Economics'. Originally in *American Economic Review 56*, 1966, pp. 1–13; reprinted in Lamberton, D. M. (1971) *Economics of Information and Knowledge*, Harmondsworth, Penguin Books.

Bradbury, R. (1953) 'A Sound of Thunder'. In Bradbury, R. (1953) *Golden Apples of the Sun*, London, Rupert Hart-Davis.

Brown, A., and Deaton, A. (1972) 'Surveys in Applied Economics: Models of Consumer Behaviour', *Economic Journal 82*, December, pp. 1145–236.

Buchanan, J. M., and Thirlby, G. F. (eds) (1973) *LSE Essays on Cost*, London, LSE/Weidenfeld and Nicholson.

Carter, C. F. (1953) 'A Revised Theory of Expectations', *Economic Journal 63*, December, pp. 811–20.

Chandler, A. D. (1962) *Strategy and Structure: Chapters in the History of the American Industrial Enterprise*, Cambridge, Mass., MIT Press.

Clarke, R. N. (1980) 'On Marshallian Economics and the Economics of Marshall—A Preliminary View', Unpublished Paper, Robinson College, Cambridge, November.

Coddington, A. (1976) 'Keynesian Economics: The Search for First Principles', *Journal of Economic Literature 14*, December, pp. 1258–73.

Cyert, R. M. and March, J. G. (1963) *A Behavioral Theory of The Firm*, Englewood Cliffs, N. J., Prentice-Hall.

Dash, J. F., Schliffman, L. G. and Berenson, C. (1979) 'Risk and Personality-Related Dimensions of Store Choice', *Journal of Marketing 40*, pp. 32–9.

Deaton, A. (1977) 'Involuntary Saving Through Unanticipated Inflation', *American Economic Review 67*, December, pp. 899–910.

Deaton, A., and Muellbauer, J. (1980) *Economics and Consumer Behavior* Cambridge, Cambridge University Press.

Debreu, G. (1959) *Theory of Value*, New York, Wiley.

Dewey, J. (1910) *How We Think*, New York, Heath.

Dewey, J. (1929) *Experience and Nature* (2nd edn), La Salle, Open Court.

Douglas, M. and Isherwood, B. (1980) *The World of Goods*, Harmondsworth, Penguin (1978, New York, Basic Books).

Dow, S. C. and Earl, P. E. (1982) *Money Matters: A Keynesian Approach to Monetary Economics*, Oxford, Martin Robertson.

Downie, J. (1958) *The Competitive Process*, London, Duckworth.

Earl, P. E. (1980) 'Characteristic Filtering: Towards a Behavioural Theory of Individual Choice', University of Stirling Discussion Papers in Economics, Finance, and Investment, No. 84.

Earl, P. E. (1983) 'A Behavioural Theory of Economists' Behaviour', in Eichner, A. S. (ed) (1983) *Why Economics is Not Yet a Science*, Armonk, N.Y., M. E. Sharpe.

Earl, P. E., and Glaister, K. W. (1979) 'Wage Stickiness from the Demand Side', University of Stirling Discussion Papers in Economics, Finance, and Investment, No. 78.

Eden, C., Jones, S. and Sims, D. (1979) *Thinking in Organizations*, London, Macmillan.

Eichner, A. S. (1976) *The Megacorp and Oligopoly*, Cambridge, Cambridge University Press (Reissued 1980 by M. E. Sharpe, White Plains, N.Y.).

Eichner, A. S. (1978) 'P. W. S. Andrews and E. Brunner's *Studies in Pricing*: Review', *Journal of Economic Literature 16*, December, pp. 1436–8.

Eichner, A. S. (ed) (1979) *A Guide to Post-Keynesian Economics*, White Plains, N.Y., M. E. Sharpe (London, Macmillan).

Engel, J. F., Blackwell, R. D., and Kollat, D. T. (1978) *Consumer Behavior*, (3rd edn) Hinsdale, Illinois, Dryden Press.

Feyerabend, P. K. (1975) *Against Method: Outline of An Anarchistic Theory of Knowledge*, London, New Left Books.

Fishbein, M. A. (1963) 'An Investigation of the Relationships Between Beliefs about an Object and the Attitude toward that Object', *Human Relations 16*, August, pp. 233–9.

Fishbein, M. A. and Ajzen, I. (1975) *Belief, Attitude, Intention and Behavior: An Introduction to Theory and Research*, Reading, Mass., Addison-Wesley.

Fishburn, P. S. (1974) 'Lexicographic Orders, Utilities and Decision Rules: A Survey', *Management Science 20*, July, pp. 1442–71.

Friedman, M. (1953) 'The Methodology of Positive Economics', in Friedman, M. (1953) *Essays in Positive Economics*, Chicago, University of Chicago Press.

Galbraith, J. K. (1958) *The Affluent Society*, London, Hamish Hamilton.

Galbraith, J. K. (1975) *Economics and the Public Purpose*, Harmondsworth, Penguin Books.

Garfinkel, H. (1967) *Studies in Ethnomethodology*, Englewood Cliffs, N. J., Prentice-Hall.

Georgescu-Roegen, N. (1954) 'Choice, Expectations and Measurability', *Quarterly Journal of Economics 68*, pp. 503–34.

Goffman, E. (1971) *The Presentation of Self in Everyday Life*, Harmondsworth, Penguin Books.

Green, H. A. J. (1976) *Consumer Theory* (rev. edn), London, Macmillan.

Hansen, F. (1969) 'Consumer Choice Behavior: An Experimental Approach', *Journal of Marketing Research 4*, November, pp. 436–43.

Harcourt, G. C. (1972) *Some Cambridge Controversies in the Theory of Capital*, Cambridge, Cambridge University Press.

Hicks, J. R. (1939) *Value and Capital*, Oxford, Oxford University Press.

Hirsch, F. (1976) *Social Limits to Growth*, London, Routledge and Kegan Paul.

Hirschman, A. O. (1970) *Exit, Voice and Loyalty*, Cambridge, Mass., Harvard University Press.

Hofstadter, D. R. (1979) *Gödel, Escher, Bach: An Eternal Golden*

Braid, Hassocks, Sussex, Harvester Press (New York, Basic Books).

Humphries, J. and Rubery, J. (1981) 'Supply Side Economics and Female Involvement in Production', Paper presented at Cambridge Journal of Economics Conference on the New Orthodoxy in Economics, Sidney Sussex College, Cambridge, 22–5 June.

Hutchison, T. W. (1977) *Knowledge and Ignorance in Economics*, Oxford, Basil Blackwell.

Ironmonger, D. S. (1972) *New Commodities and Consumer Behaviour*, Cambridge, Cambridge University Press.

Kaldor, N. (1972) 'The Irrelevance of Equilibrium Economics', *Economic Journal 82*, December, pp. 1237–55.

Kalecki, M. (1943) 'Costs and Prices', in Kalecki, M. (1943) *Studies in Economic Dynamics*, London, George Allen and Unwin.

Katona, G. (1960) *The Powerful Consumer: Psychological Studies of the American Economy,* New York, McGraw-Hill.

Katona, G. (1976) 'Consumer Investment versus Business Investment', *Challenge*, January/February.

Katouzian, H. (1980) *Ideology and Method in Economics*, London, Macmillan.

Katzner, D. W. (1970) *Static Demand Theory*, London, Collier-Macmillan.

Kay, N. M. (1979) *The Innovating Firm: A Behavioural Theory of Corporate R and D*, London, Macmillan.

Kay, N. M. (1982) *The Evolving Firm*, London, Macmillan.

Kay, N. M. (1983) *The Emergent Firm: The Role of Bounded Rationality in Economic Organization*, London, Macmillan (forthcoming).

Kelly, G. A. (1955) *The Psychology of Personal Constructs*, New York, Norton.

Kelly, G. A. (1963) *A Theory of Personality*, New York, Norton.

Kelly, G. A. (1969) 'The Autobiography of a Theory,' in Maher, B. (ed) (1969) *Clinical Psychology and Personality: The Collected Papers of G. A. Kelly*, New York, Wiley.

Koestler, A. (1975a) *The Act of Creation*, London, Pan Books.

Koestler, A. (1975b) *The Ghost in the Machine*, London, Pan Books.

Koestler, A. and Smythies, J. R. (eds) (1969) *Beyond Reductionism: New Perspectives in the Life Sciences*, London, Radius Books/Hutchinson.

Kornai, J. (1971) *Anti-Equilibrium*, Amsterdam, North-Holland.

Kuhn, T. S. (1970) *The Structure of Scientific Revolutions*, (2nd edn), Chicago, University of Chicago Press.

Lakatos, I. (1970) 'Falsification and the Methodology of Scientific Research Programmes,' in Lakatos, I. and Musgrave, A. (1970)

Criticism and the Growth of Knowledge, London, Cambridge University Press.

Lamberton, D. M. (ed.) (1971) *Economics of Information and Knowledge*, Harmondsworth, Penguin Books.

Lancaster, K. J. (1966) 'A New Approach to Consumer Theory', *Journal of Political Economy 74*, April, pp. 132–57.

Lancaster, K. J. (1975) 'Socially Optimal Product Differentiation', *American Economic Review 65*, September, pp. 567–85.

Latsis, S. J. (1972) 'Situational Determinism in Economics', *British Journal for the Philosophy of Science 25,* pp. 207–45.

Lee, F. S. (1981) 'Full Cost Pricing: A New Wine in a New Bottle', University of California, Riverside, Working Paper No. 58.

Leibenstein, H. (1966) 'Allocative Efficiency vs. *X*-Efficiency', *American Economic Review 56,* June, pp. 392–415.

Leibenstein, H. (1976) *Beyond Economic Man, A New Foundation For Microeconomics*, Cambridge, Mass., Harvard University Press.

Leijonhufvud, A. (1968) *On Keynesian Economics and the Economics of Keynes*, New York, Oxford University Press.

Leijonhufvud, A. (1973) 'Effective Demand Failures', *Swedish Journal of Economics 75*, pp. 27–48.

Levine, A. L. (1980) 'Increasing Returns, the Competitive Model and the Enigma that was Alfred Marshall', *Scottish Journal of Political Economy 27*, November, pp. 260–76.

Lipsey, R. G. and Rosenbluth, G. (1971) 'A Contribution to the New Theory of Demand: A Rehabilitation of the Giffen Good', *Canadian Journal of Economics 4,* May, pp. 131–63.

Littlechild, S. C. (1978) *The Fallacy of the Mixed Economy*, London, Institute of Economic Affairs.

Loasby, B. J. (1967) 'Management Economics and the Theory of the Firm,' *Journal of Industrial Economics 15*, July, pp. 165–76.

Loasby, B. J. (1976a) *Choice, Complexity and Ignorance*, Cambridge, Cambridge University Press.

Loasby, B. J. (1976b) 'H. Leibenstein's *Beyond Economic Man*: Review', *Economic Journal 86*, December, pp. 913–15.

Loasby, B. J. (1978) 'Whatever Happened to Marshall's Theory of Value?', *Scottish Journal of Political Economy 25*, February, pp. 1–12.

Malinvaud, E. (1972) *Lectures on Microeconomic Theory*, Amsterdam, North-Holland.

Marris, R. L. (1964) *The Economic Theory of 'Managerial' Capitalism*, London, Macmillan.

Marschak, J. (1968) 'The Economics of Inquiring, Communicating, Deciding', *American Economic Review 58* (supp.), May, pp. 1–18.

Marshall, A. (1920) *Principles of Economics*, (8th edn), London, Macmillan.

Miller, G. A. (1956) 'The Magic Number Seven Plus or Minus Two: Some Limits on our Capacity for Processing Information', *Psychological Review 63*, March, pp. 81–97.

Moss, S. (1981) *An Economic Theory of Business Strategy*, Oxford, Martin Robertson.

Pasinetti, L. L. (1981) *Structural Change and Economic Growth*, Cambridge, Cambridge University Press.

Penrose, E. T. (1959) *The Theory of the Growth of the Firm*, Oxford, Basil Blackwell, (2nd edition, 1980).

Pirsig, R. M. (1974) *Zen and the Art of Motorcycle Maintenance*, London, Bodley Head.

Popper, K. (1962) *Conjectures and Refutations: The Growth of Scientific Knowledge*, New York, Basic Books (page references are to Harper Torchbook edn).

Popper, K. (1976) *Unended Quest: An Intellectual Autobiography*, London, Fontana/Collins.

Reddaway, W. B. (1937) 'Special Obstacles to Full Employment in a Wealthy Economy', *Economic Journal 47*, June, pp. 297–307.

Reilly, M. D., Holman, R. H. and Evered, R. (1976) 'Individual Differences in Information Processing: An Exploratory Report', Working Paper No. 50, College of Business Administration, Pennsylvania State University, November.

Richardson, G. B. (1956) 'Demand and Supply Reconsidered', *Oxford Economic Papers 8* (New Series), June, pp. 113–26.

Richardson, G. B. (1959) 'Equilibrium, Expectations and Information', *Economic Journal 69*, June, pp. 223–37.

Richardson, G. B. (1960) *Information and Investment*, Oxford, Oxford University Press.

Richardson, G. B. (1972) 'The Organisation of Industry', *Economic Journal 82*, September, pp. 883–96.

Richardson, G. B. (1975) 'Adam Smith on Competition and Increasing Returns', in Skinner, A. S. and Wilson, T. (1975) *Essays on Adam Smith*, Oxford, Oxford University Press.

Richardson, G. B. and Leyland, N. H. (1964) 'The Growth of Firms', *Oxford Economic Papers 16* (New Series), March, pp. 1–23.

Ries, A., and Trout, J. (1981) *Positioning: The Battle for your Mind*, New York, McGraw-Hill.

Robinson, J. V. (1933) *The Economics of Imperfect Competition*, London, Macmillan, (2nd edn, 1969).

Rosenberg, M. J. (1956) 'Cognitive Structure and Attitudinal Effect', *Journal of Abnormal and Social Psychology 53*, pp. 367–72.

Rosenberg, M. J., Hovland, C. I. and McGuire, W. J. (1960), *Attitude Organisation and Change*, New Haven, Yale University Press.

Ryan, M. J. and Bonfield, E. H. (1975) 'The Fishbein Extended Model and Consumer Behavior', *Journal of Consumer Research 2*, September, pp. 118–36.

Schutz, A. (1943) 'The Problem of Rationality in the Social World', *Economica 10* (New Series), May, pp. 130–49.

Scitovsky, T. (1977) *The Joyless Economy* (paperback edn), New York, Oxford University Press.

Scitovsky, T. (1981) 'The Desire for Excitement in Modern Society,' *Kyklos 34*, pp. 3–13.

Shackle, G. L. S. (1943) 'The Expectational Dynamics of the Individual', *Economica 10* (New Series), May, pp. 99–129.

Shackle, G. L. S. (1949) *Expectation in Economics*, Cambridge, Cambridge University Press.

Shackle, G. L. S. (1955) *Uncertainty in Economics*, London, Cambridge University Press.

Shackle, G. L. S. (1956) 'Expectation and Cardinality', *Economic Journal 66*, June, pp. 211–19.

Shackle, G. L. S. (1958) *Time in Economics*, Amsterdam, North-Holland.

Shackle, G. L. S. (1961) *Decision, Order and Time in Human Affairs*, Cambridge, Cambridge University Press.

Shackle, G. L. S. (1967) *The Years of High Theory: Invention and Tradition in Economic Thought, 1926–1939*, Cambridge, Cambridge University Press.

Shackle, G. L. S. (1979) *Imagination and the Nature of Choice*, Edinburgh, Edinburgh University Press.

Shackle, G. L. S. (1981) Personal Letter, Shackle to Earl, 26 November.

Shackle, G. L. S. (1982) Personal Letter, Shackle to Earl, 14 March

Shaw, R. W. (1974) 'Price Leadership and the Effect of New Entry on the UK Retail Petrol Supply Market', *Journal of Industrial Economics 18*, September, pp. 65–79.

Simmons, P. J. (1974) *Choice and Demand*, London, Macmillan.

Simon, H. A. (1957) *Models of Man*, New York, Wiley.

Simon, H. A. (1959) 'Theories of Decision-Making in Economics and Behavioral Sciences', *American Economic Review 69*, June, pp. 253–83.

Simon, H. A. (1962) 'The Architecture of Complexity', *Proceedings of the American Philosophical Society 106*, December, pp. 467 –82.

Simon, H. A. (1979) 'Rational Decision Making in Business

Organizations', *American Economic Review 69*, September, pp. 493–513.

Skinner, A. S. (1979) 'Adam Smith: An Aspect of Modern Economics?', *Scottish Journal of Political Economy 26*, June, pp. 109–26.

Smith, R. P. (1975) *Consumer Demand for Cars in the USA*, Cambridge, Cambridge University Press.

Smyth, R. L. (1967) 'A Price-Minus Theory of Costs', *Scottish Journal of Political Economy 14*, June, pp. 110–17.

Sraffa, P. (1926) 'The Laws of Returns under Competitive Conditions', *Economic Journal 36*, December, pp. 535–50.

Sraffa, P. (1960) *Production of Commodities by Means of Commodities*, Cambridge, Cambridge University Press.

Steedman, I. (1980) 'Economic Theory and Intrinsically Non-Autonomous Preferences and Beliefs', *Quaderni Fondazione Feltrinelli (Proc. Seminar Economic Methodology)*, No. 7/8.

Steinbruner, J. D. (1974) *The Cybernetic Theory of Decision*, Princeton, Princeton University Press.

Strotz, R. H. (1957) 'The Empirical Implications of a Utility Tree', *Econometrica 25*, April, pp. 269–80.

Thompson, M. (1979) *Rubbish Theory: The Creation and Destruction of Value*, with a foreword by E. C. Zeeman, Oxford, Oxford University Press.

Townshend, H. (1937) 'Liquidity Premium and the Theory of Value', *Economic Journal 47*, March, pp. 157–69.

Tuck, M. (1976) *How Do We Choose?* London, Methuen.

Tversky, A. (1969) 'Intransitivity of Preferences', *Psychological Review 76*, January, pp. 31–48.

Tylecote, A. (1980) *The Causes of the Present Inflation*, London, Macmillan.

Ward, B. (1972) *What's Wrong With Economics?* London, Macmillan.

Warshaw, P. R. (1980) 'A New Model for Predicting Behavioral Intentions: An Alternative to Fishbein', *Journal of Marketing 17*, May, pp. 153–72.

Weintraub, E. R. (1979) *Microfoundations: The Compatibility of Microeconomics and Macroeconomics*, Cambridge, Cambridge University Press.

Wells, W. D. (1975) 'Psychographics: A Critical Review', *Journal of Marketing Research 12*, May, pp. 196–213.

Whan Park, C. (1978) 'A Conflict Resolution Choice Model', *Journal of Consumer Research 5*, September, pp. 124–37.

Williamson, O. E. (1975) *Markets and Hierarchies: Analysis and Antitrust Implications*, New York, The Free Press.

Winter, S. G., Jr. (1964) 'Economic 'Natural Selection' and the

Theory of the Firm', *Yale Economic Essays 4*, Spring, pp. 224–72.

Wolf, C., Jr. (1970) 'The Present Value of the Past', *Journal of Political Economy 78*, pp. 783–92.

Wolf, C., Jr. (1973) 'Heresies about Time: Wasted Time, Double Duty Time and Past Time', *Quarterly Journal of Economics 87*, pp. 661–7.

Wolfe, T. (1969) *The Pump House Gang*, New York, Bantam Books.

Wolfe, T. (1977) *Mauve Gloves and Madmen, Clutter and Vine*, New York, Bantam Books.

Wood, A. J. B. (1975) *A Theory of Profits*, Cambridge, Cambridge University Press.

Wu, Y.-L. (1946) 'International Capital Investment and the Development of Poor Countries', *Economic Journal 56*, March, pp. 86–101.

Young, A. (1928) 'Increasing Returns and Economic Progress', *Economic Journal 38*, December, pp. 527–42.

Index